DISCOURSE POWER ADDRESS

Discourse Power Address
The Politics of Public Communication

STUART PRICE

ASHGATE

Published by
Ashgate Publishing Limited
Gower House
Croft Road
Aldershot
Hampshire GU11 3HR
England

Ashgate Publishing Company
Suite 420
101 Cherry Street
Burlington, VT 05401-4405
USA

Ashgate website: http://www.ashgate.com

British Library Cataloguing in Publication Data
Price, Stuart
  Discourse power address : the politics of public
  communication
  1. Communication - Social aspects 2. Communication and
  culture 3. Meaning (Psychology) 4. Power (Social sciences)
  I. Title
  302.2

Library of Congress Cataloging-in-Publication Data
Price, Stuart, 1965-
  Discourse power address : the politics of public communication / by Stuart Price.
      p. cm.
  Includes index.
  ISBN-13: 978-0-7546-4818-5 1. Communication--Social aspects. 2.
Communication--Political aspects. 3. Mass media--Social aspects. 4. Mass media--
Political aspects. 5. Persuasion (Psychology) 6. Persuasion (Rhetoric) 7. Social
influence. 8. Rhetoric--Political aspects I. Title.

  HM1206.P75 2007
  306.201--dc22

2006025034

ISBN 978-0-7546-4818-5

Printed and bound in Great Britain by Antony Rowe Ltd, Chippenham, Wiltshire.

Contents

List of Illustrations

About the Author

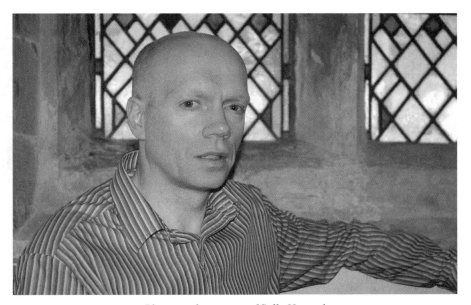

Photograph courtesy of Sally Hossack

Stuart Price is Senior Lecturer in Media and Cultural Production at De Montfort University, UK and a Research Associate in the International Cultural Planning and Policy Unit. He produced the first mass-market media studies book for the higher education sector and went on to write a series of books on communication and media. His current research includes work on rhetoric and the 'war on terror' and studies of agency, gendered identity and film.

Introduction:
Definitions and Perspectives

Directive address

The objective of this book is to examine the creation and circulation of meaning, through the study of one particular form of authoritative address. Address is used here to indicate the construction of a message which attempts to animate some aspect of a recipient's subjectivity (Price, in Ralph, Manchester and Lees, 2003, 146).[1] In other words, a proposition or purposeful statement is modeled with an imagined subject's predilections in mind.[2] Various methods are used to model the social location[3] of individuals, which amount in effect to segmentation of a marketplace or workforce. This conceptual fragmentation of the public is used to reinforce the affiliation between authority, its junior partners, and those constructed through address as subordinate.

The term chosen to describe this form of representation is *directive*. Directive[4] acts of public communication, whether commercial, political, or corporate, represent a class of event in which the primary motive for initiating contact is strategic (Habermas, 1984, 85; Fairclough, 1989, 198). Use of the category directive is, therefore, a way of identifying texts and utterances which pursue certain instrumental goals, the successful attainment of which is primarily intended to benefit those authors (individual or collective) responsible for the composition of the message concerned.

1　Subjectivity, in turn, is understood not only as a function of Benveniste's contrast between 'I' and 'you' in interpersonal address (Benveniste, in Nye, 1998, 48) but as a consequence of the 'social location' of actors, the intersection of which is determined by individual experience of space, time, moral responsibility and relational factors like class and age (Harre and Gillett, 1994, 101).

2　By predilections I mean all those personal and social preferences as they are found within the orbit of expressive existences in the lifeworld (*Lebenswelt*): the difference between its employment here and its use in Habermas, is that this position opposes the idea that the lifeworld is formed by 'unproblematic, background convictions' (Habermas, 1984, 70); in other words, belief is not regarded as unreflexive. For a progressive treatment of 'lifeworld', see Agger, 1992.

3　A term taken from *The Discursive Mind*, Harre and Gillett (1994).

4　'Directive' address is the functional form of the grammatical mood known as the 'imperative'; this study regards *all* communication as 'purposive' in that it is designed to achieve particular ends.

The type of text chosen to illustrate this mode of intentional address will therefore encompass those more clearly 'inflected'[5] examples of public intervention, including party political/election broadcasts, political speeches, corporate mission statements, advertisements and television commercials.[6]

These forms have not been identified primarily as 'media texts' (since they are not all 'mediated' to the same degree), but as products of an essentially unitary position, based on a class of discourse often described as 'monological'.[7] This concept, associated with Bakhtin and his associates (see Brandist, et al, 2004) is a form of utterance supposedly favoured by authority or the 'forces of centralisation' (Shepherd, in Hirschkop and Shepherd, 1989, 100). Dialogic communication on the other hand, at least in its extended sense, represents the mutual exchange of understanding that is produced by, and in turn regenerates, a democratic social order.

The dialogic/monologic distinction carries, therefore, significant implications for the study of power and communication, but is less helpful if confined to studies of literary genres. Bakhtin's work did indeed transcend a literary frame (see Holquist, 2002, 16), but specific claims about the relative merits of the novel and the epic, in which the former is less authoritarian because it is capable of articulating distinct positions or 'voices' (Hirschkop, 1999, 80), seem to undermine the principle that all types of meaningful expression (including the more 'elitist' genres) inevitably refer to a range of perspectives.

This is not to argue that every message strives for reciprocal gestures from an audience. Indeed, the point of this book is to identify a type of address which, however 'conversational' it may appear in *form*, or however much it refers to opposing views, amounts in reality to an act of transmission directed towards the attainment of specific social purposes.[8] Certain formal appearances can, therefore, be misleading. The modest, 'incremental' claims made in political advertising, and more particularly in recent forms of corporate address,[9] represent a drive to power

---

5   Inflection means the way in which the meaning of a spoken word may be changed through intonation, or within written texts by altering the form of a lexical item (and thus its grammatical relationship to other elements). Within my argument, inflection is used to indicate both physical emphasis (achieved through textual repetition, for example, or other techniques) and the related production of significance.

6   In the case of the last two categories, there is a difference between commercial messages which present a product and those which attempt to reinforce a brand or reputation.

7   'Monological' originates in Bakhtin but appears also in Thompson (1995, 84).

8   e.g. the discursive preparation of ground for the passage of executive decisions, or the generation of sales through the circulation of textual propositions (where a proposition is a position which may or may not be sincerely attributed to the source which promotes it; this relates to the relationship between ideology, belief and instrumental purpose, addressed below).

9   A type of interpellation freed from the more specific reference to product-sales found in commercial forms, and governed by apparently progressive principles (such as *corporate social responsibility*); see below.

masked by the *simulation of intimacy*. Such messages attempt, during the process of enunciation, to control their terms of reference and as a result try to limit the perceptual autonomy of a target audience.[10]

My contention is that conversational gambits within directive address do not represent a progressive mode of exchange, not just because there is no channel for response but, more crucially, because they make only *rhetorical gestures* towards alternative perspectives. Understanding this phenomenon is essential, because it represents a common practice within directive address: the production of caricature in order to create expedient disparities between social actors. An orator will 'bring into being' an opposing viewpoint but will not describe its true condition or cite it *on its own terms*.

This procedure, based on misrepresentation, is very far from the dialogic ideal. When, for example, the Conservative leader David Cameron acknowledged internal party opposition to his agenda for change, he described the content of critical letters as requests to 'slow down' and 'go easy' (speech to Conservative conference, 8th March 2006); in other words, conflict over direction was deliberately reinterpreted as a disagreement over pace. All such authoritative utterances and texts display this transformative impulse and belong, however personal in tone and structure, to the realm of propaganda or promotion (Wernick, 1991). Analysis of such material should, therefore, help delineate the relationship between intention, expression and models of reception as these appear in communication events knowingly produced for public consumption and scrutiny.[11]

The analytical work of the book may therefore be described as an attempt to identify, through textual evidence, the ways in which a number of 'issue proponents' (Dearing and Rogers, 1996, 2) employ a variety of generic forms to present content to *imagined* audiences,[12] within the overall context of cultural expression in 'late modernity'.[13] This will inevitably entail some evaluation of competing approaches to the study of public communication, but the interpretative part of the research is driven by relatively simple observations, taken from studies of language and applied to the truth-claims made by influential social actors.

---

10 The immediate audience may be a *professional* or expert gathering which then interprets the messages it receives for another group.

11 The material used for this study will include essential reference to previous academic interpretations of message reception, together with studies of communication acts, but will not involve audience or ethnographic studies *per se*.

12 'Imagined' in the sense that their characteristic attributes are conceived in advance and the message shaped in the light of this conception.

13 The term 'late modernity', together with its competitors, is discussed in the work on discourse and modernity; see Chapter 3, below.

Intention, public power and governance

The concept of intention[14] is central to the idea of a directive mode of address. Intention is usually presented as the everyday condition which pre-exists performance; in essence, it is seen as a purpose *held in advance* of any deliberate action. This is a reasonable definition, but has certain limitations. One point to remember is that all messages are circumscribed by the range of available discourses[15] and are partially determined by the context in which expression is made. Intention is perhaps best understood not as an individual attribute, an idiosyncratic position held by one person,[16] but as the structural reproduction of purposes whenever hierarchical relationships are renewed during communication events.

This position emphasizes, once again, the conviction that all forms of representation or utterance that reinforce authority, however affable in content or unceremonious in form, will demonstrate the structural inequality between 'legitimate' power and subordinate groups. A political speech, for example, might reveal a government initiative, or a presentation may re-brand a company, but the effect of such unidirectional communiqués is to confirm the relative positions of an author (who often 'stands in' for, or represents, a recognised *authority*) and an audience (whether or not it is physically present).

The constant renewal of hierarchical distinction between groups can be described as an economic imperative, because the state and the capitalist class both seek to extract value from the populace (Gill, 2003, 13). This goal requires, in the case of political authority, the regular projection of demands and impositions, which place the citizen-consumer in a state of obligation. In the commercial sphere, compulsion appears as a routine display of attractions, which tries to direct individuals towards a search for renewal within the 'unpredictable' mutations of cultural modernity.[17]

There are vital differences, however, in the degrees of democratic *entitlement* which should be accorded to the political and commercial realm. This is not to suggest that electoral politics is inherently egalitarian, rather that the private sector has *no formal right* to promote itself through references to a supposedly progressive 'civic' role. Gill's argument that, in most cases at least, the state 'does not seek to enter the moral realm' (Gill, 2003, 5), may need qualification (see below) but the

---

14 Although Coulthard asserts that it is quite acceptable to proceed with analysis on the basis of the hearer's understanding of speaker intention (see Coulthard, 1985, 20), this position cannot be applied to the utterances of the powerful, where there may be some distance between their purposes and the way these are 'read' by an audience.

15 The 'typical' positions, attached to particular topics, which are expressed in any structured argument.

16 In certain cases (i.e. speeches where a point of view is contested), orators may find that their immediate purposes are re-aligned or even formed during utterance.

17 Advertising is the paradigm example of a cultural form which magnifies changes in fashion and consumption, linking these to expressions of identity.

private sector, in contrast, appears to be obsessed with asserting its rights as a social actor, producing a highly visible *moral performance*.[18]

There is another important difference between these social forces. While individual examples of corporate address usually belong to a larger programme of 'reputation management', designed to display the ethical credentials of private enterprise, a political speech delivered by a ruling group is in effect *an act of governance*. Governance is a bureaucratic process of management which is meant to encompass a number of private and public interests, organized within an overall commitment to civic values; some authors see it as 'fundamentally a set of processes' (O Siochru and Girard, 2002, 15).

From an executive's perspective,[19] the inclusion of various formal bodies in a process of *consultation* can provide the necessary public legitimation for state intervention in everyday life. As a social practice, therefore, governance has become an essential weapon within the depleted armoury of social-democratic institutions. Divorced from socialist principles, opposed to traditional models of state intervention, and convinced that 'mobilising the working class' against privilege is no longer an option (Mandelson, Policy Network, 2004), 'progressive' politicians have turned to what Hansen and Salskov-Iversen call 'managerial patterns of political authority' (in MacCabe, 2002, 4).

In this situation, directive utterance is an essential tool in the reproduction of class relations, and especially effective where it takes into account the opinions of different social actors before presenting an edict. Indeed, in Gill's words, if the state can be said to 'have an essence', it lies in 'the continuing projection of public power in the pursuit of its aims' (Gill, 2003, 7). *Public power* in this example can be interpreted in two ways, as a) the exercise of an executive's acknowledged right to publicity, and as b) the demonstration of its ability to refer to 'the public interest' as a sanction for its activities.

With regard to a) above, Lichtenberg recognizes the conjunction between power and position when he remarks that governments are agents whose actions and policies have more 'exemplary significance' than those of individuals because of 'their inescapably public nature' (Lichtenberg, in Weiss, et al, 1993, 61). In the second case b), when state representatives use a public rationale for an executive action this may provide (in formal democracies at least) exactly the 'legitimate power source external to the orator' which Graham and his co-authors identify as a long-standing requirement of political discourse (Graham, et al, 2004, 199).

---

18 As this book seeks to demonstrate, private capitalism may well present a democratic façade, but its campaigns for 'social responsibility' are in effect forms of paid advocacy which by-pass the process of mediation endured by politicians.

19 An executive refers here to the branch of government which carries out acts without necessarily requiring the consent of a parliament or other democratic institutions.

Ideology and conviction

Examples of this practice are not difficult to find; in his 2005 address to the Labour Party conference, Tony Blair justified his approach to 'anti-social' conduct by declaring 'some day, some party will respond to the public's anger at the defeatism that has too often gripped our response to social disorder' (BBC online news, 27th September 2005). In this excerpt, the desire for firm action is attributed to the public, rather than to politicians. Yet, when large numbers of citizens oppose elements of government policy, they are less likely to be recognised as a 'public', and more liable to be described as individuals. Blair, responding to questions about Iraq, acknowledged dissatisfaction with his decision to go to war, by saying 'I know people strongly disagreed with it … in the end I had to take the decision as prime minister that I thought was right for the country' (BBC Newsnight interview, 20th March 2005). In this example, the interests of individualized people (with their presumably private opinions) are distinguished from 'the country', a concept used to provide public cover for the decision to support the United States' invasion.[20]

The more informal type of political utterance cited above is often perceived as marking a departure from the 'ideological', in the sense that it seems less ambitious than grand declarations founded on an invariant belief.[21] Such material can still, however, be interpreted as evidence of a consistent *position*. This highlights the difference between conviction and *footing* (Tolson, 2006, 45), if footing is understood as a stance taken on behalf of, not just an individual, but a point of view. Within a disciplined party, prominent members will be asked to supply a coherent 'line' or stance, irrespective of personal belief; in the case of New Labour, a 1997 addition to the ministerial code reveals this position, stating that 'the policy content of all major speeches … should be cleared in good time with the No. 10 press office' (Jones, 2002, 126).

Knowledge of this disciplinary measure leads to the conviction that political discourse should be studied as the projection of pragmatic aims; indeed, party leaders themselves sometimes seek to exploit public awareness of the disparity between material interest and principle. For instance, in a speech given in London, Blair argued that Britain had 'pursued a markedly different foreign policy' since his government took power, 'justifying our actions … at least as much by reference to values as interests' (Labour website, 21.03.2006). This statement was supposed to offer a contrast the government's practices with the less principled stance of previous administrations. Although the state may not be motivated by moral criteria (to return to Gill's comment, above), the typical utterance of politicians casts most decisions in ethical terms. At times, however, political figures depart entirely from such expressions of piety and reveal what the Americans call 'the bottom line'.

---

20 Blair invents a dilemma which must then be answered, ignoring the alternative view, that no decision need be taken, because no crisis existed beyond that forced by the UK and US.

21 A set of principles which would dictate policy irrespective of public or national interest.

Faced with stalemate in the attempt to create a government of national unity in Iraq, the British Foreign Secretary, Jack Straw, insisted that progress must be made, because of the coalition's political efforts and 'the huge amount of money that has been spent here' (BBC Radio 4, 2nd March 2006). At this point, the ideological character of political symbolism is stripped away. The requirements of power determine policy, while moral or philosophical consistency is discarded because it cannot provide the disciplinary constraint required by executive authority.[22]

Reference, coherence and truth: 'massive weapons of destruction'

No political or commercial intervention can make an impact, however, unless it can be understood by its intended recipients; the basic references brought into play must be recognized, before more complex values and attitudes can be represented. The need of those in authority to shape their messages in comprehensible terms carries important implications for social theory and the conduct of textual analysis,[23] suggesting that a search for linguistic and semiotic *coherence* is a productive exercise. It is clearly apparent, for example, when coherence is absent, or there is some confusion over the established order of terms.

The seemingly endless appearance of the phrase 'weapons of mass destruction', applied to the imagined military infrastructure of Saddam Hussein's Iraq, provides a good instance. On at least one occasion a significant public actor managed to produce a garbled version of the term. John Prescott, speaking on a BBC Radio 4 interview, referred to the danger posed by 'massive weapons of destruction' (BBC, 24.11.2004). This statement had grammatical integrity, but failed to make sense for two reasons: first, Hussein had been removed and no such weapons had been found; and second because Prescott seemed unable to reproduce the correct version of what had become a *standard* reference.

The example of 'WMD' shows clearly that a linguistic category *points to* something thought to exist. In other words, WMD had become accepted shorthand for a certain category of weapon, which has three distinct components; nuclear, biological, and chemical. The hope of the Western coalition was that if *any trace* of any of the three components that made up the category were to be found (or fabricated) within Iraq's borders, then the case against the regime would be proven. It was through this sleight of hand that an otherwise non-existent nuclear component was brought into prominence by smuggling it in under the larger linguistic category of 'WMD'. The West, which does possess, at the very least, a nuclear and chemical capacity, is never accused of having weapons of mass destruction, because WMD is a negative category. So, while reference indicates an accepted condition or state

---

22 There are complex arguments about what constitutes the 'ideological' as a sphere of action and belief, and to what degree it has an inclusive or 'enveloping' character; see below and in the Conclusion.

23 Criteria for the conduct of textual analysis appear at the end of the Chapter 2.

of affairs, it does not guarantee that a statement is true or that its application to a particular phenomenon is justified.

In the current work, truth is an important concept, and is considered first as a *principle* that transcends particular circumstances.[24] The pursuit of truth is useful as well as morally indispensible; it creates a set of demands which can be applied to every case of public representation. Authors or speakers must be expected to demonstrate transparency of intent, accuracy of description, and quality of provision.[25] In everyday experience, on the other hand, truth also appears as a *factual* or obdurate condition, recognized by the observation that 'it makes no profession of any kind, has no intention, does not stand for anything else' (Sheriff, 1994, 51).

The first conviction opposes the notion that truth 'never extends beyond' the particular 'domain of discourse in which it emerges' (Clifford, 2001, 31). The second is drawn from insights generated by the semiotician C.S. Peirce,[26] who described the stubborn materiality of lived experience and the ways in which individuals encounter solid, unyielding obstacles or events. In combining these points of view, the present work contests the post-structuralist emphasis on the boundless production of meaning (the notion that 'an indeterminate field of signifiers'[27] prevents conclusive descriptions of the social). I suggest instead that symbolic power exists as the *timely* exercise of 'explanation', that positions are articulated by dominant social actors for instrumental purposes. It is therefore precisely the need to produce meaning within temporal constraints that makes arguments about the impossibility of fixed or 'final' signification irrelevant.

This practical, realist perspective, in which representation is understood as an act with consequences, assumes that a text or utterance indicates the existence of something generally accepted as part of social reality. This point of view reserves judgment, however, on the *truthfulness* of the exact configuration of individual texts within wider public discourse. Phenomena that individuals are forced to recognize as real, as determining factors in their daily existence, are still capable of distorting moral principles; the existence of a financial system founded on credit, for example,

---

24 The use of 'truth' as a universal principle is very much out of favour in social and cultural theory, as it is often interpreted as a search for an impossible standard; even Dillon, in his critique of Derrida, regards it as bankrupt (see Dillon, 1995, 74).

25 By referring to provision, I mean that the thing described in discourse must be compared with the outcome provided and experienced by living individuals; if economic 'reform' produces 'redundancies', the meaning of reform can be judged by its material-symbolic effects.

26 Cobley writes about 'the realm of brute facts' manifest in common occurrences such as a door sticking during an attempt to close it, while Peirce himself talks of the condition as something 'eminently hard and tangible', a familiar state 'forced upon us daily' which is 'the main condition of life' (both in Cobley, P, 1996, 27 and 50). Dillon identifies 'a typicality to experience that allows us to recognize the unlikely and improbable' (Dillon, M.C., 1995, 168).

27 Chouliakari, L (2002) 'The Contingency of Universality', *Social Semiotics*, 12:1, 2002.

is a fact even while one of the consequences is 'a whole ideology of consumption'[28] (Baudrillard, 1998, 82). A text which advocates a consumer solution to a social problem recognizes a 'fact' but operates in a limited discursive sphere; as a result, it cannot produce useful guidance for conduct which falls outside its borders.

Reference and proposition: 'I saw communism with my own eyes'

This book suggests that the basic frame for textual analysis should begin by regarding a *reference* as the fundamental building block of address. A *reference* brings to mind a condition which is generally accepted, at the time of utterance, as reasonable, if not always beyond dispute; it usually refers to aspects of social reality which must be accepted if other, more complex notions, are to make sense.

So, when Arnold Schwarzenegger, the Governor of California, spoke to the 2004 Republican National Convention, he began by referring to events and concepts his audience could identify and understand. 'When I was a boy', he said, 'the Soviets occupied part of Austria'. The reference is therefore to boyhood and to the speaker's participation in it, an assertion which is reasonable enough since no-one would deny that, at some point, Schwarzenegger was probably a boy. Agreement with this notion may, however, lead to agreement with other features of his utterance that might be open to challenge, including the avowal that 'the Soviets occupied part of Austria'.

Schwarzenegger went on to claim that 'I saw their tanks in the streets, I saw communism with my own eyes'. Note here that the claim literally to have seen tanks is then immediately linked with the metaphorical notion of having witnessed the repressive 'communism' these military vehicles are supposed to represent. The purpose of this diatribe was to prepare his audience for a broader narrative, in which propositions about the virtues of US democracy could be built upon the more basic ideas established in the speech.

Some time after this event, a counter-claim emerged. Writing to the Washington Post on 9th September 2004, an ex-soldier described how 'I was an American military policeman stationed in Linz, Austria, in 1947, the year of Mr. Schwarzenegger's birth'. The writer establishes his own credentials as an eye-witness, describing how 'Mr. Schwarzenegger was born in Styria, which was in the British zone'. Having contradicted the idea that the young boy could have seen Soviet vehicles, the author goes on to insist 'there was emphatically no Communist government in postwar Austria' and writes that, by the time Schwarzenegger was born, 'any Soviet tanks in Austria – there were never any in Styria – were long gone'. The clear implication of these statements (see *implicature*, below) is that the 'Governator' as he dubbed himself, had not been entirely truthful.

In using reference, proposition and implicature as a system of analysis, one should recognize that they mark transitions between moods, rather than create definite boundaries between terms. The production of references, for instance, is not

---

28 A condition in which fetish-objectivity leads in turn to a sense of unreality.

always distinct from the generation of propositions, because the simpler form often contains a more complex idea. In addition, the whole point of making an intervention is to produce general propositions by the end of the speech or text. A *proposition* is, therefore, an assertion about the quality or meaning of a reference, attributing some moral status or ontological significance to an event, action or thing; the appearance of propositions marks a transition from an unexceptional, but not necessarily reliable statement, to a claim which certainly requires proof.

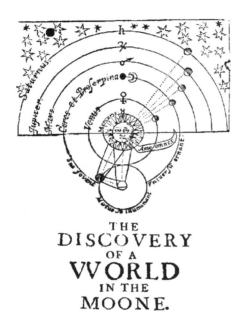

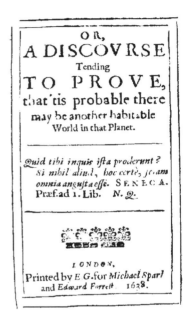

Illustration 1: Thirteen Propositions about the Moon, 1638

A treatise: 'thirteen propositions about the moon'

In rhetorical speech, one proposition is meant to lead to another, as the ideas develop into a consistent position or perspective. There is no guarantee, however, that the progression from one point to another will end up by achieving an accurate outcome. In 1638, a scientist called John Wilkins published a book called 'THE DISCOVERY OF A WORLD IN THE MOONE', with the subtitle 'A DISCOURSE Tending TO PROVE, that 'tis probable there may be another habitable World in that Planet'.

From his study of the moon, Wilkins conceived thirteen propositions. Some of these were entirely correct. For example, proposition four states that 'the Moone is a solid, compacted, opacus body'. This contrasts with the established view at the time that it was composed of gases. The fifth point argued to the effect that 'the Moone hath not any light of her owne'. Again, from observation, Wilkins made an accurate claim that the moon's radiance was reflected from the sun.

Lacking advanced technology, however, it proved impossible for the writer to verify more advanced conjectures. By the tenth statement, his line of argument had broken down. Noting the way that the reflected light seemed to have depth, Wilkins was convinced that 'there is an Atmo-sphaera, or an orbe of grosse vaporous aire' around the moon. Based on this mistake, the final proposition went on to deduce that ''tis probable there may be inhabitants in this World, but of what kind they are is uncertaine'. This early scientific treatise proceeds in the same measured way as mainstream contemporary rhetoric; analysis of its structure demonstrates how an apparently logical sequence can produce outlandish results.

The third concept in the three-part system advocated here is *implicature*, a way of suggesting or implying meaning without setting out a definite statement or point of view. An understanding of implicature is central to any appreciation of those messages which present subtle ideas or vague, indeterminate notions. In political discourse, there is often a marked reluctance to offer hostages to fortune; in other words, to make statements which can be used to attribute definite positions to a speaker who wishes to avoid being pinned down.

Journalists and interviewers, meanwhile, are often determined to force politicians to be explicit in their answers. Take, for example, the following exchange between David Dimbleby and Tony Blair, during a Panorama interview before the 1997 General Election. Dimbleby, seeking to establish the difference between the 'new' and the 'old' values espoused by the Labour leader, asked a series of direct questions designed to force this issue into prominence: 'Did you believe in CND? Did you believe in union power not being curtailed? Did you believe in nationalisation, no privatisation?' Blair's answer *could be read* as a negative response, but equally did not provide clear declarations which could then be translated into newspaper headlines. He avoided the questions by contending that, 'there were a whole series of policy positions that I adopted along with the rest of the Labour Party'. Here, the emphasis is on Blair's adherence to a collective position that was the norm in the period concerned. He immediately went on to say that 'the very process of modernisation has been the very process that I have undertaken in the Labour Party'. This does not provide a concrete denial and displays the strange circularity which is a feature of elusive or equivocal discourse.

When the interviewer pressed Blair to 'simply say' whether or not he thought Labour policies of the previous decade were wrong, the reply revealed a technique Blair was to use more than once in the future; he seized upon and repeated the key term and placed it in another context. His utterance again avoided the main point; 'I simply say what is important is to apply those principles to the modern world'. It did not take long for Dimbleby to attribute an *implied* meaning to Blair's words; 'you may be proud of what you've done now – that implies you're ashamed of what happened before'. Here, at last, the politician gave an unequivocal answer; 'I'm not ashamed of it at all'. At this point, it is worth reproducing another example of this style, characteristic of political leaders who wish to avoid difficult questions.

The exchange printed below has been taken, without comment, from a Newsnight interview of June 4th, 2001, in which Jeremy Paxman tried to elicit a response on a single issue:

> *Paxman*: But is it acceptable for the gap between rich and poor to widen?
> *Blair*: It is acceptable for those people on lower incomes to have their incomes raised. It is unacceptable that they are not given the chances ...
> *Paxman*: So it is acceptable for the gap to widen between rich and poor?
> *Blair*: It is not acceptable for poor people not to be given the chances they need in life.
> *Paxman*: That is not my question.
> *Blair*: I know it's not your question but it's the way I choose to answer it.

Chapter 1

Theoretical Background:
Critical Theory and Commercial Culture

According to critical perspectives on commercial culture all discourses, especially those which are promotional in character, share essential qualities, based upon their clear intent to achieve 'self-advantaging' ends (Wernick, 1991, 181). Such a proposition runs parallel to descriptions of political propaganda as a mode of communication which serves the interest of the propagandist (Jowett and O'Donnell, 1986, 13). Such views may suggest linear models of uninterrupted process,[1] in which a passive observer is placed as the recipient of a cohesive, 'mass produced' message (Schiller, 1986, 186). Yet these positions may also be located within a larger critical tradition, often associated with the Frankfurt School, which argued that twentieth-century media strengthened 'habits and attitudes' which made individuals and groups more susceptible to the blandishments of right-wing ideology (Curran and Seaton, 1997). The critical tradition is, according to Hearfield, characterised by 'an emancipatory interest', while traditional theory is more interested in 'the efficient control or manipulation' of existing social structures (Hearfield, 2004, 2).

The 'culture industry', a term which describes the entire organisation of culture under capitalism from Adorno's perspective, 'intentionally integrates its consumers from above' (Adorno, 1991, 55). A central function of this industry was to ensure conformity to social norms; as Adorno and Horkheimer argued, 'something is provided for all so that none may escape' (in Muller-Doohm, 2005, 285). The Frankfurt School thus seemed to regard the social meaning of all cultural products as 'entirely determined by [their] commodity status' (Buxton, 1990, 2). It is therefore possible to discern some continuity of thought between a conception of strategic communication, whether commercial or political, which is founded upon an industrial system embodying unequal power relations, and another view which characterises all conceptual or symbolic products as necessarily expressive of ruling ideas.

For example, Mills' radical critique of American society described the vulnerability of ordinary individuals as they encountered a cultural landscape dominated by media and strident forms of publicity like advertising (Mills, 1956). Later examples of critical theory seemed to concur with this view. Marcuse, for instance, believed that audiences are incorporated into mass society through a process of homogenisation,

---

1   In Herman and Chomsky's view, 'the mass media serve as a system for communicating messages and symbols to the general populace ... to fulfil this role requires systematic propaganda' (in Durham and Kellner, 2001, 280).

noting that intellectual freedom would mean the 'restoration of individual thought' which had been 'absorbed by mass communication and indoctrination' (Marcuse, 1964, 4). Using a theme which becomes more fully developed in the work of Habermas,[2] Marcuse called for the 'abolition of "public opinion"' (*ibid.*) as a means of returning to independent modes of understanding. According to this theory, consumer demands are conceived as 'false needs', the function of which is to create dependence on mediated culture, while capitalism itself is based on the reconfiguration of human desire. Agger, for example, describes the 'libidinal depths to which capitalist alienation has penetrated' (Agger, 1992, 96).

A broad characterisation of the 'culture industry'[3] as the instrument of ruling elites,[4] re-emerges in more contemporary studies as a critique of cultural imperialism. Fairclough's description of 'the power of the media to shape governments and parties' and 'to beam the popular culture of North America and Western Europe into Indian agricultural communities which still depend upon bullock-power' (Fairclough, 1995b, 2), produces a very general and rather indiscriminate conception, which implicitly compares notions of imperial and cultural force.[5]

This book, however, works to establish a more detailed conception of power, based on an understanding of social relations as these are embodied in texts and expressed through a particular form of address. Such a project requires a close explanation of the typical mechanics of interpellation,[6] but also reference to established conceptions of dominance and typifications of effect.[7] Exactly because such theories are often highly abstract in the way they model relationships of power, part of this investigation must also entail a study of the contextual circumstances in which texts appear.

'Saturation', dominance and agenda-setting

The position adopted here is that certain long-established conceptions of social control, particularly those which posit an all-pervasive media presence, obscure the true character of public address. A simple transition, from media 'saturation' to notions of dominance, is often proposed. The following, taken from an introductory

---

2   See Chapter 5 for a critique of Habermas's position.

3   Adorno, *The Culture Industry*, 1991.

4   In this model, power is exerted through either pacification or active direction.

5   A rather more balanced assessment is produced by Brooker, who notes 'the expansion of economic markets characterising developments in late twentieth-century capitalism ... while Western products and culture ... so-called 'mediascapes' ... find consumers in distant countries, these countries also serve to produce the products which are sold in the West' (Brooker, 1999, 94).

6   Althusser's term for an address which contains an authoritarian imperative; Montag speculates on its origin (see Montag, 2003, 66).

7   See Chapter 5 for examples of the tendency to attribute powerful effects to public messages.

text on media power, is an example of this tendency; 'we are saturated by media of different forms, shapes, and sizes ... the dominance of the mass media in our lives has led people to blame the media for a range of social ills' (Eldridge *et al.*, 1997). This unconvincing movement from presence to effect is repeated in other sources, compounded by theories of cultural dependence (O'Sullivan *et al.*, 1998, 19).

Another commonly cited reason for forms of dominance is at least a little more concrete; this is the process of 'agenda-setting', the notion that the media, as an instrumental force, decide which issues are worthy of public attention, or which should achieve special prominence. This issue is considered later in more detail; in the meantime, a brief overview of literature in this field finds a general adherence to a particular view of the phenomenon. The correlation of public agendas and media content was asserted by McCombs and Shaw in 1972 (in Lenart, 1994; in Manning, 2001, 213) based upon initial observations made in Los Angeles in 1967 (in McCombs, 2004, xi).

Agenda-setting developed into an essential feature of media studies, described by a number of popular authors such as Watson and Hill, who argued that the media 'set the order of importance of current issues' (Watson and Hill, 1989, 3), followed by Gill and Adams who mentioned 'the ways in which the media decide which information and which issues are most important for the public' (Gill and Adams, 1992, 6). O'Sullivan and his co-authors described agenda-setting as the process through which the media 'wittingly or unwittingly structure public debate and awareness' (1994, 8).[8] The present work finds such general descriptions unsatisfactory, also treating with caution the apparently more complex view of authors like Cohen, who famously expressed the belief that the press 'may not be successful much of the time in telling people what to think' but that it was 'stunningly successful in telling its readers what to think about' (Cohen, 1963, in Lenart, 1994, 15; in Manning, 2001, 212). As I indicate in a later chapter, the work of Dearing and Rogers (1996) and Tedesco (2005) may provide a more secure description of the mechanics of power and agenda-setting. These authors draw attention to the competition between distinct social forces and in Tedesco's case, following Gans, whether it is the source which actually leads the process (Tedesco, 2005, 198).

In the meantime, it is important to distinguish between the character of directive address as a technique, and the general degree of influence exerted by the media as an instiution. The growth of an industrialised social order in which new 'mechanisms of social cohesion' must be sought, for better or worse, in mass media forms (Robins and Webster, 1999, 131), has led to the assumption that mediated communication has come to dominate cultural expression, providing in turn a locus for theories of both domination and resistance (Hall, 1980). This perspective, which divides forms of power between competing classes or cultures, is perhaps a little crude in

---

8   The difference between knowing and unknowing transfer marks a passing recognition of two theses; that media make deliberate attempts at manipulation or that alternatively, they act as unwitting agents for ideological purposes, the source of which lies elsewhere. This issue is addressed below.

its representation of the mechanics of contestation (Price, 1998), but is at least more productive than the notion that a commodified consciousness completely negates the possible generation of progressive meaning.

Belief in the dominant power of commodification may be traced back to the conviction that the commodity is, in Mosco's words 'the most explicit representation' of capitalist production (Mosco, 1996, 141) and thus also an embodiment of its attendant values. In line with this conception, Catephores argues that what in fact dominates producers in a market economy is 'not commodities as material objects but unacknowledged social relationships set up and resolved through commodity exchange' (Catephores, 1989, 134). Goldman makes a similar point, noting that awareness of the meanings attached to goods produces commodity-signs which 'have become every bit as socially real as the products they ride upon (Goldman, 1992, 6). Thus, in rather dramatic terms, a parallel to 'natural reality' is created, which Catephores calls a 'second material reality' (Catephores, *op cit*). This is the 'world of commodities' which, escaping the control of individuals, manifests itself through the 'invisible hand of the market' to 'strike down' and dominate human subjects (*ibid.*). The origins of such a commentary lie in observations made by Marx, who used religious analogies (taken from Feuerbach) to describe the fetishistic character of 'the world of commodities' (Marx, in Hawkes, 2001, 52).

It is possible to discern in Catephores' remarks an ideological framework, in which the real conditions of existence are disguised and thus able to exert a malign and unexpected influence on subordinate classes. There are, however, other useful lessons to be learned from the notion of the commodity form. In discussing, for instance, early examples of eighteenth-century goods and symbolic power, Wernick makes a remark which provides an insight into the economic and social features of the process, noting that the sign-value of Wedgwood products became 'indistinguishable from what these products materially were' (Wernick, 1991, 15).

That the commodity is conceived as a material symbol of a social and economic system is a useful concept,[9] demonstrating the way in which objects and entities, as items of exchange, re-enter the signifying system of lived cultures as bearers of meaning (Miller, 1987, 59; Morley, 1992, 214; Dant, 1999, 36). However, the idea that such a process is merely fetishistic, making human relationships appear simply as connections between things (Barrett, 1991, 15), does not help in evaluating the cultural significance of objects or of assessing the possibility of the circulation of 'progressive' meanings.[10] When Baudrillard characterises consumption as 'the stage where the commodity is produced as a sign and signs (culture) are produced as commodities' (in Horrocks and Jevtic, 1996, 35), the structural power of representation in capitalist society is usefully acknowledged. The danger, however, is that the study of content is neglected, and the significance of particular signs is subsumed within a general law of oppressive consumption.

---

9   An issue examined more closely in Chapter 4.

10 'Progressive' is qualified here because the trappings of socially liberal positions are readily employed for authoritarian purposes; see the Introduction and Chapter 4.

Symbolic intervention and referential power

An urgent question however, concerns the status and use of 'propagandistic' address within contemporary cultural formations, and the possible fusion of politics and commercial promotion. Democracy, according to this view, no longer expresses the will of the people but offers instead 'consumer choice in the rotation of elites' (Dahlgren, 1995, 3), while the media are thought to assume considerable responsibility for shaping forms of public consciousness, or of legitimising certain values. The problem which emerges here is one of representation, both in its political character and its symbolic sense; discussion of the two is, indeed, difficult to conduct separately, as electoral representation depends upon the mobilisation of symbolic references and propositions[11] (Mazzoleni and Roper, in Kaid and Holtz-Bacha, 1995, 89).

The tensions which exist between, on the one hand, notions of powerful symbolic intervention, and on the other audience indifference to the more grandiose political claims, highlights the difficulty of attributing straightforward effects to public messages. Political advertising, for example, appears to be ineffective in securing popular approval, and seemingly powerless to reverse a current of disillusion and disengagement[12] (described by Dahlgren as 'declining levels of citizen participation', *op cit.*). Texts alone do not, therefore, offer reliable evidence for the unequivocally successful exercise of unitary address.

The present study, while acknowledging this development, does not depend for its argument upon the demonstrable achievement of textual 'objectives' (even where they can be identified), as it does not seek to prove the operation of foolproof rhetorical techniques.[13] It proposes instead the existence of a multi-discursive referential and propositional power within all forms of public communication, based upon the use by issue proponents of discourse as a *resource*. It adheres, in addition, to the argument that 'uni-directional' interventions, whatever their frame of reference, continue to be made within the context of public interaction. This recognises the persistence of hierarchical modes of social organisation and inequalities of power,[14] while drawing attention to the wide range of 'available discourses' from which coherent messages are composed.

The production of coherence must be understood in the context of a decline in the ability of authors (as originators of ideas or events) to control wider social and discursive circumstances (to realise or properly effect relations of authority through

---

11 See Chapter 5.

12 The Chapter on elections and discourse, Chapter 5, is partially devoted to examining this proposition.

13 It identifies these techniques but is not a study of audience response as such.

14 de Certeau indicates that the status of the 'dominated' in society is 'concealed by the euphemistic term "consumers"' (in Storey, 1999, 49).

persuasion as such[15]). Idealised depictions of allocution[16] have given way to ideas about the spread of conversationalisation (Fairclough, 1995a) and the production of more dialogic constructions of meaning.[17] The existence of such a complex discursive environment militates against the success of the unitary or interpellative voice, as described by Althusser (1971/1984). One consequence of this development has been a marked reluctance on the part of advertisers and politicians to maintain a paradigm of dominant address, and the production instead of a more complex representation of social goals. In the case of commercial address, these have often been marked by reference to radical politics and 'progressive' social movements (Price, 1998, 163).

Advertisers have produced representations capable of causing quite marked protest and disturbance.[18] Mainstream political groups are also capable of generating controversy (the form and content of Labour's 1992 health service broadcast is an example[19]). Competition between various forms of cultural and political authority, and the existence of cultural industries whose mode of representation is based on a dramatised rejection of behavioural conformity has, as a result, produced more dynamic *representations* of participation in public life.[20]

'Persuasion' is attempted, therefore, through the presentation of images, discourses, and auditory stimuli which make attempts to create some connection between the observer's subjectivity and the salient points of a message; in this way, 'transitional' values, those which are not yet widely accepted in society as a whole, are often circulated within commercial culture (Price, 1998, 26). What such texts 'mean' therefore, is in the first instance expressed by their appearance as appeals to common knowledge and shared attitudes, and only through these references, to action and belief. Again, the contention of the present work is that these appeals are made within a more fragmented and uncertain social context, in which *publicly expressed* relations between authority and recipient have, as noted above, become more complex. Forms of mediated address are inevitably part of the public domain, and as such can only work if they reproduce public concerns in a mode

---

15 See the Introduction for an approach which emphasises the *structural* character of dominance.

16 Allocution: the delivery of an address from a recognised authority to an assembly of followers; see Chapter 6.

17 The process of conversationalisation can be characterized as the increasingly common reproduction or simulation of the 'voices of ordinary experience' within certain mediated forms of public debate (Fairclough, 1995a, 144).

18 Yves Saint Laurent's 'Opium' ad, of Autumn/Winter 2000, featuring Sophie Dahl in a pose the company called 'a tasteful nude in the tradition of high art', caused much consternation, while the more 'vulgar' and comedic Wonderbra campaign of 1997 prompted little objection.

19 A full overview of the 'War of Jennifer's Ear' appears in Price, 1998, while other references occur in Crewe and Gosschalk, 1995.

20 'Reality' TV is one such example of an apparent shift of focus to ordinary people, though the demand for entertainment means that their activities are heavily regimented. The tendency is also present in game-shows, talk-shows and advertising texts.

of discourse recognisable as a 'sincere' expression[21] of everyday experience. Yet, in conjunction with the observation that hierarchical conditions of ownership and control nevertheless prevail, it is still possible to discern the existence of a primary source or origin[22] (an 'author', mentioned above, whether individual, collective, or institutional), despite the growth of less certain ideological positions and a multiply dispersed responsibility for message-composition.[23] This book emphasies again therefore, the continued existence of differential power relations between social actors, exemplified by the ability of certain groups to use the reproductive power of 'post-industrial' culture to make interventions within public life.

Media use and analytical frameworks

In contrast to this position, and thus essential to its description, are those theories which emphasise the efficacy of contemporary mediated culture in establishing modes of symbolic exchange between producers and audiences (Gillespie's 're-creative consumption[24]'), or which go further to argue that sub-cultural resistance negates or ameliorates the power of public spectacle.[25] While these perspectives may be understood as a reaction against 'crude' Marxism or theories of dominance (see above), which are seen to conflate economic and ideological power,[26] they fail to address the issue of institutional access, and those established rights of reproduction which are accorded to professional advocates.[27] This is not to argue that the inclusion of other groups would necessarily revolutionise, or even significantly alter currently available forms or content, nor is it intended to suggest that current paradigms of discourse are entirely unrepresentative of cultural norms. Above all, it does not mean to imply that mediated interaction and its accompanying propositions entirely encompass social exchange, leaving no space for other forms of communication practice.[28] If the latter were the case, then media forms would dominate cultural reproduction, leading to what Baudrillard calls the 'exclusion' of real culture and knowledge, and their replacement with a 'liturgy' from which all meaning is evacuated (Baudrillard, 1998, 104).

---

21 Habermas's *Wahrhaftigkeit*, a claim to sincerity which can only be validated in action.

22 Origin in this instance is regarded as an institutional, not a discursive location.

23 An account of conflict between the various agents involved in the production of advertising texts, which thus appear as an uneasy 'compromise' between different forces, is found in Fowles, 1996.

24 In 'Television, Ethnicity and Cultural Change', 1995.

25 See Fiske, 1989.

26 A position which also posits the existence of dominant ideologies *per se*.

27 Herman and Chomsky note also concentrated ownership and 'profit-orientation' (in Durham and Kellner, 2001, 280).

28 It does not attribute the realm of 'ideology' to mediated discourse, nor the domain of innocence to everyday exchange; in a society which competes at all levels of symbolic interaction, such distinctions merely act to reify the power of media forms.

I understand media use in a different way, as a meaningful expression of specially adapted and not entirely negative behaviours, in which mass communication forms become partially assimilated into broader cultural expectations and practices, in line for example with descriptions of television as a low-involvement medium (Barwise and Ehrenburg, 1988, 124), or more precisely with those domestic/social uses of media identified by Morley (1992, 142). The present study makes an additional point, however, identifying a sphere of action and interaction which lies outside technological mediation; that is to say, a space where experience of media may contribute to discursive content, but does not determine it. Adhering to this less apocalyptic account of media power[29] a number of observations can be made.

First, as indicated above, directive communication must take account of the beliefs or preferences of its audiences. Second, that to do so, considering the imperfection of market research (Wilmshurst, 1985; Brierley, 1995), an imaginative construction of an audience's social location is required.[30] Third, that the previous two conditions will act to produce complex presentations based on a variety of discursive resources. While this implies the existence of mutual cultural influence between advertiser and audience, it recognises also the hierarchical process through which this is achieved. One useful proposition in this respect is advanced by Thompson through his theory of 'mediated quasi-interaction' within mass communication forms (Thompson, 1995, 84). This theory acknowledges the ways in which meaning is circulated but also, in its characterisation of media address as 'monological', may suggest that its attempt at exchange is merely simulated.

Within this book, the creation of meaning is imagined not as the delivery of a unified core, nor as a series of deferred intertextual references, but as an emergent property of unequal social relations which at certain times and places produces textual *configurations*. These 'arrangements' of meaning constitute social actions, actions able in turn to create new frames of symbolic-material reference. The position held here is therefore relatively simple; that the reproduction and circulation of public meaning continues to be organised through hierarchical structures, even while public discourses may have been forced (partially through economic considerations[31]) to assume the tenor of informality and the representation of the 'everyday'. This, certainly with reference to established views of advertising, militates against the notion that the chief function of is to instil 'aspirational' values in its audiences (Dickinson *et al.*, 1998, 57).[32]

---

29 Models which posit a calamitous account of media dominance are perhaps inevitably associated with the work of Baudrillard, which nonetheless attempts at least to demonstrate the consequences of a pervasive media presence.

30 A term which appears in Harre and Gillett, 1994, and Benson, 2001; see the discussion below.

31 See the material on news as a practice, below; Price, on GMTV news, provides examples of this economic imperative which leads to less 'professional' and serious modes of presentation (1998, 145).

32 For a fuller exposition of this question, see the chapter on advertising.

In the study of 'monological' texts (Thompson, *op. cit.*), any working method used in analysis must be able to explain the various references, propositions, strategies, and contexts which appear within, or are suggested by, individual texts and their relationships.[33] In order to achieve this goal, the present work advocates a realist variant of critical discourse analysis (Fairclough, 1995a), allied to theories of context, strategic address, typification, subjectivity and rhetoric, founded upon a broadly realist hermeneutics (Devitt and Sterelny, 1987; Moravcsik, 1992; Greenwood, 1994; Lopez and Potter, 2001). This suggests, by extension, a realist approach to the philosophy of language (Collier, in Parker, 1998).

This mode of enquiry, concerned as it is with the public character of mediated speech events, emerges from, and shares common ground with, a number of academic traditions and perspectives:

- speech act theory, which interrogates forms of speech in the belief that utterances constitute communicative 'acts' (Austin, 1962; Searle, 1969; and Labov, 1972);
- conversation analysis, which studies the way in which speakers create a sense of social order through interaction (Sacks, Schegloff, and Jefferson, 1974);
- pragmatics, concerned with the interpretation of meaning and context and the endeavour to establish principles (such as 'co-operation') which act as a normative or moral imperative for exchange (Grice, 1989);
- modes of analysis which prioritise the study of speech events within institutional settings (Scannell, 1991; Tolson, 2006);
- and finally those forms of communication research in which certain principles of public service broadcasting are thought to persist within a more 'fragmented' public culture (Corner, 1995; Tetzlaff, 1991).

This last is characterised by the belief that some broadcast forms retain a 'civic' character, both in terms of their mode of address and through their apparent commitment to matters of public concern (Corner, 1995, 1).

This idea can be stretched a little far, producing a rather optimistic tendency which suggests that the civic principle is irrepressible, manifesting itself within whatever hybrid forms emerge within the de-regulated environment of British media production.

The theoretical perspective embraced by the present study may therefore be distinguished from both the 'dominant ideology' thesis (Abercrombie *et al.*, 1980) and other more relativist ontologies, including tendencies within post-structuralism and social constructionism (Edwards and Potter, 1992; Shotter, 1993; Harre, in Lopez and Potter, 2001). As a result of this observation, a number of issues require further exposition, including the attitude of contemporary theorists to the operational value of ideology as a concept, the realism/anti-realism debate, and the wider issue

---

33 Some aspects of context, for instance, may only be deciphered by referring to more 'visible' material.

of contested knowledge associated with the post-structuralist tendencies touched upon here.

These questions are addressed again below; in the meantime, one illustration of a competing position may suffice to illustrate how issues of method and perspective may relate. Post-structuralist critics like Connolly advocate 'deconstruction and genealogy' as the most useful modes of (in this case), political discourse analysis, on the grounds that they allow practitioners in the field to 'glimpse contingencies, remainders, resistances, and excesses in their own practices' (Connolly, 1993; vii/ix).

This approach depends upon the idea that all signs carry a 'trace' of other signs or signifying elements, producing not just the 'intertextuality' which features in this book, but an indeterminacy and what Derrida calls 'traces of traces' (Derrida, 1981a, 27). While recognising the value of analysis which is able to discover the evidence of contingent expression, in that such material may reveal competing or subordinate discourses (in much the same way that Macherey's 'act of knowing' depends on the articulation of a new discourse or the 'articulation of silence'[34]), a discursive realist perspective differs in one important respect; while assuming that the theory of traces within signs is legitimate, it argues that meaning cannot be endlessly deferred, following Dillon's assertion that 'interpretations compete in an arena of truth' (Dillon, 1995, 168). Thus the search for a 'trace' of meaning would be used to establish a record of evasions from truth, not to argue the impossibility of intra- or extra-referentiality of truth as a concept (*ibid.*, 74). At this point, the importance of text in contemporary theory must be brought into focus.

The pre-eminence of text

The study of text, in the sense of a 'meaningful cultural form' (Thompson, 1995, 37) which is subjected to analysis, has become the 'presiding unit of pedagogy and of academic criticism' (Brooker, 1999, 214). Various observations and arguments may be used to justify this statement, yet there is a sense in which such a development may be seen as inevitable. In the first place, the social organisation of 'advanced' societies depends upon the circulation of broad genres of text; this is a view of communication 'as a system of thought and power and as a mode of government' (Mattelart, 1991, x). Textual forms and sub-genres, in turn, come to represent the existence and power of institutions.

The daily appearance of newspapers, the scheduled broadcasting of drama series, and so forth, testify to the supposed permanence and predictability of the social order. Thus one reason for the proliferation of texts includes their appearance as commodified 'signs' within popular culture, attaining prominence, in the case of certain genres, through the power of industrial production (Abercrombie *et al.*, 1990; Moores, 1993). This should not be taken to mean that contemporary processes of

---

34 Macherey, 'A Theory of Literary Production', 1978, 6.

communication simply reproduce dominant ideas; if structural power is in place, then the circulation of different positions on various topics is tolerated and encouraged.

My argument is that the existence of established symbolic practices, rather than the force of particular interventions, ensures the continuation and relative stability of the system as a whole. Fiske, for example, describes 'the formal qualities of television programmes and their flow' but also emphasises the accessibility and polysemic nature of popular texts (Fiske, 1987, 16). So, although current arrangements for the mediated dissemination of knowledge and discourse are unequal and exclusive[35] (attested to in part by the way in which 'new' technologies are posited as solutions to problems within democracy), the various genres and forms of content[36] produced are meaningful in the first instance because they are *recognised*, accorded validity, and used by authors and audiences for a variety of purposes. This is partly what is meant by media use as 'social action' (Renckstorf *et al.*, 1996).

The position suggested here stands in contrast therefore to a purely 'ideological' view of textual production, in which language, as the most significant symbolic form, is presented as both the 'practical consciousness' of a society and 'inevitably a partial and false' understanding of the social world (Kress and Hodge, 1979, 6).

The present work argues that the importance of *media* texts lies not in their ability to reinforce the hierarchical divisions of a social system through hegemonic address (Tuchman, 1974; Hall *et al.*, 1980; Gitlin, 1979; Bennett, *et al.*, 1986), nor in their supposed role as a disguise for the real conditions of power, but with regard to two related functions. The first, as explained above, is their regular and thus expected appearance within a wider institutional and discursive framework. The second is the transformative capacity they represent; this refers to the way the media generate new forms of meaning based upon established sources.[37]

As Bruck observes, 'the media employ their own ... codes and conventions ... the discursive material they work with, however, is not their own' (Bruck in Wasko and Mosco, 1992, 142). Bruck, whose conclusions are based on a study of news, sees interaction between media, professional, and public domains as a process of 'active negotiation' (*ibid.*). Repeating this observation here is not intended to presage assertions about the resistive abilities of audiences, nor to create arguments about the existence of implied roles within such exchange.[38]

Rather, the point is to present two arguments. First, that it is precisely careful attention to social structure and public discourse (rather than adherence to models

---

35 This is a common observation in the work of a number of authors: see for example Schiller, 1996, 40; Price, 1998, 20; Mackay and O'Sullivan, 1999, 2.

36 For an extended discussion of form and content, see below.

37 The concept of transformation appears in Barker, 1989, 127, as the way in which structures (textual forms) mould individual items of content, and consequently generate particular meanings.

38 Theories of an 'implied' as against an 'actual' audience are treated within a realist mode of analysis not as 'fictive' but as 'imagined', because it is unwilling to concur with the view that implied audience 'exists only inside the symbolic world of the text' (Gill and Whedbee, in van Dijk, 1997, vol 1, 167).

which either presume or deny the existence of powerful media or communication effects[39]), which may help to establish some distance from the 'media-centric' trend in cultural and communication studies.[40] This is called to mind by Corner's observation that the media are too readily accorded considerable power (Corner, 1995, 4) and by Mattelart's warning, in which he cautions against an exclusive focus on 'the area of the mass media' (Mattelart, 1996, x). Within this position, media forms and institutions are not, therefore, credited with sole responsibility for the reproduction of power.

The second point is that the theory of 'predictability' outlined above, in which texts assume known generic forms, demonstrates how shared cultural understanding between source and recipient partially composes genre.[41] Though individual texts in the public domain do not achieve equal prominence, they are all subject in principle to scrutiny, and are examined by their audiences using a variety of popular (non-academic) paradigms, such as relative quality, truthfulness, interest, moral effect and so on (Alasuutari, 1992, 562; Hoijer, in Dickinson *et al.*, 1998, 162).

Texts and meaning: 'we've taken you to work in the morning'

The perspective advanced within this book is therefore that texts circulate meaning (see the Introduction), rather than simply posit world-views or 'mobilise or reinforce relations of control' (Deacon *et al.*, 1999, 149). It argues, furthermore, that they do so in the form of references, propositions and implicatures[42] *within a context* and that the ideas produced are open to active comparison with other communication events,[43] both past and present. This view, while it acknowledges the existence of established positions and inequalities of power, is alive to the appearance of fissures in apparently 'dominant' communication structures. It recognises therefore both relations of interdependence and forms of social control, and the way in which some messages seem to express both 'the logic of emancipation from all hindrances and prejudices' and 'the logic of constraint imposed by a social and productive order' (Mattelart, 1991, xvi).

This may be attributed in part to one of the central arguments of this book, that merely to make sense (leaving aside the question of effect) unidirectional messages must be created with the psychology of audiences and the conditions of reception in mind. In simple terms, the tension lies in the combination of directive form and attempts to compose persuasive content within established genres of address. This

---

39 For example, Osgood *et al.*, 1957, argue that 'we have communication wherever one system, a source, influences another, the destination, by manipulation of alternative symbols, which can be transmitted over the channel connecting them' (in McQuail, 1993, 4). Fiske in contrast states; 'Television programmes do not have an "effect" on people. Viewers and television interact' (1987, 19).

40 Note also the comments on agenda-setting, below.

41 See below for further discussion of this issue.

42 These aspects of meaning-production appear below as three categories for analysis.

43 van Dijk refers to discourses as 'communicative events'; van Dijk, 1998, 194.

point should be considered in conjunction with attention to broader structural issues, suggested in Mattelart's reference to 'a social and reproductive order' (above). Rather than reinforce what has come to be known as the 'dominant ideology thesis', in which a common culture 'functions to integrate the social system' (Abercrombie *et al.*, 1980), the preference here is for a model which admits the existence of an (albeit circumscribed) democratic process which sets limits to the production of political address, and the growth of corporate interventions which try to ease the entry of product-images into public consciousness through imitations of face to face exchange.

Therefore, it is the contention of the present work that certain commercial forms have assimilated the codes of 'public' communication. This is the process identified by Fairclough as the '*converstionalization* of ... public language' (Fairclough, 1995b, 9). Fairclough recognises the ambiguous nature of this development, on the one hand entailing the growth of 'a new public prestige for 'ordinary' values and practices' (*ibid.*, 11), and on the other suggesting 'a link between conversationalization and marketization' (*ibid.*, 12). Although Barker argues that the 'private sphere' of mediated communication and consumption may produce texts which 'in small ways embody resistances to the prevalent forms of public authority' (Barker, 1989, 132)[44] this applies to commercial texts and narratives, rather than political interventions (such as manifestos and election broadcasts. An important difference is that advertisements and television commercials, for example, occur 'as forms, not as overt arguments' (Barker, *ibid.*).

The differences and resemblances within and between 'private' and 'public' texts, together with other general points about argument, tactics and structure, may therefore be illustrated through a *contextual analysis* of two different types of material. The examples which appear below are taken from a television commercial and an election manifesto. At this stage, before analysis proceeds, the notion of context should be described.

At the most fundamental level, context refers to the conditions which 'provide structure for any act, statement or event' (Price, 1997, 55). It is often the case that the process of placing a text in its location is actually a matter of 'recontextualisation', because the text is no more than an excerpt used for purposes of close study, or because some element of its character has been masked. The first example given here is an extract from a longer text, and demonstrates the point just made:

'We've taken you to work in the morning
And we've taken your mother to church
We've taken you to the beach
And we've taken you home again'

Without the presence of other necessary elements, and greater knowledge of the structure of the act itself, this could qualify as one of any number of 'speech events'

---

44 Barker's study is based on an analysis of comics.

or written passages. It could even be, judged by the way it is set out here, a form
of blank verse. However, certain lexical items still generate meaning. Even without
knowing the source, the 'speaker', or the intended audience, it could be understood
as a series of references to shared understandings of various human activities;
references to work, to religious observance (connected to family), to leisure activities
and to home. These all establish human activity as the general frame of reference,
but provide no detail through which they might be evaluated.

The material does not constitute a narrative,[45] however, and appears more as a
catalogue of events (Branigan, 1992, 7); there is no necessary causality which can
be traced between the four declarations. They are all connected rather as 'outcomes'
of the same motive force which is indicated by the presence of the unknown 'we'.
The central proposition of the passage, on the other hand, can only be discovered
by following the whole sequence; it is simply that some force or power seems to be
responsible for the movement of the addressee between the locations specified. The
second part of the text confirms the genre to which it belongs:

> 'As Europe's biggest car retailers, Network Q help you go
> Wherever you want to go, whenever you want to go there
> Ah well, onwards and upwards
> Network Q, raising the standard in used car quality'

This addition suggests an inevitable re-assessment of the material set out above.
It demonstrates that Network Q as an organisation has not literally taken the person
or persons addressed to various places; in fact they represent one element in a process
of enablement. Yet the claim presented here represents a transfer of significance, in
that a commercial transaction (buying a used car) becomes an act of social solidarity
(supplying essential transport). It represents the enactment of public values. The
missing part of the advertisement provides more information about the production
of meaning:

> 'We've taken you to work in the morning
> [*lone red car seen from far above, passing over a junction devoid of other vehicles;
> various shots of a smiling man in a fishmonger's shop serving a middle-aged woman;
> clear blue light – slow pace*]
> and we've taken your mother to church
> [*car seen from above pulls up to a church amid rolling wheat-fields; man, woman, older
> woman enter gate against a blue sky; interior, baby with priest, couple and mother with
> another older child; mother crying with happiness*]
> we've taken you to the beach

---

45 A narrative is a 'presentation of a sequence of events from a particular point of view
or perspective' (Georgakopoulou and Goutsos, 1997, 44) or 'a way of organising spatial
and temporal data into a cause-effect chain of events with a beginning, middle, and end'
(Branigan, 1993, 3). Branigan emphasises causality whereas Georgakopoulou and Goutsos
merely indicate the presence of a sequence. Branigan's description is preferred in the present
work.

[car from bird's eye view on deserted road alongside empty beach: couple and two young boys on the beach: slow motion shot]

and we've taken you home again

[car seen from above on winding road, clear of traffic, set in green hills with a lake in the distance]

as Europe's biggest car retailers, Network Q help you go wherever you want to go, whenever you want to go there

[ferry crossing calm water with a single car on board]

ah well, onwards and upwards

Network Q, raising the standard in used car quality

[car again in mountainous landscape; anthem with Network Q flag across screen][46]

A form of visual implicature appears to be at work, reinforced through the combination of music, sound and image. Sound, so often neglected in the consideration of text (Price, 1998; van Leeuwen, 1999), creates an atmosphere suited to the oddly depopulated idyll which surrounds the family life depicted in this advertisement. Images are reinforced by the contextual explanations they are accorded. Intertextual reference, in turn, draws upon an established convention used in car advertising; the representation of clear roads set in beautiful countryside. The car is thus of itself a social benefit; its destructive effects on the environment to which it provides access, or its more commonly expected appearance in crowded cities, forms no part of the tale which unfolds in this example.

'Absence' and structuralism

The comment made at the end of the last paragraph resembles those theories which offer 'absence' as the key to discovering presence, following Macherey's assertion that 'the object is never given but progressively discovered' (Macherey, 1978, 5). Close adherence to a search for absence in texts, conceived as the non-appearance of an element which might be expected to appear in a certain place or position, is one of the hallmarks of structuralism.

In structuralist theory, patterns are created through the relationship of elements. While this is not denied within the present exposition, the elevation of 'absence' as the key to some kind of ideological subterfuge is rejected; instead, detailed awareness of elements which do appear are taken to indicate other attendant ideas. The range of implicit meanings can only be identified by referring to those understandings and experiences called to mind by the situation represented. This explains my preference for a theory of implicature over that of absence. The material 'points away' from itself to other experiences, against which it will inevitably be compared. It represents a model of social relationships, particularly between an 'enabling' authority and a resolutely conformist addressee, pictured in the commercial itself and supposedly reflected in an 'overhearing' audience.

---

46 Transcript made by the present writer.

A further reason for emphasising the importance of social context, rather than paying attention to the arrangement of internal elements alone, may now become more obvious; it allows a more empirically grounded approach to develop, which attempts to bring into focus the moral, intellectual and economic conditions under which these kind of propositions about social use are made. There are certain differences between the advertisement cited above, for example, and ones centred entirely upon a clearly identifiable product; in this case, the model of the car is never revealed, as it is not the function of the used car company to concern itself with particular types of vehicle, but rather with the general principle of their availability. This has other consequences in the field of representation, or perhaps happily coincides with the other aim of the narrative, which is to show access to places which, taken together, constitute a realm of freedom; the car is always seen from a great height or distance.

At one level, the text represents a single narrative, yet its intertextual range extends far beyond the genre within which it is delivered. Such material (idyllic social settings centred on community, nuclear families, heterosexual relationships and fulfilling work) manifests itself in other guises; for example, the whole visual and aural repertoire of this example bears a strong resemblance to the Conservative party's PEB of 1992, 'Did the Sun set on Britain?',[47] and to the Abbey National's 1995 production 'Changing Tides', which represents a fishing community in peril.

These texts use the same lush or rugged countryside, close family relationships and calming musical interludes; most significantly from the viewpoint of the present work, all three examples use a benevolent authority which offers solutions to broader social problems. Thus all three genres (advertisement, election broadcast, and corporate video) compose a similar picture of reality, producing a coherent 'social' narrative (the term this book uses as its central description of discourse as it appears in textual form).

Political discourse: 'we want to set people free'

In the extract from an election manifesto[48] (see below), a conscious attempt is made to position its audience, by manufacturing references which if recognised, are supposed to lead to an acceptance of the propositions offered. Once again, a benevolent authority addresses a subordinate group, in this case the electorate:

'We present here the most ambitious Conservative programme for a generation.

Its aim is to release the wisdom, decency and enterprise of British citizens. We can achieve that by handing back to individuals and their families the ability to shape their own lives and communities.

---

47 A partial transcript, and an analysis of this political broadcast appears in Chapter 6.
48 The Conservative Party manifesto of 2001; 'Time for Common Sense'.

We will free entrepreneurs to build businesses and to create prosperity, free those who use public services to choose what is best for them and free those who work in our schools and hospitals and police service from endless political interference.

We want to set people free so that they have greater power over their own lives'.

A number of observations can be made. In the first place, there is the use of the rhetorical technique known as the 'inclusive we'. This represents in the first instance the Conservative party, but may at any time change its range of inclusion to encompass more broader groups, from 'we' as a political organisation, to 'we' as a nation, transferring the supposed values of one entity to another. Concepts such as 'freedom' play a pivotal role in the construction of political address. Yet its referential power conflates, for example, the 'economic' freedom of the business man or woman (which is assumed to 'create prosperity') with other types of power over the everyday experiences of work and community.[49]

The advantages and disadvantages of employing 'ideological' as opposed to more broadly discursive approaches, can be summarised briefly, even from the material examined so far. Ideology provides a means of describing the connection between structures of various kinds, and the production of meaning; in its traditional manifestation as a controlling hegemonic power, ideology suggests at the very least the composition and delivery of a powerful 'external' address.

The work of Althusser, in particular his theory of interpellation, links the utterance of authoritarian address with an instantaneous recognition. Although this may seem overly deterministic, Althusser draws attention to the subjectivity of the oppressed. From this, it may be possible to imagine a system of messages which does more than merely bring the individual to order, but makes in addition a more persuasive attempt to present a case. This may therefore provide a model of inter-discursivity based on shared recognition of the power of certain terms within contemporary social systems. In sum, this initial explanation for the ubiquitous presence of texts, describes their existence as a product of modernity (see Chapter 3) and as a condition of and pre-requisite for social cohesion;[50] such cohesion is understood, however, as the production of 'interpretable' common knowledge,[51] rather than unitary belief.

This attention to shared understanding is imagined within the present work in a particular way; as that set of common perceptions circulated between various authors or 'issue proponents', between authors and 'receivers', and between different segments or rather configurations of audience. This does not imply the abandonment of a basic principle in media and cultural analysis; the attachment to the question

---

49 For a comparison with another Conservative party text, Chapter 6 on elections and discourse.

50 This does not exclude the notion that the social order itself is organised within a system of unequal class relations; see for example Poulantzas, 1974; Laclau, 1977.

51 References to this and related notions appear in Morley, 1992, 97; Bosman and Renckstorf, in Renckstorf *et al.*, 1996, 44; and throughout the volume produced by Gripsrud, 1999.

'what in this case is being said or enacted?', and in conjunction 'what values are being presented?' At the same time it has become particularly important to recognise that any study concerned with a search for value and meaning must face attacks from quarters which have emphasised the 'intractable contingency of experience' (Coles, in Simons and Billig, 1994, 38) and which have, moreover, shown marked hostility to realist principles in general (Lyotard, in Brooker, 1992, 150).

Relativism, realism and the 'linguistic' turn

It seems that broadly relativist positions (and in the case of discourse analysis, social constructionism) have become easier to compose since discourse itself came to be accorded socially constitutive powers; for example, Parker insists that 'a good working definition of discourse' is that it is 'a system of statements which constructs an object' (Parker, 1992, 5). Yet whatever the origins of this tendency, the current situation is one in which academic enquiry has been re-cast within a number of competing paradigms. Instead of the pursuit of 'certainties' or at least demonstrable proofs (in knowledge, reference and conduct), a generally more 'localised' or provisional activity has been proposed, one in which normative goals and realist perspectives are replaced by more modest, relativist models of enquiry. Such perspectives seem nonetheless to require some referential boundaries in order to make their arguments tenable.

In the case of social constructionist critiques, the field of analysis is sometimes based on adherence to the values and activities of 'community' (Shotter, 1993, 11), as an alternative to dependence upon reference to a world of 'things and substances' (*ibid.*). This principle avoids crude empiricism but seeks to establish referential boundaries by indicating the existence of consistent human practices (Price, 1996, 57); it also carries with it certain implications for the conduct of textual analysis. If social constructionism really appears to prefer 'the local effectiveness of particular kinds of argument' (Coles, *op. cit.*), then such a perspective would be impossible to use as an instrument to secure more general conclusions about reference or meaning.

The nomination of collective human practices as one reference point against which the validity of social enquiry can be measured, has thus appeared in works of constructionist psychology exemplified by Shotter (see above) and Edwards and Potter, who draw attention to the importance of 'the contexts of everyday life' (1992, 21). Within enquiries into mediated communication, interest in group behaviours is reflected in numerous studies,[52] in most cases concentrating upon 'receivers' or audiences. Attention to professional collectives is less common, but is considered in Scollon's work on news practices, which combines media studies with the post-modern search for alternative standards of academic conduct, outlined above.

---

52 See for example Lazarsfeld, Berelson and Gaudet, 1948; Hovland, *et al* 1949; Klapper, 1955; Blumer and McQuail, 1969; Ang, 1985, 1996; Liebes and Katz, 1993; Alasuutari, 1995.

While the present enquiry would certainly accept the existence of 'communities of practice', professional groups which create media texts with the approbation of other proponents in mind (Scollon, 1998), it regards the further elevation of such intra-group conduct to the status of a primary frame of analysis as a serious mistake.

Scollon's belief that the 'public discourse of news journalism' can be seen as 'primarily a discourse of and among journalists', with the public as witnesses to events staged only partly for their behalf (Scollon, 1998, 216), is reasonable only if one first accepts the general notion that journalists as a group are really primarily interested in the judgement of a closed circle composed of their own colleagues and associates. It would certainly be to use this observation as a guiding principle for the study of textual meaning or audience response. Even if the first condition were to be fulfilled, there is a sense in which the production of texts with 'publication' in mind, in other words as intentional interventions in the public domain, renders the supposed professional consensus which Scollon constructs irrelevant, becuause the texts are evaluated within a larger realm than the professional. In the case of news and other related material, the public nature of reception suggests that in-group behaviours will not be perceived as the most important aspect of individual texts, but rather as a visible part of the working mechanics of media presentation. It may be the case that audiences or readers are interested in the relationships between individual media professionals (especially in view of the use of reflexive frameworks within news and documentary programming, the rise of 'celebrity' newscasters and the growth of 'youth' programming[53]) but they are more concerned with the ways in which the regular appearance of generic material is presented for their benefit, gratification or use, however such activities are theorised (Barker, 1989, 244; Hietbrink in Renckstorf *et al.*, 1996, 126).

The task of academic analysis is not, according to the perspective of the present work, to take issue proponents at their word, nor to treat their practices as sacrosanct. Above all it advocates the principle that academics must avoid imagining that particular relationships between authors can provide secure frameworks for the interrogation of meaning. Scollon's call to prioritise channel and participant above topic not only marks a departure from the thrust of critical discourse analysis (despite the sympathy for increased attention to 'routine' categories like channel which this view displays[54]), it produces as a result distinctly muted observations about politically virulent tendencies like the 'privatisation' of public discourse (Fairclough, 1995a; Cameron, 2000). The 'colonization' of medical discourse observed by Musson and Cohen (2000) and other realms of public life,[55] becomes in Scollon's terms the rather

---

53 For the latter, see Lury, 2001.

54 Scollon's belief in attending to relationships as they are expressed in texts is also relatively 'progressive', in tune with the work of theorists like Nofsinger who call upon academics to consider what roles, identities, and relationships are revealed by speech-based actions (Nofsinger, 1991).

55 A tendency observed in education and other spheres; Fairclough,1995b; Cameron, 2000.

oddly dispassionate 'significant interdiscursivity between enterprise and medicine' (Scollon, 1998, 253). Here, the constitution of power relations becomes no more than mutual exchange.

The issue which introduced this chapter, the salience of text, may also be related to the 'turn to language' as a particular feature of academic enquiry. Within many disciplines, including audience studies and ethnography,[56] a preoccupation with written or spoken 'evidence' may be described as a movement away from other more traditional modes of analysis.[57] This 'new' development is sometimes associated with the linguistic concerns inherent within structuralism but, in its social constructionist mode, is chiefly characteristic of post-structuralist thought (Deacon *et al.*, 1999, 147). The advantages and drawbacks of this tendency, may not relate immediately to the overall importance of text as a social and cultural phenomenon, but the crux of the matter may be summarised in brief; it turns on whether such interest demonstrates a retreat from essential matters of academic responsibility (Simons and Billig, 1994, 17; Mosco, 1996) or whether in contrast it offers a theory of language sufficiently 'realist'[58] to make it a useful tool for the conduct of a more concrete social theory. In the meantime, a closely related development has been the movement of the concepts discourse and text to the centre of many academic disciplines. Mills, for example, refers to the 'common currency of the term "discourse"' (Mills, 1997, 2), thus anticipating the possibilities of a mode of analysis shared by various fields of enquiry.

Yet it is the concomitant extension within these disciplines of what *qualifies* as a text, which has ensured the increased circulation of the concept itself. It should become clear therefore, that texts proliferate partly because various forms of public communication are allowed to 'assume' the status of the textual,[59] as in the case of 'talk' and its subsequent formal analysis (Scannell, 1991). Thus it is possible to identify a significant expansion from text as a traditional literary form, to encompass 'any system of signs which can be "read"' (Branston and Stafford, 1999, 450) or indeed 'any product of authorship (single or multiple) embodied in a recognisable structure ... and which is the site of cultural interpretation' (Price, 1997, 228).

Branston and Stafford's use of inverted commas around 'read' (above) indicates these authors' unwillingness to be drawn into the older conception of text as the fixed accomplishment of literary production; yet the increased use of such general

---

56 See for example Alasutaari's description of his ethnographic practice; 'the focus shifted to the distinctions that people made in their speech as well as to the broader systems of distinction that provided the general structure and organisation of their everyday life' (1995, 163).

57 At another level it should be noted that, particularly in the case of linguistic forms, their suitability for academic analysis is based on their comparative inexpensiveness; they remain 'economically viable' as objects of study and enquiry.

58 'Realist' here is a broad reference to a position which emphasises the performative quality of language, in conjunction with an attachment to so that language is both 'socially shaped and socially constitutive' (Fairclough, 1995, MD, 55).

59 They may even perhaps eventually attain the next stage, the *canonical*.

description is also a recognition that texts have become 'multi-semiotic' (Fairclough, 1995b). This concept is not identical to Barthes's notion of the availability of 'polysemic' meanings, but indicates rather that texts contain a variety of 'signs', including everything from linguistic content, visual design, and illustration to the 'spatialised ideas' presented in web-sites[60] (Barnet, 2000). Individual 'genres' of text thus seem automatically to extend an already flexible criteria of definition, setting and then fulfilling as it were, their own terms for inclusion in an ever expanding category.

In parallel with the processes described above (both scholarly and more broadly social), the need to search for 'raw material' in academic study, ensures the production and maintenance of categories to which texts may be allocated for analysis. Yet despite the exalted position which the concept 'text' has supposedly achieved (the assertion made by Brooker at the start of this chapter), the precise way in which an act of communication *becomes* 'textual' is the subject of disagreement. The comments made above suggested that academic activity itself works to produce, if not texts themselves, then certainly a process of 'recognition', acts of categorisation which allow disparate material to become the legitimate object of study. In suggesting answers to the question of textual genesis, attention should be drawn to descriptions of text as an individuated product or category, which has so far received less attention here than the various reasons for its prominence.

Text, purpose, and genre

Closer study of the origin of the concept text, therefore, provides useful information about its character; the Latin root of the term is 'textere', which means 'to weave' (McArthur, 1996, 951; Green and LeBihan, 1996, 8). This suggests a coherent product, the expression of a creative impulse given a material form. Yet the very recognition of a discernible pattern depends partly on the existence of established, pre-structured generic forms, such as newspaper articles, speeches, advertisements and so on. Within the period of their consumption, individual texts cannot be recognised as such without the appearance of enough of the requisite elements currently accepted as characteristic of particular genres. Texts which fall within their scope or which share enough 'family resemblances' (Wittgenstein, in Price, 1996, 183), are thus recognised as characteristic of the larger category or genre of media event. The issue of recognition demonstrates another aspect of genre; this is its character as 'systems of orientation, expectations and conventions' (Neale, 1980, 19). Following the first of these observations, it might seem that all symbolic components must be subsumed under the generic conditions of their expression; in other words that the presentation of symbolic content is subjected to the discipline of the form in which it appears. Such a position would, however, fail to account for the generation of 'hybrid' forms; in essence it could not explain how form and content interact. As Neale observes,

---

60 See the work on corporate power and new media forms, below.

a conception of texts as 'products' rather than processes makes form and content appear as a dichotomy, rather than operating in a more productive dialectical relation (*ibid.*, 13). In more advanced theories, the form which content 'assumes' becomes inseparable from the whole ensemble's *presentation* of meaning; this may help to explain why, for example, tabloid stories are habitually received as examples of 'sensation'[61] over and above their particular message or stance.

Whereas Fairclough at one point argues that 'meanings are necessarily realized in forms' and 'differences in meaning entail differences in form' (Fairclough, 1995b, 57), the missing part of the equation here is necessarily content. In another volume of theory, Fairclough notes instead that if content is to 'enter the realm of practice, it must do so in formal clothing' (Fairclough, 1995a, 74). It is possible to argue then, that the parameters of form are re-configured by content, just as content is shaped by form, so that texts as types of expression must assume or become the technical means of their own accomplishment. The next point to make is that texts are produced both routinely and intentionally; that is, by the conjunction of both convention and intention, producing a configuration of elements which owes its existence to both general established practices, and particular goals.

The constitution of text, imagined as a product of this process, may have helped to sustain theories which emphasise the structuring effect of 'dominant discourses', discourses which work towards the 'closure' or limitation of meaning (Fiske, 1987, 94).

Linked to this view of structural determination, is the assumption that 'hidden' processes work to create a set of 'implicit themes' (Billig, 1988, in Parker, 1992, 5) which may in turn reproduce a set of unconscious 'ideologies' or beliefs. Fairclough also pursues this line, calling for analysis of 'implicit content' and linking this with notions of 'common sense' and the realm of the ideological (Fairclough, 1995a, 74). Common sense appears here as the bugbear of those theorists who see it, after comments made by Gramsci, as a barrier to clear or even more exalted 'scientific' thinking (Price, 1997, 51).[62]

As an illustration of this point, Deacon *et al.* take the view that 'people are not usually conscious of the assumptions and conventions on which they draw in their linguistic interactions' (Deacon, *et al.*, 1999, 149). Cooke, citing the example of film, discerns the existence of 'less evident, even invisible' ideologies which, owing to the use of subterfuge (their 'natural' appearance within narrative), are able to reinforce unequal relations 'without the subordinate groups recognising the degree of their subordination' (Cooke, in x 1996, 298). Hayward, also within a discussion of mainstream cinema, argues that 'whatever form the closure takes, almost without exception it will offer ... a message that is central to dominant ideology: the law

---

61 See for example the objections of Williams, 1997, to the tendencies of the popular press.

62 For a fuller discussion of 'common sense' and its place in theory, see this chapter under 'the power of speech'.

successfully apprehending criminals, good gunmen of the Wild West routing the baddies, and so on' (Hayward, 1996).

This approach to the reproduction of belief, in which ideology is conveyed both through what Cooke calls 'overt propaganda' (*op. cit.*) and through 'innocent' modes of entertainment, and in which social actors are presented as unaware of the sources of their own perspectives, is not supported by the argument advanced in this book. Although the present work presents intention as an important factor in the production of meaning and subjectivity, it is nonetheless alive to the proposition that directive address does not always achieve unalloyed success, as Buxton so ably argues when he remarks that 'no ideological project, regardless of political tendency, is sufficiently coherent to survive the ordeal of figuration totally intact' (Buxton, 1990, 18).

Forms and contents

The current work attempts however to demonstrate how forms and contents work in the construction of objective positions, without assuming that such positions will be achieved. So for example, a political slogan requires a symbolic form commensurate with its purpose as a language-based intervention in the public realm; one would expect therefore a spoken, written or electronic appearance of intent. Political utterances like 'tough on crime, tough on the causes of crime',[63] are thus intentional in the sense that they *make a show* of representing policy (action may not necessarily follow such declared intent).

They may also be regarded as intentional because they are composed in the expectation of their re-appearance in parallel forms of discussion and documentation, feeding also into the production of new texts, the contexts of which will no longer necessarily remain under the control of the original authors. Particular references or propositions are not, therefore, fixed within specific boundaries, so that material delivered in a speech can become an election broadcast, or indeed may appear within a newspaper commentary.

This demonstrates the movement of ideas between related forms, which implies the existence of two subsequent notions. First, that purposive address works not through disguise but through intertextual reference, suggesting in turn that it picks up other ideas in the process of exposition (and thus that it cannot achieve a 'pure' representation of some unitary belief). Second, the recognition of such movement between texts implies in turn that there are boundaries between genres which, while difficult to describe, are nonetheless recognised by audiences. Where genres are understood as 'discourse types', there is still the sense that, as demonstrated above, their boundaries are set by 'norms, conventions, rules of use, schemata and ... expectations' (Georgakopoulou and Goutsos, 1997, 33). These elements may be described as agents which contribute to the production of form.

---

63 New Labour election slogan, 1997, based on Blair's dictum as Shadow Home Secretary; see Fairclough, 2000, 8; Toynbee and Walker, 2001, 153.

Thus a more developed perspective, to which the present study is sympathetic, suggests that a text 'is primarily defined by its possession of an identifiable purpose' (Trask, *op. cit.*), but not that this purpose remains uninfected by other currents of thought or other objectives. It is certainly possible, however, to observe a development from text as 'the main body of a printed or written work' (Collins dictionary, 1987) to a more complex product based upon purpose and socio-cultural value. One insight into this process is the idea that a text is essentially 'the topic or subject of a discussion or work' (*ibid.*), reminiscent of the declaration 'I take as my *text*' made by a minister of religion; this refers not merely to form or location, but to the point or the moral of the work. The moral, or alternatively functional aim or intention, can therefore be described as the purpose of the text. Textual meaning is clearly based therefore on *significant* content; the problem of deciding what exactly is of importance, especially when certain authors declare that 'there is no analytic method' (Potter and Wetherell, 1987, 169), is a question which can only be answered by proposing consistent methods of analysis.[64]

Indeed, the conviction that some parts of content are more important than others, explored by Brown and Yule (1983, 107), may be attributed to speaker or authorial intention, despite Gumperz's observation that interpretations of intent are 'unstable' and much less amenable to study than referential meaning (Gumperz, 1982, 32). However, it is exactly through the study of reference and the associated categories detailed below, and their articulation within an extensive model of context, that intention may be discovered. This involves asking fairly obvious questions, such as 'why was this said', and 'why were such words used?' (Parker, 1992, 4).

In addition, it is useful to know the location of the actors and the event itself, in both physical, temporal and moral terms; that is why election material makes a useful study, because the overall structure and purpose is known. *Directive text* may thus be seen as *a performance* or dramatisation of goals *for an audience within a context*. Following this insight, text may be described in Barthes' terms as 'a process of demonstration', which is produced in accordance with, or in reaction against, a set of rules (Barthes, 1977, 157) or, as it might be understood within recent studies of discourse, a temporary conjunction which is achieved through a dramatised relationship between competing positions,[65] or what Howarth calls the production of meaning within 'particular systems of significant differences' (Howarth, 2000, 101). Text is therefore a product of discursive or procedural rules, and could be portrayed in Luthar's words as both 'a piece of objectified culture' and in turn 'a producer of specific identities'[66] (Luthar in Drummond, 1993, 44).

---

64 See for example Parker's 'seven criteria' (Parker, 1992, 6) and the proposed frames of analysis which appear below.

65 Rhetoric, in particular, dramatises positions and beliefs; see the chapter on elections and discourse and van Dijk, 1998.

66 Luthar recognises that texts can be composed from many divergent sources, especially the popular; for example, she argues that 'we can all remember several canonical texts in our own national literary tradition, as well as films, serials and hit songs which act as mnemonics to a stock of knowledge' (Luthar, in Drummond, 1993, 44).

The individual text is thus seen as more than an account of one particular position or 'world-view', to be accepted or rejected in the course of the communication process; it attains the status of a social relationship made, in Bernstein's terms, 'visible, palpable', so that it should be possible to 'recover the original specialised institutional practice' through the use of analysis (Bernstein, in Chouliaraki and Fairclough, 1999, 118).

The circulation of texts as cultural artefacts, often but not exclusively in narrative form, may therefore be seen both as evidence of existing social relations, and as opportunities for reflexive identification (Murray, in Shotter and Gergen, 1989, 177), even if the prospect of a 'recovery' of an original practice or meaning, as suggested above by Bernstein, is a little optimistic. Nonetheless, texts are clearly repositories of value, in the sense of recognised and shared cultural worth. The notion of value, in turn, has led some commentators to the conclusion that it is possible to describe a 'textual economy', based on Marx's conception of a capitalist system which produces abstract standards of economic value (Shankar, 2001). Such a conception imagines a social system in which texts assume the behaviour of commodities, moving from potential use value, through exchange to actual use and thus finally the realisation of their original potential; in Marx's terms, this is the point at which goods drop out of the sphere of exchange and enter that of consumption.

Text, discourse and power

Within linguistics and cultural theory, text bears a relationship to consumption and 'commodified' meaning, but its primary frame of reference is to discourse *per se*. This connection is not, however, always fully theorised. Some commentators do not even distinguish between the two, while to others text is merely the product of discourse (Trask, 1999, 312). Fairclough also recognises text as a product, but confirms the common perception that discourse must remain a larger concept, representing a whole process of interaction, including meaning-creation and interpretation (Fairclough, 1989, 24). In this case, text 'carries' or represents aspects of discourse, but cannot encompass all its elements; yet it should be noted that individual texts not only reveal aspects of discursive practice, but re-compose their elements in new formations.[67] Stubbs notes that a distinction is often made between interactivity (discourse) and monologue (text), followed by the observation that a discourse is often delivered at greater length (Stubbs, 1983, 9). This, however, does not advance the issue, creating instead rather arbitrary barriers between concepts; for example, the practice of distinguishing between 'dialogic' and 'monologic' texts,[68] inherited from Bakhtin,[69] makes it difficult to construct more narrow characterisations of text. Kress and van Leeuwen produce more useful insights into the nature of the relationship, beginning

---

67 Implying, in turn, the production of new individuated discourses; see Bruck, 1992 above, and see below.

68 Whatever the flaws in the categorisation of these genres.

69 See Vice, 1997, Chapter 2; also Brandist, *et al*, 2004.

with the interpretation of discourse itself. To these authors, all texts, of whatever nature, are sites where discourses occur; by the same token, discourses appear in many different forms but must have an existence which is separate from 'their mode of realisation' (Kress and van Leeuwen, 2001, 24). Jaworski and Coupland seem to concur with this important view, when they state that 'discourses are sometimes held to be abstract value systems which will never surface directly as texts' (Jaworski and Coupland, 1999, 7).

Howarth, in turn, examining the concept of 'discursive fields', notes that they are characterised by a 'surplus of meaning' which can never be fully represented by 'any specific discourse' (Howarth, 2000, 102), while Parker believes that discourses as such are never found, only 'pieces of discourse' (Parker, 1992, 6). Although these writers do not specify how discourses assume such large dimensions, or how they maintain an independent existence, the essential point is the difference between actually existing texts and a domain of ideas, concepts and references which is both brought to light by textual expression and which remains a resource for its production. This book proposes therefore the notion that an extra-textual field may be understood to be *a necessary act of idealisation* or *typification*, in the same way as an analyst of a distinct ideology, like political conservatism for example, could represent or list its essential qualities, typical practices, and attendant beliefs, without necessarily being able to account for all possible textual permutations, and without being able to anticipate all future developments (the appearance of new, related representations of belief).

Such a process would acknowledge that discourse, as an abstract universal, must represent the sum total of all that is expressible and capable of being understood. A 'global' concept of this nature would depend in essence on the extrapolation of possible meanings from discursive practices, and equally the representation of underlying attitudes from textual evidence. In this sense, the purpose of analysis is two-fold; to detail the particular referential and propositional qualities of texts as 'outward manifestations of communication events' (Bell and Garrett, 1998, 3), as these are expressed in the context of their utterance, and to identify the systems of thought from which such expressions might emerge, and with which they might engage. None of this can be applied to the actual analysis of text unless there is an understanding of the multiple meanings which attach to the term discourse itself; therefore, it is important to return to the definition of the concept.

Definitions of discourse

Discourse, at its most basic level, refers to verbal expression and thus, as a study, suggests the evaluation of speech and 'ordinary' modes of conversation.[70] In all descriptions, it seems to be recognised that discourse cannot be constituted by a single utterance alone. It is formed rather by talk, exchange, conversation in general

---

70 Together with its supporting modes of inflection such as intonation.

(Mills, 1997, 2) or a particular instance of such interaction; yet within discourse analysis, the object of study may also be 'unidirectional', such as for example a source like a newspaper report (van Dijk, 1997, 4). Nonetheless, the principle of exchange is impossible to eradicate from even the most 'monologic' product;[71] as Stubbs notes, 'discourse often implies interactive discourse' (Stubbs, 1983, 9). Where interaction does not take place, there is nonetheless the assumption that, to a greater or lesser degree, some form of wider cultural exchange is taking place.[72] If this principle holds true, then distinctions between 'readerly' and 'writerly' texts become irrelevant (Barthes, 1977; Fiske, 1987, 94), as all texts must simulate some type of interaction. Discourse appears *within* certain forms, whether as a presentation or conversation, but in the case of the directive or persuasive material studied in this book, always contains a dialogic principle.

Within this field, the basic assumption must be that everyday exchange is particularly significant, in the sense that it enables social actors to achieve specific tasks. Stubbs asserts that discourse analysis is important because it is founded on the realisation that 'language, action and knowledge' are inseparable (*ibid*, 1). If this is the case, an urgent question must be the issue of power. This is not however always addressed in relation to speech or conversation (the basic configuration in which discourse appears), with the consequence that the problem is deferred until institutional or more broadly social matters are brought into focus. When the study of power is confined to its operation at a supposedly more complex level, important insights into the mechanics of influence and authority, demonstrated within everyday interaction, may be lost.

Even reasonable assessments of media power tend to over-emphasise its appearance as a social and cultural force; Livingstone, for example, argues that 'the modern mass media possess a hitherto unheard-of power to encode, preserve, manipulate, reproduce and circulate symbolic representations of knowledge' (Livingstone, in Gripsrud, 1999, 91).

While there is some truth in this judgement, the unfortunate consequence may be to neglect other forms of communication in which relations of power are evident. As Deacon and his co-authors realise, 'relations and structures of power are embedded in the forms of everyday language use' (Deacon, *et al*, 150). In addition, all forms of public communication, as argued above, are necessarily based upon an interactive model, both in the sense of providing shared 'cultural references', and in the habitual use of techniques learned from face to face exchange.[73]

The essence of the question here is that conversation represents an act of communication for a purpose, and as such constitutes the pursuit of particular goals, however ordinary or limited in scale such aims may seem in comparison to mediated events. This attribute of personal interaction is noted by writers like Nofsinger,

---

71 See the Introduction.

72 See Barker on Volosinov and 'talk' as essentially 'dialogue' (Barker, 1989, 263).

73 Stubbs notes that 'communication is impossible without shared knowledge and assumptions between speakers and hearers' (1983, 1).

who observes that conversation is 'a rational activity having a strategic dimension' (Nofsinger, 1991, 6/7). Wrong takes another step towards a more balanced assessment of power in these situations, when he argues that 'people exercise mutual influence and control over one another's conduct in all social interactions; in fact, that is what we mean by social interaction' (Wrong, 1979, 62).

The usefulness of this observation to the present enquiry lies in its location of power in apparently ordinary, uninflected exchange; the principle must therefore be that power exists within interaction in all its guises, rather than being confined to a more specialised use of discourse alone, in for example what Fairclough calls 'unequal encounters' (Fairclough, 1989, 44). From these comments it is possible to discern an important feature of ordinary exchange; that it is not wholly 'innocent', and need not be constructed as an opposite pole to a media characterised as entirely 'strategic' in its acts of communication. Such a reassessment can lead to a more precise delineation of the concept of power itself, and thus may offer an important perspective on the meaning and operation of discourse. To demonstrate this point, it is possible to recall (if discourse remains confined for the moment to its simpler forms of utterance or exchange), the well-known phrase 'the power of speech'.

The power of speech: 'do you see those colours?'

The power of speech means the possession of a general faculty, or a physical capacity which can be used to produce sounds which can be interpreted as meaningful utterances. The power of speech may also refer to an individual ability to 'perform'. In both cases, this suggests that the power of this elementary type of discourse depends first on *capacity*, but also that there is a relationship between what Chomsky called 'competence' and 'performance' (in Coulthard, 1985, 2). The second part of the process (performance) more closely concerns the question of power as *use*, in this case the deployment of linguistic resources for specific purposes. Therefore, while competence is regarded as the larger 'abstract' background resource, or the underlying knowledge of the 'ideal speaker-hearer' (Coulthard, *ibid*), performance remains the domain of individual production. In fact however, the first quality can only be revealed through a study of the second, just as text reveals the attributes of discourse (see above). Speech or utterance may now be characterised as a product of two elements; composed by 'power to' (as in potential) and 'power over' (as in effect).[74] This characteristic is expressed as the 'performative' function of speech, in which an utterance embodies an action (Austin, 1962), a class which includes acts like 'promising, denying, and ordering' (Stubbs, 1983, 152). Amongst established examples of this phenomenon are 'I name this ship' and 'I give and bequeath this watch to my brother' (Coulthard, 1985, 13).

However, other conditions are required to make such remarks effective. Knowledge of the existing conventions or contexts which govern the use of such

---

74 See Price, 1996, 228, for an account of power.

utterances is essential (for the speaker as for the analyst). In addition, this knowledge can only be employed by an appropriate individual, i.e., one who has the recognised authority to make the performative utterance effective. As Coulthard notes (*ibid*, 14), it is impossible to enact a divorce by declaring 'I divorce you', and equally marriage cannot be secured by saying 'I marry you'; such outcomes can only be secured by the exercise of recognised authority within an established context. Discourse as speech has the potential therefore, under the correct circumstances, to achieve an illocutionary force, to create an effective act performed in an utterance. Ultimately, however, it is difficult to identify linguistic features which 'unambiguously distinguish' performative from non-performative utterances (*ibid*, 15); that is to say, all language use is in some sense an attempt at the performative, geared to the achievement of particular aims.

In addition, as seen above, discourse is not confined to the 'linguistic' alone, or put another way, linguistic considerations are themselves actively connected with and productive of social actions and relations. The realisation, however, that effective speech can only be attained under certain conditions, may also be used to extend the definition of power employed in the instance of 'simple' discourse as it is described above. The reference here is to the partial dependence of successful performance on the exercise of recognised authority, which is an important issue within the concerns of this book. For example, it would not be possible in normal circumstances to persuade or compel individuals to risk their lives in pursuit of particular goals. In the right context, however, where a speaker is known to have the moral or formal authority to utter instructions, such extreme appeals can be acted upon. In looking more closely at power in use, it may be possible to glean more information about the character of discourse.

The example here is an historical one, taken from an account of an event which took place during the American Civil War. On the second day of the battle of Gettysburg (fought between the first and third of July, 1863), the Northern army was attacked as it occupied a defensive position on the outskirts of the town. During the battle, Union General Hancock saw the approach of Wilcox's Confederate division, some 1,200 strong, which threatened to break through a gap in the Federal position (McPherson, 1988, 660). He approached a small, under-strength regiment that stood in line of battle and spoke to the commanding officer. A contemporary account reproduces the following exchange:

Hancock:	What regiment is this?
Colvill:	The 1st Minnesota.
Hancock:	Colonel, do you see those colours? (*indicating the enemy flags*)
Colvill	(*nodding to indicate that he did*)
Hancock:	Then take them.

Lieutenant William Lochren, writing a description of the incident in a letter, recalled 'every man realized in an instant what that order meant; death or wounds to us all, the sacrifice of the regiment to gain a few minutes' time and save the position'. Two hundred and sixty-two men charged forward, and only forty-seven only remained fit for combat at the end. The attack succeeded in allowing Hancock to close his defences (McPherson, *ibid*). Although the linguist Firth said that language is 'a way of behaving and making others behave' (1951, in Coulthard, 1985, 1), the successful use of speech and writing must depend upon the fulfilment of specific conditions, and the character of discourse must be understood as both a matter of 'compulsion' and 'agreement'. The Union soldiers mentioned above were part of an army which had been, in its early years, notoriously difficult to discipline (made up as it was of many volunteers), but by this stage in the conflict between North and South, had acquired a shared perception of the cause for which it fought; combatants did not merely obey orders from what is sometimes called 'blind obedience'. Hindess distinguished between power as 'a kind of generalised capacity to act' and as 'a right to act' (Hindess, 1); in the case cited above, Hancock's authority was founded on the recognition of the 'right to act'. Hancock uses key terms to suggest an order which is actually not made directly. Thus a form of implicature is employed, which reveals an attitude or position shared by Hancock's subordinates and brought into effect through an established hierarchy.

Chapter 2

Discourse and Ideology

Ideology, 'common-sense' and discourse

Suspicion of authoritarian address is common amongst critical analysts, but similar misgivings seem to exist concerning everyday speech and exchange. Deacon and his associates, for example, seem to represent this position, when they argue that the analyst must 'stand back and investigate ... the common-sense basis of the ways we communicate with each other and the ways the media communicate with their audiences' (Deacon, *et al*, 1999, 150). These two examples, the interpersonal and the mediated, are run together to suggest that some form of general 'hegemony' is at work, applying both to interpersonal and mediated discourse.

Fairclough is another writer who attacks what he sees as 'common sense' assumptions, calling them 'the conventions according to which people interact linguistically, and of which people are generally not consciously aware' (Fairclough, 1989, 2). The idea that individuals are unaware of the informal rules that govern their own language behaviours, seems doubtful, especially if the outcome of this ignorance is unwitting belief in dominant values. If common sense is 'a category of practical knowledge which is found in the ordinary exchanges of everyday life' (Price, 1997, 51), then academic hostility to the use and possession of such knowledge must be explained.

Gramsci is chiefly responsible for the proliferation of this attitude, describing common sense as 'the "folklore" of philosophy', and 'a conception which, even in the brain of one individual, is fragmentary, incoherent and inconsequential' (Gramsci, 1971, 419). Contemporary theorists depart from this in two important respects; they regard its existence as more systematic and its exercise as positively harmful. Hartley, in a contribution to a popular dictionary, argues that the media in particular 'have colonised this concept, and use it to "prove" that the unequal distribution of wealth is ... actually only explicable as common sense' (O'Sullivan *et al*, 1994, 49).

The move here is from the identification of common sense as ordinary, to a general condemnation of its use as *ideological*, promoting (through some unspecified mechanism) a deliberately distorted world-view.

Fairclough's observations are at least a little more empirical, describing how 'the conventions for a traditional type of consultation between doctors and patients embody "common-sense" assumptions which treat authority and hierarchy as natural' (Fairclough, 1989, 2). The reasons Fairclough offers for this state of affairs is that doctors know about medicine and patients do not. Doctors are therefore in a position to decide how a health problem should be dealt with, while patients cannot make a judgment. This certainly confirms the existence of differential knowledge and power relations. This explanation, however, does not necessarily support the conclusion that doctor-patient relations are either *masked* by a 'naturalised' form of discourse, or effected only through professional structures of speech.

The point here is that both doctors and patients know that they are engaged in a certain type of rule-bound exchange, the formal qualities of which are partially designed to effect or carry through what is always a potentially difficult interaction. In other words, there is a reason for the exercise of 'common sense' in such situations, which although expressed within the context of an inequality of power and expertise, is also marked by elements of co-operation designed for mutual benefit; both participants know the 'language game' in which they are engaged. Therefore, Fairclough's assertion that 'practices which appear to be universal and common-sensical' actually 'function to sustain unequal power relations' (*ibid*), may have correctly identified the issue of power, but misconstrued the question of footing in the discursive strategies used. Fairclough maintains that 'existing social relations and differences of power' are legitimised 'simply through the occurrence of ordinary, familiar ways of behaving which take these relations and power differences for granted' (*ibid*).

The context of power

The existence of behavioural conformity does not necessarily prove that inequalities of power are simply taken as the natural order of life. In the example given at the end of the previous chapter, the 'common sense' offered to the troops at Gettysburg, is one that all ranks share and, in carrying out the suicidal attack, recognise as legitimate. This is not to deny the existence of power, but to place it in context and to separate its exercise from theories of ideological subterfuge. The brief excerpt contains enough allusions to established notions of battlefield necessities, and is clearly made within the immediate context of action, to carry forward the event as a whole.

It might be helpful to recall Heritage's suggestion that all intentional messages are subject to a dialogic process, so that the participants must act within 'updated implicit understandings of what is happening in social contexts' (Heritage, 1984a).

From a wider *contextual* point of view, the analyst must also consider the historical meaning of warfare in the period concerned, acknowledging the contradictions inherent in the conduct of the war. The North was forced through practical necessity to pursue the cause of anti-slavery, while at the same time attempting to dominate indigenous peoples within its borders.

Hancock's words, however, bear the marks of another mode of discourse, that in which a specialised form of language, following a set of rules and conventions, employs 'typical statements or phrases' in a structured way (Price, 1997). This could be defined as 'any regulated system of statements' (Henriques *et al*, 1984, in Parker, 1999, 10/11). What regulates statements in such cases is more than the situation or the participants, it is the *institutional* framework in which utterance takes place; there is an essential difference which should be understood here between structure and form, as structure refers to 'the organisation or articulation of both form and content' (Georgakopoulou and Goutsos, 1997, 11).

Instances or traces of a professional or institutional mode of speech in the battlefield example, include therefore reference to rank, questions about the origin of the regiment, and descriptions of the enemy position through associated terms (their 'colours'). This more advanced use of the term discourse is one which suggests a formal treatment of a subject; a typical example is the 'discourse' of the law, or of medicine, or indeed of military authority as suggested above. Other instances of formal genres are found in a variety of structured situations, such as classroom interaction.

Discourse, cohesion and coherence: 'more police, cleaner hospitals'

At this point, therefore, it seems to have become possible to describe a formal difference between discourse as utterance or speech, fundamentally constructed as at least *representations* of interaction, and discourse as system or genre or *structure*. In effect, as mentioned above, discussion of the simpler meaning leads immediately to issues which feature in more complex definitions. The enquiry made so far has already brought to light Foucault's distinction between three types of discourse; as 'an individualizable group of statements', as the 'general domain of all statements', and as 'a regulated practice that accounts for a number of statements' (Foucault, 1972, in Jaworski and Coupland, 1999, 2). As an initial exercise at least, it may appear quite difficult to identify within texts the relationship between 'an individualizable group of statements', and the 'general domain of all statements'. However, it should be possible to link a collection of individual statements with particular 'positions', in the sense of identifiable beliefs (however incomplete and contradictory the expression of such ideas may be in practice).

Take, for example, the distinctive (apparently hand-written) assertions used by the British Conservative Party on the front page of its election manifesto, in the 2005 General Election (11th March 2005):

> More Police
> cleaner hospitals
> Lower Taxes
> school discipline
> controlled immigration
> Accountability

These statements were followed by the question 'ARE YOU THINKING WHAT WE'RE THINKING?' and the declaration 'IT'S TIME FOR ACTION'. An overall political position is suggested by the way in which these elements point to an attitude; taken alone, or produced in another combination, their meaning would be different. They are meant to be examples of 'common sense' (see above) but could only be produced in a political culture in which certain perceptions have become the social norm; in other words, they are generated by an attitude which could produce other, related statements. The Conservatives attempt here to reinforce pre-existing positions that are, for instance, inimical to immigration *per se* (or else it would not need to be 'controlled'). The relationship between distinct utterances and ideology is taken up later in this chapter (see the analysis of the Tory election broadcast, 1993, below). The immediate usefulness of such observations lies in their potential as modes of analysis. For instance, examples of speech or expression, whether or not they constitute true examples of face to face exchange, always create meaning through *cohesion*; this is usually described as 'textual cohesion', recognisable in elements like surface lexis (the arrangement of words), grammar and, dependent on these, 'propositional development' (Stubbs, 1983, 9). In relation to Foucault's first category above, texts ('an individualizable group of statements') make sense or demonstrate cohesion because they are regulated by grammatical rules.

Cohesion is thus produced by 'cohesive ties', in which grammatical forces such as demonstratives and comparatives[1] 'indicate the semantic identity of an item with another' (Georgakopoulou and Goutsos, 1997, 12). Similarly, an 'anaphoric element'[2] such as a pronoun 'is treated as a word which substitutes for, or refers back to, another word or words' (Brown and Yule, 1983, 24). Bell describes cohesion as 'linkages ... between the sentences or events' (Bell and Garrett, 1998, 80). Such ties keep the text in order and also enable the re-organisation or interpretation of a text in a new form, while retaining the same meaning.[3]

Thus cohesion represents the 'texture' of texts (Brown and Yule, 1983, 191; Georgakopoulou and Goutsos, 1997, 13), or in other words the *property* of being a text.

Some perspectives, however, locate textual meaning not in 'rules' such as the supposedly automatic reference between pronouns and previous examples of noun phrases (anaphoric reference), but in the *expectation* of the analyst or reader that there is an intended meaning.[4] In terms of the relationship between cohesion and intention, it may as a consequence be clear that what the 'textual record' means is 'determined by our interpretation of what the producer intended it to mean' (Brown and Yule, 1983, 25).

At this point, it seems that cohesion as a concept is based entirely on either verbal or lexical elements. Yet it is the larger issue of semantic relations, or the production of meaning, which emerges from the notion of a 'cohesive text'. Internal cohesion

---

1   Demonstratives indicate the thing or person referred to, while comparatives express a higher degree of a particular quality.

2   An anaphoric term refers back to a previous statement and thus gains its meaning from the original element.

3   The full list is composed of reference, substitution, ellipsis, conjunction and collocation (Georgakopoulou and Goutsos, 1997, 13).

4   Morgan, 1979, holds this view; see Brown and Yule, 1983, 25.

of the kind outlined above, can only be recognised by a reader or analyst because grammatical relations refer, either directly or indirectly, to a world of significance, a domain of structures, events and experiences known in advance of the act of reading or analysis.

As Brown and Yule discover, it is possible to find grammatically meaningful texts (what they call 'contiguous sentences') which actually display very few explicit markers of 'cohesive relations' (Brown and Yule, 1983, 196). Semantic relations are therefore very often assumed, especially where material is *presented* as a text (see the Conservative PPB,[5] below). Formal cohesion is not enough to guarantee coherence, but in a sense this does not matter; readers or in a broader sense audiences, make connections which, although partly based on grammatical consistency, depend also on generic expectation[6] and the ability to make links based on possible configurations of meaning.

The use of the term 'configuration' here has been chosen to represent this book's preference for understanding texts as 'alignments' of various themes, mobilised to serve certain purposes, rather than necessarily representing expressions of unitary belief. Texts are therefore seen to be composed of linguistic rules, 'contextual' intentions and generic conventions.[7] My argument is that realms of experience and action are re-imagined in the course of expression and consumption. This suggests a movement from models of internal 'cohesion', to a more secure notion of socially referential 'coherence'. Fairclough describes coherence in a similar manner, calling it a connection between 'the sequential parts of a text' and between parts of a text and 'the world' (Fairclough, 1989, 78).

This observation may be re-applied as a mode of analysis. The study of text may be seen as the relationship between internal 'textual' structure, and external social forces (including audience perception of meaning), which produces 'discourse coherence'. Discourse coherence is the perception of a unifying theme or themes within and between individual speech acts, and their place in a larger world of meaning. It is also possible to compare individual texts with the notion of ideology as a specialised mode of explanation and coherence, the 'general framework' of all those beliefs which offer an interpretation or critique of 'things as they are' (Price, 1997, 111).

Discourse, statements and analysis: 'Britain's prisons are overcrowded'

From the perspective introduced above, discourse types seem to be characterised by the appearance of semantic coherence and by the production of specific themes or topics, organised by intention and generic convention. Kress writes that 'a discourse

---

5   Party Political Broadcast.

6   Simply, the kind of statements anticipated in particular settings; political speeches, product launches, public relations events, are all genres which produce anticipation about form and content.

7   Processes are the 'contingent' part of meaning-production.

provides a set of possible statements about a given area, and organises and gives structure to the manner in which a particular topic, object, process is to be talked about' (Hodge and Kress, 1988). Yet it is also possible to generate positions from individual utterances. In simple terms, a perspective may generate statements, while statements can also generate a perspective (van Dijk, 1998).

So, for example, if an initial utterance is made to the effect that 'Britain's prisons are overcrowded', this reveals first a conviction that such institutions exist, as well as expressing certain ideas about the condition they have attained. This demonstrates the notion of *reference*, what van Dijk calls 'the ways discourse and its meanings are related to the real or imaginary events that people talk *about*, namely its so-called *referents*' (van Dijk, 1998, 10). In other words, a discourse has to measure up against something and is automatically compared to experience, and thus against other possible ways of representing the world.

This first utterance does not, however, reveal or even implicitly suggest a distinct position on the issue of incarceration. If, however, this statement is followed by or linked with the utterance 'we need a more effective rehabilitation programme', then a liberal discourse or position may be indicated. Or again, if the initial declaration is connected with the statement 'those convicted of murder should be executed to make space', then a very virulent right-wing agenda may lie behind the speaker or author's remarks.

An awareness of the movement from ordinary utterance to a larger, 'ideological' frame can be found most clearly exposed in certain types of political material. The use of an ordinary utterance which embraces common sense and is also, implicitly or explicitly, aligned with a particular point of view, is seen as one way of leading the viewer from his or her own position to a realisation that he or she is a 'natural' supporter of one party or another.

For example, a Conservative Party Political Broadcast of 1993 entitled 'What do you want for Britain?', shows a series of individuals (differentiated by age, gender, ethnicity and class) making statements on a variety of political issues. As they do so, a handwritten date appears at the bottom of the screen:

Old affluent white female in marketplace: I know that criminals are a problem in the cell, but they're *much* more of a problem in the street (8th October 1993)

Young black male in street at night: We need to crack down on hardened criminals who ask for bail, get it, and commit crime all over again (4th June 1993)

Middle-aged white male in a smart bar: It's stark-staring obvious to me that if children *are* staying out of school, they're not learning what they should be, and probably learning what they shouldn't (6th March 1993)

Middle-aged white male in daytime street: We don't need reams and reams of complex papers that take hours for teachers to handle. What we *do* need is simple pencil and paper tests (8th October 1993)

Young white female: If someone belongs in prison, then that's where they should be (4th June 1993)

Second old affluent white female: Far too much well-meaning theorising nonsense is poked at our children in schools! (11th June 1993)

Second young black male: Well the recession's over, but it's left it's scars. What people are concerned about is their livelihoods, security, family and prospects (15th November 1993)[8]

All these statements, and the ones which follow, seem to *exemplify* certain attitudes about crime, education and the economy. Taken individually, they qualify as explicit propositions, or as utterances which carry 'truth values' which may therefore be tested for their veracity. In addition, they may also be read as a collective set of statements, indicating 'position' or belief. As such they may relate to more abstract representations of meaning (Stubbs, 1983, 203); in other words, the ideas which they contain could be expressed in a number of different forms.

This can be seen in Ayer's answer to the charge that the concept of a proposition is unnecessary, as it supposedly indicates little more than would a term like 'sentence'. Ayer notes that 'proposition' makes it possible 'to express what is valid not merely for a particular sentence ... but to any sentence to which it is logically equivalent' (Ayer, in Nye, 1998, 78). Here, as with the concept of discourse, the existence of a large source of possible statements, is based on the notion of a consistent set of ideas which are able to generate, or at least provide a source for, such individualised utterances.

This perspective is supported by Pinker in his discussion of the difference between the 'representations underlying thinking' and 'the sentences in a language' (Pinker, 1994, 78).[9] So, for example, the utterance 'if someone belongs in prison, then that's where they should be' (which sounds tautological), could be expressed in an alternative manner as 'those who deserve prison must be locked up', with the implication that 'criminals should not be allowed to go free', suggesting in turn that some political forces in Britain encourage mistakenly liberal attitudes about allowing malefactors to gain parole or early release. Thus, we may encounter the use of 'declarative' sentences which carry the same broad meanings (Stubbs, *op cit*).

The statements above, taken individually, do not seem to be examples of 'directive' communication. Taken together, however, they could as noted above, be understood to represent a consistent position, illustrating van Dijk's observation about the relationship between positions and utterances. It is the *form* in which these statements appear, that provides the directive utility of this act of communication;

---

8   Author's transcript 2001 of Conservative PPB, 1993.
9   Price disagrees, however, with the next stage of Pinker's argument, about the existence of an 'intention' which language can misrepresent, making an alternative case to the effect that what is said becomes what is meant, and advocating a theory of 'contextual intention' (Price, 1996, 99).

a Party Political Broadcast is intended to establish or consolidate support for one particular group or philosophy.

These statements are implicit invitations to share the positions expressed; yet the whole broadcast rests uneasily between its supposed representation of personal values, and the fact that the individuals who speak are clearly actors, rather than real citizens interviewed about beliefs they actually hold. Towards the close of the piece, some of the statements are re-deployed so that they appear to be spoken by people other than those who originally appeared to be responsible for each utterance. This curious interchangeability of persona and statements leads to a revelation at the end of the broadcast, in which the following appears on screen; 'Every word you have just heard was spoken by the same person'.

Images of John Major speaking to schoolchildren are shown. His signature is revealed, being written across the screen; 'John Major. Speaking for Britain'. This 'closure' (Branigan, 1992; Hayward, 1996; Price, 1997) is interesting because of the implied contradictions it contains. It attempts to demonstrate, on the one hand, that many people share Major's world-view (if it can be accorded such a cosmopolitan status), by allowing his words to be spoken by a variety of very different individuals. Major is thus an 'everyman'; yet all the proofs that have been provided are no more than his own utterances, extracted from political speeches, press statements, and so on, and re-attributed to 'real' people in everyday situations, individuals who are actually quite obviously professional actors.[10] Therefore, one possible reading of this broadcast is that the implied composite power of Major's 'common sense' is no more than a highly individual point of view.

Discourse and ideology

Such material is ideological in the sense that it produces a coherent, but necessarily incomplete 'version of events'. It might be described as ideological, according to McLennan's three conditions (McLennan, 1991, 111), because it constitutes a recognised, coherent system (of thought, of expression) which is shared by (or projected onto) a significant number of individuals, and which is connected in some way to the use of power in society. There are however certain qualifications which need to be made here. Taking the last question as a starting-point, the relationship of ideology to power does not actually help to distinguish it as a specialised form of meaning-production.

As McLennan recognised in a later work, every system of signs and symbols is 'implicated in an asymmetrical distribution of power and resources', suggesting that ideology is ever-present in the realm of the symbolic (McLennan, 1995, 83). In addition, the notion of a belief-system qualifying as an ideology only where it is shared by a 'significant' number of people, is ultimately a little unreliable, since

---

10 No outstanding ability need be attributed to these actors, through the use of the term 'professional'.

many of the most important ideologies no longer command the kind of extensive adherence they once seemed to attract.

This is not simply a question of the 'death' of ideological thought, the supposed consequence of the defeat of state-sponsored alternatives by a victorious market capitalism (Agger, 1992, 3; Mills, 1997, 29). It is rather partly a matter of the bureaucratisation of politics and a turn from an 'activist' base to a professional mode of organisation in which specific 'lines' or positions are crafted by parties for their representatives to parrot (Jones, 1999, 76), with, at the same time, use of more ambiguous language-formations (Fairclough, 2000). Some professional politicians have taken this development to suggest not only that political engagement is less evident, but that parties should in effect accept the advent of an entirely new representative environment, mediated through the availability of new technology.

An example of this view was expressed by Peter Mandelson in May 1997, when he spoke at a meeting of German politicians. He argued, according to Observer journalist Nick Cohen, that ballot boxes and Parliaments were elitist relics and that 'today people want to be more involved in government' via the superior instruments of plebiscites, focus groups and the Internet. He also declared that 'it may be that the era of pure representative democracy is slowly coming to an end' (Cohen, *Observer*, 28th November 1999).[11]

A more productive description of this problem, concentrating on the role of ideology and belief, rather than the question of engagement and activity *per se*,[12] may be to admit a decline in the significance of public support for identifiable political perspectives, but also to advance the notion that such beliefs continue to represent 'part of the legacy of organised ideas' (Price, 1997, 110), distinct doctrines which still act as reference points within public debate.

Ideologies, therefore, must be meaningful explanations, even where they are not held as convictions. One important proposition, used above, is that ideology represents nonetheless an incomplete explanation of social reality. Chouliaraki and Fairclough call ideologies simply 'one-sided' (Chouliaraki and Fairclough, 1999, 26). The reasons for this 'incompleteness' may be summarised as follows: first, because the social order itself is contradictory; second, because all descriptions of relationships in the world are necessarily presented as abstractions; third, because only certain aspects of available 'evidence' which might be used in support of a case, are actually produced, with the consequent omission of other parts of reality (Price, 1997, 111).

According to this position, it is in the nature of ideology to present a limited conception of the world, exactly because it is divided between the requirements of accurate description (correctly identifying events, beliefs, issues and objects in

---

11 Mandelson's German audience was shocked; Wolfgang Schable, a Christian democrat, said 'I absolutely do not believe that' (Cohen, *op cit*). Many governmental organisations present interactive electronic media as a supplement to established means of representation (Guterres, 1999), but more extreme views present it as a replacement.

12 An issue which is covered in the chapter on elections and discourse; see below.

order to be taken seriously) and the demands made by its own political goals, which require an essentially propagandistic mode of address, or at least the presentation of certainty. Ultimately, the former must be subsumed within the requirements of the latter.

A similar theory appears in Mannheim, who presents the idea that ideologies are 'situationally transcendent ideas which never succeed *de facto* in the realisation of their project contents' (Mannheim, 1957, in McLennan, 1995, 39). The difference here, however, is that ideologies are presented as particular types of belief-system, ones which are incongruent with the period in which they appear. They fail therefore because they wrongly describe social relations, prevent individuals from adapting to their circumstances, or refer to confusing myths or ideals (McLennan, *ibid*). Mannheim appears to be more interested in the social power of Utopian ideas, a concept explored below.[13]

The two positions described above suggest that discourse, when used to describe both the social process of creating meaning, and the end product of that process, must encompass smaller practices and more restricted instances of address. This has a bearing on the conduct of textual analysis itself. van Dijk speaks of the 'discursive expression and reproduction of ideologies' (van Dijk, 1998, 199), yet discourse is an 'unreliable' mode of utterance (Price, 1997, 76/77), in that when made into an *address*, it must appeal to more than the precepts it wishes to represent: it must consider what its audience believes and will tolerate, quite besides the vital requirement to demonstrate an awareness of common knowledge and understanding. At certain times, a political party (for example), will tailor its message to gain support from groups which do not constitute part of its 'natural' constituency, in which case, new policies or initiatives will appear to provide concrete evidence for the utterances made in advance of legislation.

Toynbee and Walker provide interesting examples of this tendency, citing the behaviour of New Labour ministers in the first Blair government; Blunkett in the case of schools, and Straw with regard to crime (Toynbee and Walker, 2001, 53 & 154). This does not mean to say that issue proponents merely ape the ideas they find in other domains; they re-present their precepts. Discursive *practice*, therefore, is always 'reproductive and transformative', because the 'particular configuration of discourses' and their articulation produces 'a new, changed, transformed arrangement'; in these new conditions, individual discourses which contributed to the arrangement of meaning, are themselves re-cast (Kress and van Leeuwen, 2001, 32).

To van Dijk, discourses also lie at the centre of social theory; they are in his view the most important 'ideologically based social practices'. Ideologies appear therefore as 'discursive manifestations' (van Dijk, 1998, 6). Although van Dijk does not mean

---

13 Some support for this perspective may be found in historical examples such as the strength of attachment to 'impractical' ideas during the English revolution; however, these appear to be more clearly articulated as 'myths', another category of which Mannheim is suspicious (see Hill, 1975).

to present ideology as a negative conception, preferring instead to characterise it as 'the basis of social representations shared by members of a group' (*ibid*, 8), it is still true that he seems prepared to tie discourse as a concept very closely to this idea of 'representation'.

Forms of ideology

Discourse, according to this view, is created by 'underlying' ideological forces.[14] The present work, however, argues that discourse cannot be identical to ideology. One reason why this is the case, is that ideology manifests itself through other material or symbolic forms, besides that of language. German fascism used speeches, articles, books, marches, images, symbols, behaviours, all in the service of an ideology. van Dijk certainly recognises this in another example, when he explains that 'forms of everyday discrimination against women and minorities' are certainly manifestations of 'sexist and racist ideologies' (van Dijk, 1998, 6).

However, he attributes most power to those discourses which explicitly 'explain, defend, legitimate, motivate or otherwise "formulate" fragments of the "underlying" ideologies' (*ibid*). Yet there is a problem here which must be addressed with care. It is important to emphasise van Dijk's proposition that it is only through discourse that ideology can be 'explicitly formulated' (*ibid*, 317), in other words that it can achieve the kind of coherence which allows its successful reproduction. There are two responses which might be offered to this position.

In the first place, taking the example already introduced above, German fascism was certainly, to a degree, ideologically 'identifiable', in the sense that an analyst or witness could point to its main precepts in general terms; racism, militarism, authoritarianism, populism and so forth. However, explicit Nazi ideology is also marked by inconsistencies and silences. For instance, the project to exterminate the Jewish people is hedged about with euphemism and evasion. In other words, the explicit content of fascism is not always coherent, and has to be recognised in a more general context.

It was therefore sometimes more clearly and truthfully expressed through the actions of its adherents and the associative power of its symbols, for instance the construction of concentration camps and the ubiquitous presence of the swastika. Thus, when van Dijk argues that 'if we want to know what ideologies actually look like ... we need to look closely at their *discursive manifestations*', this can only be true *if the discursive is taken to be a term which includes all processes of meaning-creation*. The second point made in response to van Dijk's view, has been discussed before. This is the difficulty of formulating precise ideological propositions in discursive terms, exactly because of the persistence of the 'primary' function of discourse: interactive exchange in speech.

---

14 Just as, in Parker's opinion, 'the term 'discourse' is sometimes used to refer to patterns of meaning which organise the various symbolic systems human beings inhabit' (Parker, 1999, 3); in such perspectives, both discourse and ideology have a 'generative' capacity.

Ideologies are thus imagined, within the terms of this book, to be less coherent than van Dijk suggests, while discourse in turn is seen as an unreliable and unwieldy instrument of ideology.

van Dijk asks how it is possible to know 'how discourse expresses or reproduces underlying ideologies' (*ibid*, 193) but also asserts that ideologies 'cannot be reduced to discourse' (*ibid*, 317). This means, as I mentioned before, that ideologies appear in other social practices besides discourse, but it should also suggest that discourse is not capable of being reduced to an effect of ideology. This would more comfortably accord with the characterisation of discourse as a *resource* for individual and collective expression, textual or otherwise. Understood thus, it is therefore larger not only than identifiable examples of expression, but also clearly bigger than particular instances of belief or ideology. Eagleton is helpful in this respect, when he presents ideology as 'less ... a particular *set* of discourses, than ... a particular set of effects *within* discourses' (Eagleton, 1991, in Mills, 1997, 46).

The present work contends therefore, that the analyst can only discover the 'ideological' if careful attention is first devoted to the study of reference, proposition, implicature and resultant patterns of meaning.[15] Individual discourses may therefore be reconfigured in new formations which inevitably remove certain essential signifiers from the 'fixed' place Eagleton believes they are assigned in their original ideological firmament (*ibid*). The position offered within this book, therefore, identifies forms of unidirectional address, but emphasises that they operate within wider conditions of cultural interaction; they cannot avoid contributing to debate and controversies which may be conducted in more inclusive spheres than the commercial or that pertaining to formal politics.

This suggests in turn the existence of potentially democratic practices with regard to meaning-production, but not in the mechanics of delivery, which remain hierarchical. The context in which this enquiry is conducted retains, however, a critical perspective on both structure and content (see below). The developments set out above, from text as the product of discourse, as singular or general purpose, and as a repository of social and economic value, do not however help to define more closely those 'internal' qualities which must be noted in preparation for analysis, and which allow authorial purpose to be recognised.

Linguistics and the background to analysis

Traditional linguistics, though it shows little awareness of the ideological realm or of new genres of textuality, is nonetheless useful when a description of internal structure is required, attempting to 'account for the recognisable unity or connectedness of stretches of language' (Stubbs, 1983, 9). Halliday and Hasan search for such 'cohesive relationships' both within and between sentences, patterns of connection which as noted above, create texture (in Brown and Yule, 1983, 191). Texture, as

---

15 See below for a detailed explanation of these terms.

the product of these unifying relations, is brought about through the employment of various formal markers that relate what is about to be said or written, with what has gone before (*ibid*).

Although it is clear that cohesion does not work in quite such a mechanistic fashion (see above), unavoidably reproducing wider social and cultural references, the identification of 'co-referential forms' (*ibid*, 192) can help to focus the analyst's attention on important sequences of meaning. These types of references direct the reader, observer or hearer to 'look elsewhere for their interpretation' (*ibid*). It is the need to look in other places, within and beyond the text itself, which provides *the first productive link between descriptive linguistics and the identification of the wider context of 'ideological' values*, vital to any enquiry which uses the frame of *context* to interrogate reference and meaning.[16]

The types of co-referential elements listed by Brown and Yule are as follows: where interpretation can only be made outside the text, the relationship is 'exophoric'; where internal, it is said to be 'endophoric' (*ibid*).[17] The internal production of meaning is divided into two further types: anaphoric (introduced above), those signifiers which *look back* in the text for their frame of interpretation (created through four types of marker; additive, adversative, causal and temporal); and cataphoric, elements which *look forward* in the text.

All discourse *strategies*, the essential modes of expression common to all attempts to effect even a co-operative outcome, must proceed on the basis not only of individual linguistic competence, but on the assumption that socio-cultural knowledge is shared between participants, or between 'speaker' and audience (Gumperz, 1982, 3). This assumption has long been a staple of textual analysis, just as it must impinge on the consciousness of those whose role it is to compose forms of public address (discourses which become texts).

For example, Zeitlin notes the necessity for the speaker in antiquity to 'try to identify himself with his audience', which was moreover 'standard practice in the rule books of oratory' (Zeitlin, 1990, 160). Ober and Strauss, in their work on Athenian society, argue in a similar vein that the public speaker 'is constrained to take the opinions and attitudes of his audiences into consideration', with the useful consequence that modern theorists can use the 'analysis of political rhetoric' to provide 'a window on the attitudes and opinions – the ideology – that informed the relations between ordinary and elite citizens' (Ober and Strauss, 1990, 238).

Using, therefore, simple knowledge of internal and external reference, the analyst can provide the structure for detailed enquiry into those ideas and values brought into play during attempts at directive or persuasive address. It is also possible to investigate the productive tension between two levels of structure; textual cohesion

---

16 For the four levels of context used in this book (taken from Price, 1997), see below.

17 These authors actually regard this distinction as unrepresentative of the actual processing involved in reading through a text, preferring instead to use a cognitive model of internal 'mental representation' against which information is checked (Brown and Yule, 1983, 199).

(see above), originating in lexical rules and made manifest in grammatical and propositional development, and discourse coherence, an attribute which underpins meaning, linking together individual speech acts (Widdowson, in Stubbs, 1983, 9). The relationship is essentially between the requirement to make sense (obeying the principles of semantics) and a larger issue, the question of 'composition', the way in which an utterance or speech or advertisement is 'put together', choosing certain aspects of publicly available discourses to serve this end.

In building upon this general overview of text, three other concepts should be summarised and more firmly established. The first is *reference*, a term traditionally glossed simply as 'words refer to things' (Lyons, in Brown and Yule, 1983, 28). However, Lyons revised this relationship to advance the idea that reference is the *act* of referring, tying its meaning to the volition of a speaker and not to an empiricist model of a direct relationship between words and objects (*ibid*). Searle also maintained that reference is not an inherent property of expressions but 'a speech act' (in Cruse, 2000, 305). Reference is used in this book to indicate an act, intentional or otherwise, which creates a link between the context of address and the realm of shared knowledge, ideas and beliefs.

The next concept, *proposition*, will be treated as an attempt to create more definite meanings in the course of making statements; propositions attribute 'some property to an entity' (Cruse, 2000, 25) and in this sense have truth-values, as seen above (Stubbs, 1983, 203), whether or not these can ultimately be reliably established. Adherence to the existence of truth as a category which may or may not validate what is said or written, is however of importance because of my preference for a realist account of meaning and reference (see below). The third concept used in this exposition is *implicature*, the practice observed in conversation and public address, of creating meanings through suggestion or implication rather than literal forms of description (Grice, 1975, 44).

Thus, as in the case of rhetoric, the observation of actual practices can provide the analyst with categories which can be re-applied to new texts. Throughout the various accounts given above, there is the firm acknowledgement that texts consist of systematic arrangements, rather than random collections of phenomena. Another key issue may be repeated, to the effect that texts are constructed with audiences, consumers, recipients, and readers in mind, so that the meanings apparent in the text can be interpreted by others within the same broad cultural milieu. Luthar's 'objectified culture' (above) is thus something set apart from the everyday by certain boundaries or conventions, but which is then able to re-enter the circulation of meaning, exactly because it is 'read' and understood. As Benveniste asserts, 'language is marked so deeply by subjectivity that one might ask if it could still ... be called language if it were constructed otherwise' (in Nye, 1998, 48).

A list of functions and effects

If texts are produced by the conjunction of intention and convention, producing a configuration of material, the outcome of which is a 'meaningful cultural form', analysis may include consideration of all possible symbolic functions and structuring effects, described within this chapter and the Introduction. Only a broad presentation of these factors will allow a more precise method to be applied to texts which appear within this book. The analyst must therefore show an awareness of discourse as *a social practice*, a definition Fairclough and Wodak explain as the way discourse is both 'socially constitutive' and 'socially shaped', so that it produces situations, objects of knowledge, and social identities (Fairclough and Wodak, in van Dijk, 1997, 258). Discourse as a social practice manifests itself:

in texts;
as the regular appearance of texts within a wider institutional and technological framework; their circulation as commodities; their generic qualities; the transformative capacity texts nonetheless represent (the production of new themes from 'sedimented meanings');[18]

as forms;
in the appearance of generic forms, within which apparent content is presented (both the connotations of symbolic and lexical items, and their shape, font, size, position, execution, arrangement and design), so that texts 'assume the technical means of their own accomplishment', becoming a *physical* 'configuration' of elements;[19]

within 'rules';
in the existence of rules for the production of linguistic significance, including morphology, grammaticality, syntax and semantics; the presence of cohesion and coherence; types of co-referential elements and internal and external reference;

as purposes;
as the principle of contextual intention or purpose, as it appears in concrete forms of address (where address is composed in the light of the subject's imagined subjectivity and may thus assume an 'interpellative' form); relationships of power between participants in communication; the production of elements intended to achieve particular 'resonance' with an audience, including appeals to common knowledge, shared values and 'transitional' ideas (see Introduction); the 'reflexive' nature of contemporary existence;

as narratives;
as the composition of narrative through the production of symbolic content, where narrative is the organisation of spatial and temporal data into a cause-effect chain of events; the existence of systems of statements and by extension of 'social narratives', stories which offer interpretations of events or broadly plausible explanations for events in the social world,[20] or which demonstrate some 'ideological' preference in their composition;

---

18 See Barker, 1989, 267-272.
19 What Kress and van Leeuwen call 'multi-modal' texts.
20 (Price, 1997, 74).

as strategies;

as the use of *reference*, the production of language or image or intonation to point to objects, events, shared concepts, or other cultural knowledge; *proposition*, a statement which offers explicit points of view or opinions; *implicature*, the existence of more 'covert' references within content (the force of which depends on readers or hearers recognising the use of conventional modes of utterance or textual form, and producing suppositions as to the intended meaning); strategies of speech, including the appearance of key terms, and the use of rhetorical and conversational devices; the production of 'speech genres' and 'evaluative accents';[21]

as structures;

the concept of abstract value systems or discursive fields which have an existence separate from their mode of realisation; the presence of discourse as an emergent property of unequal social relations; the presence of competing ideological positions; the use of intertextual reference; and the significance of context as those conditions which give structure to any communication event, and which entail an understanding of the place of texts within the social organisation of 'late modernity'.[22]

Modes of analysis

Following these observations, the method of analysis employed in this book first identifies text as an arrangement of physical elements. Put another way, text is understood as the site of symbolic or other content of one or more type, brought into a relationship or 'designed' for a communicative purpose. The next issue is to recognise the existence of generic forms that act as structuring agents for the appearance of the various 'components'.

The forms might include advertisements, political broadcasts, newspaper articles, and so on, while the constituent parts are likely to appear as lexical or other symbolic items, or as *less directly referential material*, such as music, sound, intonation, inflection, etc. This suggests in turn that there must be in each case a technical means of accomplishment, and a set of established practices that allow the overall procedure to be effected to an acceptable standard. The technical capability and the skills required to achieve the desired outcome (a recognisable product of sufficient quality) is usually the responsibility of professional organisations which have the capital, resources and authority necessary for such enterprises. These structures, together with the generic content they mediate, act to re-configure the apparent purposes suggested by the material itself.

---

21 See Barker, 1989, 267-272.

22 Four levels of context are proposed here, including 'functional' (the purpose of an event and its subject matter), 'situational', (the immediate physical and temporal circumstances within which any event is played out), 'discursive' (the general range of ideas and opinions which the participants are able to draw upon when they interact), and 'social', the wider condition of the society itself (including inherited forms of language, social customs, and the state of political and economic development (Price, 1997).

The next point to consider is discourse as a practice and as a form of representation, which derives from and relates to established positions or points of view ('available discourses'). In textual form, discourse appears as a mode of evaluative description employed in an attempt to convey something about the particular quality or essence of the ideas it represents; text is therefore a configuration of referential and propositional elements which are brought into alignment by an overall purpose. This does not mean that individual parts of the text are always seamlessly presented in the service of a consistent objective; individual statements, for example, refer to more than simply the material which surrounds them.

Intention here can be understood in the words of the Introduction as 'the structural reproduction of purposes whenever hierarchical relationships are renewed during communication events'. This means that intention is already shaped by anticipation of the conditions of expression and reception, including the generic form in which the text is to be cast (in the course of election broadcasts, for example, speakers sometimes acknowledge the limitations of the genre).[23] As the Introduction argued, texts are 'knowingly produced for public consumption and scrutiny'.

Therefore, intention must be understood as a multiply constituted category; in composing messages, authors must attend to models of reception and subjectivity. In turn, the overall determination of an author or authors can only be gauged through attention to supposed purposes as these are expressed in the course of exposition, yet these must be estimated *in turn* through both cumulative effect and the relative importance which seems to be accorded to individual elements. Texts as discursive phenomena may be said therefore to express *contextually sanctioned* purposes.

Notice, however, that the realist variant of critical analysis continues to identify the existence of agents, multiple or otherwise, whose purposes can be revealed in texts, whatever the complexity of the interventions themselves. In addition, although it recognises that texts are not merely objects but 'practices', it continues to maintain that individual examples also represent an accomplished product of internal and external structures.

As a result of these observations, the study of text must encompass close attention both to internal 'cohesive' techniques, and to 'external' reference to those events, ideas, and discourses, which lie beyond the scope of the text but which are brought to mind through its power of suggestion. This means that a more subtle form of 'content analysis' is required, one that does not readily assume that the process delivers an objective quantitative tally of elements. Although it can be used to record individual occurrences for the purposes of later judgement and comparison, its genesis must always remain theoretical, as Leiss and his co-authors note (Leiss *et al*, 1990). Essentially therefore, critical discourse analysis provides a more reliable method, exactly because it makes its aim (the search for both referential force and 'ideological' inflection), apparent from the start. It assumes that discourse expresses relations of power, *however mundane the textual 'event' itself may appear*, and seeks to demonstrate how power is directed to the attainment of ends, concensual or not.

---

23 John Cleese, Alliance Party Political Broadcast, 1987.

This differs somewhat from Fairclough and Wodak's position, in that it shows less concern that 'discursive practices may have major ideological effects' (Fairclough and Wodak, in van Dijk, 1997, 258). Rather than instituting a search for such evidence, this book attempts to account for the strategies found within textual configurations, relating these in turn to a theory of language which posits its aim as the achievement of 'resonance' through various communication strategies. Resonance, once employed by Gerbner (1977) to describe the concurrence of viewer expectation and media content, is used in this book to refer to a quality called forth by successful address (Price, 1997, 199), in which an audience recognises and appreciates (in both cognitive and emotional terms) the 'cultural references' (Eco, 1960), provided by the source. The creation of resonance is, in the view of the present work, a critical aim of any intentional communication act, and depends upon the appropriateness or suitability of content and delivery to the 'event' (whether in actual time, or in the case of mediated interaction within the context of a 'structured break'[24] in communication).

The conduct of analysis must also take into account the character of reference itself. An approach (sometimes suggested by the cruder forms of semiological analysis) which posits only an exact correlation between sign and 'significance', would fail to represent the pressures brought to bear on a text's symbolic resources. The process of expression is essentially creative, since ideas require *elaboration* if they are to convince audiences of their validity. Symbolic resources of various kinds may be mobilised, but concrete utterances can only attain significance through their power or range of reference. To some degree then, the goal of referential accuracy (the extent to which a purposive discourse is able faithfully to represent the position it advances), *comes into conflict* with the need to establish the propositional and rhetorical qualities needed to locate the utterance within a broader discursive universe.

Discourse therefore, embodied within a number of symbolic/expressive forms besides language, is understood as the existence of terms, statements, propositions, observations, images and narratives which *taken together* within a particular alignment or context, may present or suggest some form of 'meaning-coherence'.

Such coherence need not necessarily constitute a complete perspective, or a precise ideological conjuncture, or even represent an entirely logical or consistent position. The point is, despite theories which emphasise the 'contingency' of language (and by implication the conditional status of all representation), symbolic expression produces a range of meanings at particular times and places which both sanction and enable the production of a range of actions and outcomes, events which may themselves in turn be linguistic or symbolic in character, providing points of reference for future discursive activity. In the light of this statement, the existence of other more ambiguous positions must be acknowledged.

---

24 See Thompson, 1995 for the difference between mediated and face-to-face interaction.

The context of academic enquiry: deconstruction vs. *timeliness*

Certain developments, together with the assault upon the 'grand narratives' of social theory, have created an intellectual atmosphere in which 'radical pessimism' and anti-rationalist interpretative strategies have achieved notoriety (Reicher in Wheeler, 2000; Bennett, 2001).[25] Considering the challenge such relativist tendencies pose, it is important to offer a brief response. The following discussion should be understood, therefore, not as a diversion from but as an essential contribution to the investigation of directive address.

In the field of post-structuralist philosophy, deconstructive technique suggests, in Derrida's words, that no text is a 'finished corpus' of writing, but instead a 'differential network, a fabric of traces referring endlessly to something other than itself' (Culler, 1985, 84). Such analysis posits the impossibility of meaningful or at least incontestable reference. Nash refers to the 'obliterative indeterminism' of deconstruction, as all utterance or reference indicates only textuality not 'things', and ultimately 'speaks against itself' (Nash, 2001, 9). Clifford describes the 'self-consumption' of concepts in the work of Derrida (Clifford, 2001, 159). The deconstructive position is therefore usually recognised as a perspective which opposes realist accounts of textual intelligibility. Deconstruction, employed as an *analytical* position, seems to be assisted by the wider postmodern and post-structuralist project in which it is set; yet this larger context seems to the present author to be, in essence, a *dramatisation* of existing social and cultural trajectories.

In an admittedly wide postmodern domain, some strands of theory appear not only to defer to the prevalent trajectory of aesthetic production, but to abandon any position which might provide an independent locus for assessing the meaning of cultural change, exactly because they adopt the tenor and discourses of the objects under study.[26] This is not to deny the genuine existence of developments which have engendered such perspectives. Nash, for example, traces the postmodern critique to 'the loss of trust for the systems of signs sustaining human communication' (Nash, 2001, 259). It appears, however, that the postmodern treatment of what a realist would regard as empirically-verifiable events (a loss of trust, for example, attributable to political corruption and the concentration of economic power), sets such experiences within narratives which emphasise the dissolution of traditional social formations (Baudrillard, 1990) and the erosion of faith in the consistency and usefulness of experience.

On the other hand, some postmodern arguments seem to depend upon the exaggeration of empirical evidence[27] or the assertion of conditions for which only

25 The methods of analysis used by, and the conclusions reached within the broad practices of this tendency, appear to have disrupted but not entirely undermined the Enlightenment project (Sarup, 1988; Sim, 1992).

26 Billig notes, for example, that the social critique advanced by Baudrillard appears to coincide with themes in the novels of DeLillo (Billig, in Simons and Billig, 1994, 153).

27 See for example Bogard, and his account account of surveillance, 'The Simulation of Surveillance', 1998.

fragmentary supporting material is cited, sometimes apparently with the deliberate intention of both demonstrating and embodying the hypereal and the hyperbolic (Baudrillard, 1988, 7). A significant issue therefore, from the viewpoint of a study primarily concerned with the circulation of meaning, is the growth not only of 'decentred' theorising, but of those cultural developments which provided academic observers with their first intimations of practices which were then cited as evidence for the onset of the postmodern. The existence of intertextual, ironic and self-referential semiotic strategies, particularly in the field of advertising (Fowles, 1996), is thus often regarded as an example of such an aesthetic. These approaches do seem to represent real shifts in cultural orientation, and appear as one consequence of the increased availability of multiple sources of representation, brought into being by the social and cultural fragmentation, and subsequent re-alignment identified by authors like Tetzlaff (1991) and Stallabrass (1996). Such manifestations may also be attributed to the simple and necessary search for novel representations or startling propositions which will capture the attention of consumers or voters (albeit in the context of multiple forms of reference and specularity).

Timeliness and the production of *alibis*

The present work advances the argument that postmodern aesthetic and theoretical tendencies do not necessarily lead to the debilitation of all referential systems, yet do represent an intellectual and procedural dead-end (see Smith's summary of deconstruction's opponents, in Smith, 2005, 103). Texts do contain multiple possibilities. They are, however, active interventions for specific purposes, intended to be effective within a particular set of circumstances; of course these texts/utterances begin to 'decay' upon expression! A New Labour diatribe on the NHS, made for consumption in 1997, would be a severe embarrassment if repeated in an election held in 2008 or 2009.

My argument here turns on the concept of *timeliness*, which may be understood as follows. First, the process of refining power relations *within* hierarchies must be seen as a permanent process, taking place *behind closed doors*. Second, decisions are taken which then require public alibis. Third, actions (initiatives, declarations, adjustments) are required to meet contingencies. The aim of the authoritarian speaker/author is to generate meaningful explanations (clear references) at specific times, irrespective of their success as persuasive devices. A timely intervention meets, therefore, all the requirements of publicity, the production of a *rationale* after the fact, while journalists mistakenly regard public statements as *matters of record*.

Timeliness is the generation of appropriate alibis within a hierarchical frame that keeps democratic demands at arm's length. While Derrida dissects the 'arrow's flight' or concentrates on the difference between the present and the 'not present', in an attempt to demonstrate how the 'instant' is governed by alterity (Smith, 2005, 37), authoritarian speakers are chiefly concerned with making an impact and then moving on with the *business* of governance or commerce.

Rhetoric is the technique which creates the *alibis* mentioned above, the provisional interventions which, if necessary, can later be qualified. There were no 'WMD's' in Iraq? 'We' were sincere in this erroneous belief; this can be translated as 'we used this ruse and now it has served its purpose', or 'we thought this at the time, now it is *time* to move on'. Interventions are not serious attempts at truthful explanation, but rather 'required formalities within a hierarchical system which is *known* as democratic' (Price, 2006a, 19). What then does it matter if texts cannot, 'ultimately be fixed or stabilised'? (Burke, Crowley and Girvin, 2000, 223). From the authoritarian point of view, it is better that they cannot. From this book's perspective, texts work best as tools for purposes within a spatial and temporal context; the task of the analyst is to trace the convoluted relationship between footing, belief and utterance, in the interests of truth. Attacking 'specific closures of meaning' which are composed 'in the service of hegemonic projects' (Chouliakai, 2002, 92) is a waste of effort because closure is impossible and hegemonic projects can live perfectly well with inconsistency and contradiction; they depend, ultimately, on other forms of entrenched power.

Illustration 2: The Mobilisation of Identical Themes: Childhood, Nationality and Political Allegiance
Source: Conservative and Labour websites, 2004.

Configurations of meaning and ideology

This is why texts are described in the present work as configurations[28] of meaning, 'locations' of significance set within a larger category or genre. A number of points may be developed from this observation. The first is that the process through which this representational agenda is taken forward, represents the necessary confluence of form and content, an interplay between broad genres of communication event, and the production and reception of individual texts. This must nonetheless be seen within the context of wider social and economic forces which act as reciprocal structures in the creation of meaning.

---

28 After Buxton's observation, 1990.

Familiar persuasive techniques continue to be deployed in an attempt to prompt 'typical' responses, at least within the 'life' of the configuration itself. Audiences will thus anticipate the sequence or pattern of references which constitute meaning.[29] The existence of such foreknowledge can in some circumstances be advantageous, in the sense that the group or institution which composes a message is able to assume a mutual awareness of shared codes or 'cultural references' (Eco, 1960).

This goal has important implications for an understanding of ideology, and departs from one established current of critical discourse analysis, abandoning the latter's preference for a negative conception of ideology, and proposing instead a model which describes it as a general framework of ideas and beliefs which offer a coherent but incomplete critique of the world (Price, 1997, 111; see above). The negative character of ideology is attributed in the first instance therefore to its function as an instrument of partial representation; yet the development of this idea must recognise the greater issue of context, in the sense that these incomplete accounts are made in the service of an instrumental purpose. In other words, there is always a tension between their use as *accounts* or *descriptions*, and their status as persuasive interventions. In line with this conception, discourse becomes a resource, a system of statements (Parker, 1992, 5) suggesting in turn the production of 'social narratives' from a range of different material (Price, 1997). Discourses are therefore, in Howarth's words 'relational entities' the identities of which depend on 'differentiation from other discourses' (Howarth, 103).

Inconsistent discourse

The impossibility of an ideologically consistent discourse may therefore be explained by the difficulty of composing 'pure' messages *per se*, but include more specifically the following: the structure and nature of language itself (grammars, categories, implicatures, rhetorical formulae, fashions of speech, strategic techniques etc.); the existence of a discursive environment composed of these features; the active modelling of audience through address; and the structuring effect of social forces which, though experienced partially through symbolic representation,[30] are nonetheless also felt in the 'brute' facts which constitute everyday experience.[31] This book gives discourse a central place in the circulation of meanings, assuming that 'speech' or language is able to recompose the salient features of those phenomena it is employed to represent; Bain describes the composition of new combinations or aggregates of meaning (in Greenwood, 1994, 20).

---

29 This may demonstrate how form and content are inseparable co-elements which reconstitute one another, producing a particular configuration of text.

30 The question of the reality or otherwise of 'structure' as an affective force is discussed below.

31 Pierce's second level of phenomena (Jensen, 1995, 23; Cobley, 1996, 27), or the 'brute matter' which Collier presents as the partner of consciousness.

The realist perspective offered in these pages follows Collier's dictum that language 'is a pointer' and that to study it 'without reference to what it points to' is to make a fundamental error (Collier, in Parker, 1998, 48). This remains true even when language points, as it were, to itself. The proviso here is that language is not endlessly self-referential and that in Jensen's words, 'no social structure ... could exist without procedures for ending language games' and instituting collective action (Jensen, 1995, 11). Dillon, in a similar mode, argues that 'words could not refer to other words unless they also related to things' (Dillon, 1995, 167). As a consequence, following Price's argument that post-structuralist theories which postulate 'chains' of reference fail to do justice to the complexity of communication networks, it is possible to imagine an alternative model in which intertextual reference reinforces rather then debilitates the performative character of language use.

Another important point is that language itself is not the only, nor indeed the ultimate location of meaning (Collier deems language 'not even the first runner', in Parker, 1998, 47), and that there are recognisable phenomena which human subjects use to negotiate a passage through existence: sights, sounds, states of mind, and physical self-awareness, to name a few.[32] Dillon contends that language is a means of describing and evaluating the world, and that where such linguistic constructs compete, it is possible to measure their worth against the world itself (Dillon, 1995, 170). One test of this position is immediate experience; Dillon's argues that misery and suffering, for example, 'transcend signifiers and cultural boundaries' (*ibid*, 170).

This study therefore posits the existence of a world composed of objects, people, events and so on, which are subject to mediation through the manipulation of symbolic forms (a process through which things make 'sense' or achieve coherence), but which would continue to exist whether described or not; phenomena of all kinds exist outside discourse, and endure beyond the figurative power of symbolic systems. Yet it must also be recognised that the notion of a world which is not described and re-configured through language or symbolic forms, emerges only as a consequence of the debate over realism and its categories; as a singular proposition, it is distinctly odd. Such a world would lack entirely those aspects of meaning from which the social is composed; as Chouliaraki argues, when explaining the position of Laclau and Mouffe, 'the domain of physical materialities ... only becomes intelligible ... once it enters a particular field of signifying relations' (Chouliaraki, 2002, 92). This is what is meant when social reality is ascribed to the field of human agency. Particular kinds of *social* meanings are thus activated and enacted through the human faculty of symbolic expression. Chouliaraki's statement here, again written in relation to the position espoused by Laclau and Mouffe, cannot be bettered; 'discourse ... *is* the materiality of the social' (*ibid*).

---

32 While it is true that theoretical description, to take one instance, can call into being linguistically objective accounts of 'unobservables' such as the behaviour of atoms (Greenwood, 1994, 17), discourses cannot of themselves build physical structures. They present interpretations or accord social meanings to things.

The concept of discourse: constructionism and realism

To argue that studies of discourse should be conducted within a broader field of enquiry than the discursive alone, in effect that they ought to be set within the context of a wider-ranging and more inclusive social theory, seems at first sight an entirely rational proposition. Yet it may seem to imply that the concept of discourse is often conceived quite narrowly. This concern appears especially significant in the light of misgivings about the effects of a 'turn to language' within contemporary disciplines such as cultural studies and, more significantly for the critics of 'semiological reductionism' (Dillon, 1995), within social and critical theory in general. Reservations about this development were perhaps most notably expressed by Bourdieu, who identified the core intention of linguistics as an 'intellectualist philosophy' which treats language 'as an object of contemplation rather then as an instrument of action and power' (Bourdieu, 1991, 37). Despite the fact that it is exactly the contribution of theorists like Bourdieu which has helped to produce a social view of language, disquiet over the effects of the linguistic approach continues to appear.

Renegger for example traced the 'death' of political philosophy to the rise of the 'linguistic turn' and an associated growth in 'behaviouralism and positivism' in political and social science (Renegger, 1995, 2).[33] Barrett also notes how the onset of textuality in its deconstructive mode at least, has subverted traditional philosophical enquiry, in which language was once used to convey, as clearly as possible, unambiguous meanings (Barrett, 1991, 125). The tendency is again identified by Howarth, who draws attention to the blurring of a once important distinction between an 'objective ... empirical social science' and approaches which emphasise 'interpretative' methods of enquiry (Howarth, in Scarbrough and Tanenbaum, 1997, 268). Garnham argues that models of a 'broadly discursive, hermenuetic, post-modern type' have used linguistic theories 'without argument' (Garnham, 2000, 139). Mosco, in addition, describes how 'cultural studies', using textual and discourse analysis, has produced a sustained critique of science and has been attacked in turn for, amongst other offences, 'relativism' (Mosco, 1996, 11).

Yet, as this book argues, realist currents of critical discourse analysis oppose relativist tendencies like social constructionism, supporting instead the viewpoint Mosco himself expresses, that the realist 'gives equal weight to theoretical and empirical considerations' (*ibid.*, 2). It would appear that different perspectives within the field have been on occasion unhelpfully conflated, producing a narrow reading of more complex developments (see for example Chouliaraki's analysis, 2002). This need not have been the case, considering the existence of fairly early enquiries which prepared the ground for studies of discourse within its social context; Kress and Hodge, for instance, in proposing an enlarged project to encompass 'relations between language and society and language and mind', were at pains to avoid charges of 'academic imperialism' in their expanded version of linguistics (Kress and Hodge, 1979, 3).

---

33 Specifically, the political philosophy of the '1950's and 1960's' (Renegger, 1995, 2).

At the same time, it would appear that realist positions have been forced together with empiricist points of view. So, for example, the use of Wittgenstein to defend the constructionist position that 'words are not mimetic simulcures of an independent world but derive their meaning ... from their use', neglects to mention that Wittgenstein made this point in order to demonstrate the inadequacy of empiricist accounts of meaning, which depended upon the notion of a relationship between language and 'private mental images' (all in Greenwood, 1994, 41).

Nonetheless, there have been indications of more progressive developments; in the same year that Mosco's assessment of cultural studies appeared, Harris greeted the 'linguistic turn' in social theory in much more positive terms, arguing that the study of 'language in use' is more profitable than attempts to investigate 'individual consciousness', where the overall purpose is an attempt to consider the operation of ideology and culture (Harris, 1996, 65).

Following therefore the insights of Chouliaraki and Fairclough, transformations in theory observed within the condition of 'late modernity'[34] can indeed be attributed partly to changes in language, but these developments are also recognised as taking place *outside* discourse (Chouliaraki and Fairclough, 1999, 4). Put another way, alterations in the social order are often pre-figured, accompanied and followed by explanations for the particular effects they may entail. This process could be illustrated by any number of examples, but may be represented here by excerpts from a speech given by the British Labour leader Blair, at a Confederation of British Industry dinner, held on 16th May 2000.[35]

As the 21st century opens, the central challenge for governments the world over is how to provide opportunity and security amidst fundamental economic, social and technological change.

The 'arrival' of the twenty-first century is not something this speech has created, though of course in recognising its significance (and not, for example, the 'alternative' beginning of the new millennium, proposed as the onset of 2001), it helps to legitimise its place within a particular culture's social reality. In addition, the 'fundamental' change to which Blair refers, is not brought into being by the remarks themselves, though they represent one determining factor in the way such developments are understood. Economics, to take one example from Blair's list, is made up of more than discourse; it may be characterised as a combination of 'brute' facts (this commodity is imported, that activity is subsidised) and the meanings, rules and discourses which attach to these phenomena. There is a relationship or reciprocal impact therefore between the activity and its representation. Poulantzas addresses this question when he argues that the economic apparatus reproduces political and ideological relations so that in effect, 'not everything that goes on in "production" involves the "economic"' (Poulantzas, 1975, 32). In the course of Blair's speech,

---

34 For a discussion of nomenclature and the 'modern', see Chapter 3.
35 Transcript taken from 'info@new.labour.org.uk'.

in keeping with the way New Labour wishes to characterise 'change' as inevitable, rather than as a potential catastrophe, he declares that:

> Our job as a government is not to resist change but to help people through it. Our duty as a government is to take no short-term risks with economic stability.

Using the approach outlined in the previous chapter, the *reference* is to economic developments as though they are an irresistible force. The *proposition* is that this particular government will assist in the process of adaptation. The *implicature* is that resistance to change is unwise because it risks economic stability, while the undeveloped content, which both underpins and makes sense of the whole perspective, is the harshness of capitalist social relations. Such discourses, while similar to those produced by the Conservative Party, are nonetheless generated by New Labour's commitment to a particular position. This is the concept of the 'Third Way', which in Fairclough's words is 'constituted and reconstituted as a discourse in the documents, speeches, interviews, etc. of New Labour' (Fairclough, 2000, 9). The 'Third Way' is a project which attempts to provide a supposedly 'social democratic' path between on the one hand, classical social democracy and on the other, neoliberalism. Giddens, the foremost academic advocate of this tendency, produces sweeping statements which declare 'the final discrediting of Marxism', and the 'death of socialism', while acknowledging that 'whatever Thatcherism may or may not have done, it certainly shook up British society' (Giddens, 1998, vii, 3, ix). The 'Third Way' appears, therefore, as a linguistic and policy-driven intervention intended to reinvigorate one of the central political creeds which has both shaped and explained late modernity. Fairclough argues that it 'both draws attention to assumed incompatibilities, and denies them', bringing together terms from what might seem to be opposing traditions of thought; he cites in particular the link made between 'enterprise *and* fairness', as one example of an attempt to present 'the potentially fatal contradictions of New Labour as its greatest strengths' (Fairclough, 2000, 10/11).

The discursive and extra-discursive

With regard to theories of discourse and expression, and from the ideas outlined above, the present work accords sympathetic treatment to Foucault's distinction between two separate (though related) modes of experience, the discursive and the 'extra-discursive' (Foucault, 1980). The alternative is the removal of this dichotomy, suggested in the work of Laclau and Mouffe (1985, 146) and explained by Chouliaraki as bringing physical materialities 'too close to discourse' (Chouliaraki, 2002, 93).

The consequences of over-emphasising the discursive, for the study of language and action, would be considerable. In its most extreme form, such a move would entail the conceptualisation of a universe which cannot exist beyond its mediation by symbolic forms[36] (a position avoided by Laclau and Mouffe).

Or, to examine the problem in a less dramatic light, it may suggest a strictly constructionist account of language and its effects, in which social reality is the creation of symbolic activity alone, and is not generated by other material practices.[37] However, some care needs to be exercised in order to establish the exact parameters of the argument. If Laclau and Mouffe contend that all objects are 'constituted as objects of discourse' (in Howarth, 2000, 104), this suggests that they become meaningful by virtue of their description within a symbolic system, allowing their appearance as elements of *social* reality, denying not their independent existence as such, but instead their ability to create *autonomous meaning* beyond the referential powers of signifying systems.

Distrust of a re-invigorated linguistic tradition on the grounds of its supposedly relativist character (noted above), may have had an impact on the concept's development as part of what van Dijk calls 'broader sociocultural structures and processes' (van Dijk, 1997, 21). The social or more performative function of language would be as a result underestimated; in other words, the discursive realm could be imagined as an inherently limited part of social reality, circumscribed by supposedly larger forces, such as the economic, or the more broadly cultural, for example.[38] Its role in the partial constitution (or at least the public representation) of such structural phenomena might then be overlooked.

The countervailing and perhaps equally flawed alternative to the dominance of an extra-discursive world, has already been suggested; the proposition that all social life is mediated through symbolic forms to the extent that nothing can be represented (and thus brought into existence), beyond the bounds of the symbolic itself.[39] It is not the intention of this book to promote either a circumscribed, nor an all-encompassing view of discourse, since the goal of the study is actually to provide a theory of contextualised meaning-creation which acknowledges the material power of language use.[40] This perspective finds support in those theories which conceive the 'linguistic turn' in more even-handed terms. So, for example, it may be

---

36 The notion that all human experience is mediated rather than 'direct', symbolic rather than lived, appears within social theory from the Frankfurt School to Giddens, suggesting a kind of enveloping tyranny of symbolic forms; see for example Adorno in Bernstein, 1991, 3.

37 Collin notes that the regulation of human activity has an impact on more than the physical environment individuals inhabit; human groups bring into being 'social relationships, social structures, and institutions – in brief, *social reality*'.

38 See Parker, 'Discourse Dynamics', Chapter 2 (1992).

39 For a fuller discussion, see below.

40 Material in the sense that expression is imagined here as a response to environmental conditions, which are in turn affected by what I call 'expressive actions'. This position is sympathetic to, but not an exact recapitulation of the established Marxist perspective, in which 'ideological phenomena are determined by material causes' (Barrett, 1991, 6). Instead of a one-way process, it adheres to a conception of ideology and expression as integral parts of material existence.

reasonable to propose in Lovell's words that 'the social world is ... not the product of theoretical work' but on the other hand to point out that it 'cannot be *known* without the work of theory construction' (Lovell, 1983, 9). A comparable way of imagining the relationship between discourse and the 'material world' is proposed by Pujol, *et al.*, who argue that the 'discourse/material assemblage' represents the actual nature of human experience of social reality and subjectivity (Pujol *et al.*, in Burr in Parker, 1998, 20).[41]

A position such as critical realism (Bhaskar, 1978), relevant to the present enquiry, accepts many of the differences which theorists of all persuasions have identified between the contents of 'social and natural science' (*ibid.*, 9), including ideas about the constitution of social reality, but maintains nonetheless that reference cannot be reduced to language or the symbolic realm, on the grounds that the end product would be an enclosed and self-referential symbolic order. Rather than search for an absolute 'unity' of knowledge to offset this tendency, one alternative is to treat different traditions of enquiry (what Cassirer calls the 'various branches of science') as a complementary process (in Fiumara, 1992, 9). This, in essence, is a theory of epistemological strength achieved through diversity.[42] Whereas all knowledge is indeed 'historically produced', it does in this model attempt to represent an external reality and in this sense is provisional yet also practical (Shotter, 1992, 27), constituted by social relations yet always motivated by the desire to establish and test truth-values and what Chouliaraki calls 'truth effects' (Chouliaraki, 2002, 93). The realist and 'dialectical' methods employed by such tendencies may help to reveal what Mosco calls the '*concrete totality* of integration and contradiction that constitutes social life' (Mosco, 1996, 33).

Transformation and symbolic power: 'all persons held as slaves'

This book takes the position that changes in the social order are accompanied and, to some extent, driven by 'transformations in language and discourse' (Chouliaraki and Fairclough, *op. cit.*). This is not the same as insisting that they originate solely in the realm of discourse or the symbolic. When Lovell states that the whole complex structure of social relations is 'produced by the dominant mode of production and reproduction of material life' (Lovell, 1980, 9), the present work is in agreement. Yet the question remains, what is the 'dominant mode'? While not concurring with those views which characterise contemporary Western societies as functioning without

---

41 Potter and Lopez offer another useful proposition when they maintain that the real significance of a broader application of linguistics to social theory, is that human society, as 'an object of investigation' possesses features 'analogous to language', not simply that theory and knowledge themselves are simply 'language-borne' (Lopez and Potter, 2001, 8).

42 Cassirer notes that 'the unity of knowledge can no longer be made certain and secure by referring knowledge to a ... transcendent prototype ... a new task arises: to gather the various branches of science ... into one system, whose separate parts precisely through their necessary diversity will complement and further one another' (in Fiumara, 1992, 9).

visible means of support,[43] it does seem apparent that changes in global capital have allowed 'cultural' and thus symbolic production to attain increased significance within Western economies. As Dodd observes, postmodern theory marks a departure from the 'production' paradigm, favouring a description of 'a new era of exchange and circulation', but of signs rather than commodities *per se* (Dodd, 1999, 11). Baudrillard's intervention marks a fusion of both, describing 'a generalised system of exchange and production of coded values' (Baudrillard, 1998, 78). Garnham, in an overview of the various explanations which have been offered for the growth of such phenomena, refers to 'post-industrial' theories and the creation of global markets (Garnham, 2000, 31). Yet he also recognises the enduring power of the symbolic in all social formations, asking 'what is the status and function of these ... miraculous entities that both stand for other material realities and cause action at a distance?' (*ibid.*, 138). In this view, symbolic power is both material and performative, providing a basis for the study of expression as essentially *meaningful*.

A useful example of such power, causing action 'at a distance' may be found in the variety of declarations made by states which, at first sight, are 'merely words' and as such could cause little consternation to their neighbours; yet they are taken to heart as statements of intent. So, for instance, during the American Civil War, the Emancipation Proclamation of 1863, made by President Lincoln, had to be taken seriously by the Confederacy, which depended upon the institution of slavery. However, it precipitated an immediate crisis not in the Southern states, but in the North, reducing the efficacy of the war effort for at least six months; soldiers had joined the army to reinstate the Union, not to free the slaves (McPherson, 1997). The proclamation, which eventually proved fatal to the war-effort of the South, read in part as follows:

> ... on the first day of January, in the year of our Lord one thousand eight hundred and sixty-three, all persons held as slaves within any State or designated part of a State, the people whereof shall then be in rebellion against the United States, shall be then, thenceforward, and forever free.

Another strange material effect of this text, intended from the outset, was to allow slavery to continue (at least in name), in those states which held slaves but which remained within the Federal camp; the proclamation was careful to ensure their precarious loyalty. In the late modern era, symbols and references are employed in order to reap the benefits of their significance. In the post-communist Russian state, this was done in order to retain useful associations from the past; a mix-and-match policy for the creation of unitary address. 'The Times' of 1 January 2001 reported that President Putin had 'approved Russia's new civilian tricolour', retained Alexsandrov's tune for the national anthem (with different words), reinstated the red banner as the military standard, and 'in a nod to monarchists ... has confirmed the

---

43 i.e. that having lost those structures erected by more traditional, production-based activities within a clearly bounded nation-state, they depend on symbolic exchange.

Tsarist double-headed eagle as Russia's coat of arms'.[44] Such strategies had been adopted, earlier in the previous century, by Franco in Spain, who adopted the Carlist red beret and the Falangist blue shirt to signify the unity of movements (Preston, 1995). 'Meaning' here is created through both linguistic and non-linguistic modes of reference. Rather than object to the reality of secure reference and the generation of shared meaning, a strategy adopted by some currents of postmodern thought, Baudrillard accepts its existence but argues that 'the objective of information is always to circulate meaning, to subjugate the masses to meaning' (Baudrillard, 1980, 142). There is no sense of democratic potential here, or support for Fairclough's suggestion that media forms at least offer 'a new public prestige for 'ordinary' values and practices' (Fairclough, 1995, 11). In Baudrillard's view, networks of communication act as a uni-directional force, the goal of which is not persuasion, but simply dominance through the provision of meaningful discourse.[45] If meaning itself is an instrument of repression within modernity, then it follows that effective resistance must answer in terms which debase the meaningful. Baudrillard insists that 'the masses remain scandalously resistant to this imperative of rational communication' (Baudrillard, 1980, 142), and imagines the deployment of 'fatal strategies' (Baudrillard, 1990). In other words, resistance becomes disengagement.[46] Tetzlaff, who presents cultural fragmentation as the guarantor of power[47] (in effect, a successor to Fordist centralisation), maintains that the postmodern project tends to assert that 'the bounds of subjectivity are torn away by the networks of information' (Tetzlaff, 1991, 11). Yet there seems to be a definite continuity between the postmodern belief in phenomena such as, to take a related example, reference without definitive meaning, and some of the established canons of modernist social theory. A particularly germane example would be the conviction, from the Frankfurt School on, that contemporary experience is largely 'mediated' rather than direct, suggesting an apparent belief in the tyranny of symbolic forms. Giddens, for his part, writes that 'virtually all human experience is mediated – through socialisation and ... the acquisition of language' (Giddens, 1991, 23). The problem lies in separating experience from the symbolic realm in this way, as though the former is sullied by its refraction through the medium of language. This is to alienate experience from

---

44 'The Times', 1 January, 2001.

45 Eventually, however, all articulate discourse is reduced 'to a single, irrational, groundless dimension, in which signs lose their meaning and subside into exhausted fascination' (Baudrillard, 1980, 142-3).

46 He identified a new form of oppression, 'ambience', in which a society is controlled through its inclusion in the spectacle of consumption; 'individual choice is the ideology of the industrial system. Freedom of choice is imposed on the consumer'. According to this view, the sign is 'an agent of abstraction' while meaning functions as an 'alibi' to allow signs to circulate in exactly the same way as commodities'.

47 'I suggest that mass-produced culture does contribute mightily to the maintenance of the social order in late capitalism, but that it does so more through social and semiotic fragmentation than by forging any sort of ideological unity among the subordinate' (Tetzlaff, 1991, 10).

language, an act as dangerous to an understanding of the relationship between the two as their conflation, setting language at some distance from the everyday, and underestimating its ability to both represent and reflexively develop experience.

Adherence to Lovell's observation (above), combined with a recognition of the role of symbolic power in the reproduction of social relations, is the first step in the move beyond what Bourdieu calls 'economism and culturalism' to his vision of 'an economy of symbolic exchanges' (Bourdieu, 1991, 37). This suggests in turn that the way in which social change is both described by, and sometimes anticipated through the use of symbolic forms, can affect the precise configuration of social relations. Cameron, for example, calls language 'an instrument as well as an object of cultural change' (Cameron, 2000, 3).

A similar perspective is found in Giddens, who proposes the existence of a society which is highly 'reflexive'; that is to say, one which generates information about itself and the world in general (Giddens, 1991, 244). The application of such knowledge to everyday life ensures continued change in the human environment, though this is not presented by Giddens as a necessarily progressive development. It is his contention that 'the reflexivity of modernity actually undermines the certainty of knowledge' in all domains of enquiry, even the core sciences, partly because these obey what he calls 'the methodological principle of doubt' (*ibid.*, 21). The reflexivity of practice itself suggests that 'all practices have an irreducible discursive aspect' (Chouliaraki and Fairclough, 1999, 26). This model places discourse at the heart of all activity, but does not subsume action within discourse.

Parker departs from the apparent simplicity of this solution, declaring somewhat bluntly that reflexivity and discourse analysis, as solutions to the problem of knowledge and reference are 'specific to our time and place in Western culture'; he suggests (in a vein reminiscent of the debate which initiated this chapter), that academic preoccupation with language is 'an evasion of the material basis of oppression' (*ibid.*, 21), yet is also prepared to recognise its necessity in politicising everyday life. If language, and therefore discourse, is able to alter the consciousness of individuals, part of its power may lie in its 'transcendent' quality, recognised by Giorgi when he argues that it is not wholly determinative, but capable of generating new ideas and insights (Giorgi, in Semin and Gergen, 1990, 79).[48]

The question to ask therefore is what practical implications this quality, and the material action of language in general, carries for the analysis of texts. The argument advanced by Chouliaraki and Fairclough is that one discursive practice may 'appropriate' another. The example given is the growth of managerial ideologies in education, which appear to have colonised traditional discourses, providing new resources for the ordering of speech. Through new configurations of reference and proposition, certain types of understanding are established and particular forms of conduct sanctioned. However, all modes of discourse within contemporary society,

---

48 I disagree, however, with his statement that linguistic evolution can only take place when speakers respond to something 'non-linguistic' (Giorgi, in Semin and Gergen, 1990, 79).

whether on education, 'race', equality, crime, conflict, the environment and so forth, are articulated within a particular spatial and temporal understanding of the society as a whole; whether this shared conception is entirely accurate, or indeed whether it is really a universal feature of public perception, are questions which can be tested through the use of discourse analysis.

However, considering that a central task of this book is to investigate the material character of discursivity in general, and the associated usefulness of 'realist' textual analysis,[49] it seems appropriate that it should begin by considering an essential concept, which can be regarded both as a structure within which discourse operates, and as an instance of contemporary discursive practices. This concept is that of 'modernity' itself.

---

49 See the Introduction to this book.

Chapter 3

Discourse and Modernity

Modernity as structure and practice

A study of the term modernity appears immediately to reveal the operation of competing theories of the social. Developments in political, economic, cultural and social life are identified through the use of an uncomfortable combination of conceptual and temporal signifiers, such as modern, late modern, 'high' modern or post-modern. The use of such terms enables theorists, policy makers and academics to employ a series of competing narratives that promote radically different versions of social reality, often entailing quite divergent ideas about public conduct.

A common point of agreement, however, is that 'modern life' is markedly different from earlier social formations;[1] another shared tendency is therefore a preference for descriptions of the social order which emphasise flux and traumatic change. However unstable and contingent, the existence of modernity (in its discursive and extra-discursive form), cannot be theorised without tracing the root of the term from which it has grown. The English word *modern* emerges from the French *moderne*, which came from the late Latin term *modernus*. Its origin, in turn, is found in the classical Latin *modo*, meaning 'recently' or 'just now'. Williams notes that the earliest English meaning was closest to the idea of the 'contemporary' (or co-temporary), 'in the sense of something existing now, just now' (Williams, 1988, 208).

The word thus refers to a very recent past, and by implication a state of affairs at least old enough to be identified as separate from (though still intimately related to) the immediate sensations of everyday experience. Yet it also suggests a kind of *on-going recency*, which reveals the difficulty of making references to the transitory moment, the elusive yet constantly 'renewed' present. As the concept of 'the modern' began to be applied to a particular era, so it became increasingly laden with value. In Lefebvre's 'Introduction to Modernity' (written from 1959 to 1960) the author draws attention to a familiar habit of speech, when he notes that the term modern is employed by people who 'think they know what they are talking about and that there is nothing more to be said' (Lefebvre, 1995, 1). Here, it is the idea that the concept is self-explanatory, and self-evidently positive, which Lefebvre wishes to question. It is also clear that this author identifies 'modern' as an operative term within everyday exchange, a locus of discourse which closes down, rather than opens up, possibilities for dialogue or critique.

---

1   See the discussion below.

Such unreflexive utterance also demonstrates the connection between ordinary expression and larger systems of belief, indicating in a negative sense the existence of what Deacon and his co-authors call 'the relationship between language use and social structure' (Deacon *et al.*, 1999, 146). Modernity is certainly a powerful theme within advertising texts of the period. For example, the effects of the compression of space and time within air travel, became an increasingly common experience, and thus something which advertising addressed. In a TWA airlines advertisement of 1964,[2] below a photograph of an aircraft interior, the following printed text appeared:

> One movie ... and 1,000 miles slip by. You're there before you know it on TWA, the airline that knows America best. There's only one way you lose time on TWA. You lose awareness of it – and we help you every minute of your trip to the U.S.A.! Besides wining and dining, there's an absorbing, full-length feature film presented by Inflight Motion Pictures ...

Analysis of such textual expressions and the contexts in which they appear, should also help to establish 'how relations and structures of power are embedded in the forms of everyday language use' (*ibid.*, 150).[3] It is possible to suggest, therefore, that the presentation of a single (modern) era as the ultimate and most desirable state of affairs, as though no further development, alteration or decay is possible, may be responsible for the vehement rejection of 'grand narratives' by post-structuralist writers, and indeed may explain their hostility to the 'project' of modernity itself. As Norris writes of Lyotard, '[he] argues that the philosophic discourse of modernity is now historically redundant' (Norris, 2000, 10). Ashcroft, writing about postcolonial developments, believed that the representation of modernity as 'a major revolution ... in world society' was to 'employ the historical consciousness which is a characteristic of modernity itself' (Ashcroft, 2001, 32).

There is a difference, certainly, between the complacency noted by Lefebvre in the early sixties, and the resonance set up by current usage of such terminology. Although it is possible to encounter references to the 'modern' in contemporary speech and writing, and in many forms of 'corporate' or formal address (such as advertising and political broadcasts), the range and values of the term has changed since Lefebvre made his observations; a positive connotation is no longer always assumed. Therefore, its referential power as a clarion-call for progress has been cast into doubt.

The same quality of events may be signified, but the concept itself suggests, rather than unquestionable confidence, a rather more circumscribed outlook. It is possible to think for example of the reservations which seem to be associated with

---

2   The ad appeared in 'Woman's Weekly' of 21 November 1964.

3   The difference is that it is not my intention to argue, as do these writers, that language necessarily contributes to 'the legitimation of existing social relationships' (Deacon, 150); such a position would suggest an attachment to the 'dominant ideology thesis' (analysed by Abercrombie *et al*, 1980; 1990) which the present work does not support.

the term 'modern art', the scepticism attaching to the idea of 'modern architecture', or the exhaustion and ennui implied in references to 'modern life', all of which may indicate that modernity is no longer the phenomenon which 'justifies its own existence merely by moving' (Lefebvre, *op. cit.*).

In plotting the contours of modernity as both discourse and structure, therefore, reference to the 'present' alone will prove less than enlightening; the term can be used to indicate any number of situations, with no guarantee that one set of events (soon to be 'overtaken' by the next wave of occurrences) will reveal the salient features of the modern epoch. Therefore, any study of contemporary language and society which concentrates on the mere coincidence of the most 'recent' events, will fail to reveal the true character of the period from which they emerge. The root of the problem, that 'modernity is a form of historical time which valorises the new' (Osborne, 1995, xii) means that it cannot help but create, through the process of self-identification, value judgements about its own status; this in turn implies a degree of superiority to other eras. Blumenberg for example goes so far as to claim that, 'modernity was the first and only age that understood itself as an epoch' (Blumenberg, 1983, 115), and as a result of this awareness actually 'created other epochs' (*ibid.*). Acceptance of this position requires a refusal to believe that other periods could ever engage in temporal/spatial self-identification.[4]

Considering the position on discourse and reflexivity presented above, ideas which propose the retrospective 'creation' of earlier epochs also invite a close appraisal of two other notions, the first of which may be regarded as a reasonable and productive proposition, while the persuasive force of the second is more doubtful. The first associated idea is that social formations may be brought into being as reflexive entities through a form of what may be called 'discursive action', where discourse is understood as a material resource and action is deemed to encompass speech as both an organisational tool and as a 'projective' instrument (Harre and Gillett, 1994).

This is not to suggest that social reality extends no further than linguistic categorisation (other symbolic forms are also employed in the life of a society), but rather that members of a social order employ language to describe situations and imagine transformations in their condition of life.[5] The *essential difference* here when compared with Blumenberg's assertion (that the constitution of previous epochs may be a *contemporary* exercise of symbolic description), is that a mediated public culture has in effect simply brought into focus a 'compositional' and even

---

4   It is certainly reasonable, however, to argue as does Mattelart, that there is a 'possible kinship between the first attempts by topographers of routes and waterways to control territories in the seventeenth and eighteenth centuries, the normalisation and classification of individuals and regions undertaken by the pioneers of "moral statistics" ... and the targeting of "consumption communities" by modern marketing in the twentieth century' (Mattelart, 1996, ix/x). In other words, the epoch of modernity is characterised by attempts both to describe and to rationalise the conditions of life.

5   Witness for example Barker's reference to the purpose of fairy-tales as transformative depictions of peasant life (Barker, 1989, 132).

a projective quality of reflexivity and discursive action which has *always existed* in human societies. The second implication drawn from Blumenberg's position is less satisfactory, at least in the sense that it disallows further development. This is the problem identified above and which keeps recurring; the notion that modernity has become the pinnacle of history, the refinement of all other social formations, doing so not only by representing the 'now', but by creating a comparative system of representation in which it itself is the benchmark whenever an advanced form of social organisation needs to be identified.

A complex of processes

The difficulty in attaching a particular 'label' to contemporary experience is that modernity must be recognised as a 'complex of processes' (Murdock, 1993, 523). Modernity is thus characterised by a number of phenomena, identified as: the continued dominance of capitalism as an economic system, a secular rather than religious approach to knowledge and meaning, an attachment to rationality as a guiding principle in public conduct, the existence of the nation-state and, in Murdock's words, 'a more fragmented and contested cultural field', in which 'contending discourses struggle for public visibility and authority' (*ibid.*). Murdock's description finds an echo in Hall's temporal perspective on this subject, where he notes that processes unfold 'according to different historical time-scales, whose interaction led to variable and contingent outcomes' (Hall *et al*, 1992, 1). He identified four processes; political, economic, social and cultural, though it should be understood that all developments in advanced societies appear as composites of these forces.

Agreement concerning the broad character of modernity may be shared by a wide variety of writers, but there is far less accord about the status or condition of the forces which produce the phenomenon itself, and about the pace, direction and significance of their development. One of the consequences of the drive to revise the social order which accompanies the 'reflexive' principle is, as we have seen, that modernity 'can have no respect even for its own past, let alone that of any previous social order' (Harvey, 1990, 11). If the aim is of modernity is *modernisation*, then anything perceived as redundant (an idea, a social practice, an institution), is under threat of replacement or alteration. One manifestation of this tendency may be found when certain types of public behaviour are identified as 'outmoded'; this, for example, has been a feature of the state's response to those forms of social solidarity which provide some defence against the operation of the free market.

While 'modernity' does indeed refer to the condition of life in contemporary society, including the symbolic, political, cultural, social and economic forms through which that life is expressed, it must do more than merely describe the attainment of a particular state. It should also suggest a dynamic process, an evolution towards the desired/feared outcome of becoming modern.[6] Murdock's description

---

6   See the Chapter on Advertising.

of modernity, which introduced this section, recognised that the processes which characterise it as a phenomenon, 'detached societies from the economic, social and cultural formations we now characterise as "ancient" or "traditional"' (Murdock, 1993, 523).[7] Murdock's observation is important because he notes that modernity is 'best seen as a set of dynamics rather than as a condition, a continual process of becoming rather than an accomplished state of being' (*ibid.*). Wagner argues that the meaning of 'modernity' relies on 'a basic distinction between these social formations and 'traditional' societies', yet it is 'immensely difficult to both exactly define the characteristics of modern societies and to show when they actually broke with traditional social formations' (Wagner, 1994, 3). This in turn might indicate that modernity has a starting-point, though in common with the assertion found in Genesis ('in the beginning was the word'), the moment of inception itself remains obscure.

The character of modernity

Considering the variety of forces which together produce the modern condition, and the different importance accorded to each by various writers, it is not surprising that there is no exact agreement about the timing of modernity's emergence. The eighteenth-century Enlightenment is often cited as the era that most closely represents the beginnings of the phenomenon, though other periods, such as the early sixteenth-century, are also identified as significant. Hall, for example, locates the onset of modernity not in the growth of nineteenth-century industrialism, but rather with the 'rapid and extensive social and economic development which followed the decline of feudalism' (Hall, 1992, 1).

Outram, concentrating upon the eighteenth century, refers to the establishment across Europe of 'new institutions and organisations where ideas could be explored and discussed', together with a growth in population and the expansion of communication systems, but in so doing refers to the 'stagnation of the previous century' (Outram, 1995, 15). Such differences of opinion about the quality of epochal development may be considered in the light of their exposition through contemporary orders of discourse, and the values they appear to reveal; in the meantime, however, it should be noted that the outstanding features of modernity are hardly 'settled' or agreed upon, in the sense that the entire condition is often described as contradictory (see below).

As a category which designates an historical period, modernity takes on what Osborne calls 'a peculiar dual role' (Osborne, 1995, 13). The appearance of the term indicates its contemporary status by being identified with a particular epoch (the 'modern'), while registering this contemporaneity 'in terms of a qualitatively new, self-transcending temporality' (*ibid.*). Modernity thus becomes 'permanent transition' (Osborne, 1995, 14). It attains therefore an apparently impregnable status,

---

7   See Murdock; 'Communications and Modernity', in 'Media, Culture and Society', October, 1993, 523.

in which dramatic alteration of its own configuration, far from undermining its claim to pre-eminence, serves only to reinforce its position as the 'ultimate' social order.

A distinction has already been suggested between 'modernity' as a term (used to describe the current social formation), and those references to 'modern life' which merely seek to establish temporal markers between contemporary existence and a largely undefined past. While the modern period does show clear differences to earlier types of human organisation and constitutes a break with 'traditional' social forms, the contention of the present work is that this break can be over-dramatised.

For example, the opening paragraph of Martin Shaw's study[8] makes a bold claim about 'historic transformations' in human society; 'for the first time since human beings inhabited this earth, it is possible to describe comprehensive networks of human relationships which include all people' (Shaw, 3). The idea that society has recently experienced particularly significant social and political change, has indeed formed a constant refrain in contemporary theory. The notion that social forces like the media and the concomitant development of 'mediated interaction' (Thompson, 1995), have brought about near-universal contact may begin to stretch credulity; to claim that this development represents the establishment of 'comprehensive networks' of 'human relationships' is perhaps to misapply both terms.[9]

The pre-modern and the modern

Caution should therefore be exercised when references to modern life emphasise its far-reaching or uniquely 'advanced' character. The effect is, as stated above, to suggest that development is at an end, and that previous social formations have been completely superseded; but it also implies that every aspect of past experience (technological, cultural, moral and so on) has become redundant. Thus even the modes of conduct associated with the past may be mistakenly regarded as curiosities, as though they are in all respects entirely dissimilar to the ordinary conduct of life in modern societies.

This is partly because, as Peter Wagner argues, social theorists 'describe a new social state and the process towards it in terms of an earlier state', without paying proper attention to 'the adequacy and consistency of the concepts and terminology used to characterise the earlier state' (Wagner, 1994, x). The danger is that 'pre-modern' societies will thus be presented as wholly primitive, emphasising again the supposed superiority of the modern social order.

Lefebvre also noted the tendency to elevate the status of the contemporary world, drawing attention to the fact that 'for a long time the "modern" has been seen as the opposite of the "ancient"' and that modern is a word 'which for centuries the new and the here-and-now have used in triumphalist self-justification' (Lefebvre,

---

8   See 'Global Society and International Relations'.

9   Such optimism is matched by Negroponte's evaluation of new media, in which a complete conversion from analog to digital systems will bring about the dawn of a new social order (Negroponte, 1995).

1995, 168). There is a certain laziness apparent in much use of the juxtaposition modern/ancient, as though the ancient acts as a mere contrast to the contemporary, with little sense of what Calinescu declares to be 'the distinction between *antiquus* and *modernus*' which 'seems to have always implied a polemic significance, or a principle of conflict' (Calinescu, 1987, 14).

Above all, there is no one identifiable moment in which traditional societies became modern. Instead, a gradual transformation took place, with a number of social forms existing side by side, though centuries of development could be overshadowed by more traumatic periods of change. If the modern period does show marked differences to earlier types of human organisation it is important to ask what distinguishes the present social formation from what has gone before. To do this, some knowledge of both modern and 'pre-modern' society is required.

However, the brief description of pre-modern societies which follows must be treated with caution, because it is easy to imagine that each was superseded by the one which follows next on the list; in fact, these forms could be found at various times and in a variety of places, and no single example is necessarily more 'advanced' than another. In addition, any summary of this nature is bound to oversimplify the internal dynamics of any society.

Giddens (1993, 43) sets out four types of pre-modern society: *hunter-gatherer* societies in which relatively small numbers of people live by hunting, fishing and the collection of edible plant material; *agrarian* societies consisting of small rural communities which rely upon agriculture; *pastoral* societies which depend on the possession and use of domesticated animals; and finally *traditional* societies where agriculture is the mainstay of life, but where trade and various branches of manufacture also take place.[10]

The first three modes of life mentioned above have declined and only exist in a few isolated areas. No *traditional* form of civilisation has survived into the twenty-first century, in some cases as the direct result of contact with what Giddens (1993, 50) calls 'Western influences'. This may be true where two societies, one advanced and the other traditional, 'collide'; but it is also the case that modernity itself developed from traditional forms of social organisation.[11]

What distinguishes modern from traditional societies? One typical answer is the development of technology and the process of *industrialisation*. Industrialisation is the application of machine technology to production. Bradley notes that 'industrialisation in Britain was a long, slow and uneven process' dating from 'about

10 Catephores calls one of the dominant forms of production in pre-capitalist or traditional societies *simple commodity production*, This form exists where *local* rather than long-distance trade is of particular importance. Its main features can be summarised here: specialised division of labour; small-scale production by individual specialists; self-employment; a mixture of money and barter as a means of payment; and lack of co-ordination over the economy overall. (Catephores, 1989, 20).

11 It is the 'internal' transition from one configuration to another which is the main focus of this brief study; therefore, the analysis of traditional societies should provide clues to the comparative status of modernity.

1780' (in Hall, 1992, 191). She also explains that the establishment of an industrial economy was not secured until 1850 or later. Even at this date, there were still 'three times as many agricultural workers as textile workers' (*ibid.*, 193). Industrialism therefore, cannot account for the entire character of modernity. Industrial society was given its particular shape by the social and economic system within which it developed – capitalism.[12] Yet the basic principles of capitalism existed before industrialisation gathered pace, taking agrarian and mercantile forms, for example.

While Postan described mediaeval England as pre-industrial, noting that most of its population was engaged in agricultural production,[13] he makes a point of emphasising that industrial and commercial activities were not insignificant; exchange between regions was fairly commonplace as was trade with other countries, undertaken in order to obtain commodities such as salt and spices. Postan's work demonstrates that mediaeval economies were not as 'primitive' as some post-war historians believed. In fact, he goes further, arguing that 'no society known to us, however remote in time or backward in economic development, was wholly incapable of exchanging commodities within itself or with other societies' (Postan, 1972, p. 206).

He notes that 'for all the periods of pre-history in which men lived in social groups ... archaeologists have found evidence of men exchanging, sometimes over long distances, their surplus produce' (*ibid.*, 207). Exchange of this nature relies upon communication, which in turn depends upon the physical maintenance of public highways.

The main thrust of Huizinga's famous volume, 'The Waning of the Middle Ages', which first appeared in 1924, is rather different. A study of human relations and culture in fourteenth and fifteenth century France and the Netherlands, its purpose is exactly to emphasise the difference between existence in pre-modern society and the nature of contemporary experience. The key to this difference lies, according to Huizinga, in social behaviour, thought, and artistic expression; in all those forms which together create the public ambience of existence. It is not, then, an assessment of economic development.

Huizinga in the first instance argues that, in the mediaeval period 'every event, every action, was still embodied in expressive and solemn forms, which raised them to the dignity of a ritual' (Huizinga, 1924, 9). This would include not only the 'great facts' of birth, marriage and death, but everyday events such as journeys, tasks and visits. He also contends that 'calamities and indigence were more afflicting than at present', while illness and health 'provided a more striking contrast' (Huizinga,

---

12 One of the most difficult problems which faces the student of modernity, is how exactly *Industrialisation* and *Capitalism* have affected one another. It is possible to approach this question from a different direction, by asking if capitalism would ever have attained its global influence without the power of industrial production, or if industrial society could have taken more democratic forms had co-operative models of social organisation been established during the transition to modernity.

13 The numbers occupied in trade and industry 'formed a relatively small proportion of the total ... even those ... often combined their industrial and commercial occupations with some agricultural pursuits' (Postan, 1976, 205).

1924, 9). While Huizinga's account is well-written and persuasive, there are certain points which require caution. In the first place, industrial modernity, at least in its mid-nineteenth century manifestation, did a great deal to worsen the prospects of life of the urban worker, and to make existence more traumatic and dangerous; therefore, calamitous experiences do not simply indicate the existence of pre-modern formations. The second point concerns the question of ritual, described by Bloch as 'invariant ... unclear' with 'little possibility for individual innovation' (Kuper and Kuper, 1985, 699). It is also characterised as 'anti-intellectual' (*ibid.*). While ordinary events in the contemporary world may not be attended with what Huizinga calls 'a thousand formalities: benedictions, ceremonies, formulas' (Huizinga, 1924, 9), they nonetheless involve certain formulaic behaviours.

Ritual, as a 'dramatic commentary on life' (Bloch, in Kuper and Kuper, 1985, 699) is a feature of all societies and does not disappear with the onset of modernity; rather, it assumes new forms and is taken up by agents of public mediation (the mass media and related institutions). The point is not to argue that pre-modern ritual has been over-emphasised, nor to assert that contemporary society ever reaches the same intensity of ritualistic public behaviour. Rather, it is to avoid seeing the 'proud or cruel publicity' described by Huizinga as a unique feature of mediaeval society, creating thus a barrier between social formations, and making it more difficult to understand how one society developed from the traditions of another.

When Giddens contends that '... modern social life is characterised by profound processes of the reorganisation of time and space, coupled to the expansion of disembedding mechanisms – mechanisms which prise social relations free from the hold of specific locales, recombining them across wide time-space distances' (Giddens, 1991, 2/3), it is clear that he assigns a particular quality to pre-modern or traditional life. In simple terms, he reinforces the common idea that social relations are bound to a single locality. The notion of a largely static society, in terms of both physical movement and the relationships between individuals, is found also in Huizinga, who notes that 'the conception of society in the Middle Ages is static, not dynamic' (Huizinga, 1924, 56). It appears in Burke, who declares that the lives of mediaeval people were 'regular, repetitive, and unchanging' (in Crowley and Heyer, 1995, 80). Such statements suggest a social order somehow deficient in imaginative perspective.

The picture presented in Bloch's 'Feudal Society' is however rather more complex. He takes the view that communities were not isolated in quite the way envisaged by more casual commentators; 'though poor and unsafe, the roads or tracks were in constant use ... no institution or method could take the place of personal contact ... to control a country there was no other means than to ride through it incessantly in all directions' (Bloch, 1962, 63). A host of individuals, including vagabonds, clerics, nobles, merchants and pilgrims, passed through the various social locations of mediaeval society.

Speaking again of modernity, Giddens emphasises 'the reorganisation of time and space' which 'act[s] to transform the content and nature of day-to-day social life' (*op. cit.*). Such transformation does not apply to the traditional order, but it was certainly less moribund than might be supposed. Bloch agrees that the 'ordering of the scheme of human relations' in this period was 'quite different from anything we know today', but mentions also that 'there was scarcely any remote little place which had not some contacts intermittently through that sort of continuous yet irregular 'Brownian movement' which affected the whole of society' (Bloch, 1962, 64).

The difference between traditional and post-traditional orders lies, according to Giddens, in the idea that pre-modern societies derive their power from 'externally referential systems', meaning 'the natural order, the sanctity of tradition or custom' or God (O'Brien, 22). By contrast, in Giddens' opinion, the power of modern societies is to be discovered in 'internally referential systems' such as 'accumulated or scientific expertise, procedural rationality or efficiency, and ... trust relations' (*ibid.*). Here, we begin to see the concept of reference groups ... 'an individual or social grouping which either sets or maintains standards for the individual' or 'a frame of comparison relative to which the individual compares himself' (Urry, in Kuper and Kuper, 690). Max Scheler maintained that 'the mediaeval peasant prior to the thirteenth century does not compare himself to the feudal lord, nor does the artisan compare himself to the knight ... every comparison took place within a strictly circumscribed frame of reference ... in the 'system of free-competition' on the other hand ... aspirations are intrinsically *boundless*, for they are no longer tied to any particular object or quality' (Urry, in Kuper and Kuper, 691).

Modernity and reflexivity

If modernity is not merely a name given to mark the succession of one epoch by another, but a phenomenon which continues to generate change, then it could be described as the orientation of a society towards the *goal* of modernisation, a continual process shaped by present need and a particular conception of the future. This book illustrates the idea through reference to political and commercial rhetoric. One of the terms used to describe the forward-movement of modernity as a project is, of course, 'reflexivity', already discussed above. Not only can the modern era be described as 'forward-looking', but the future itself can be imagined to be, in Giddens' words, 'continually drawn into the present by means of the reflexive organisation of knowledge environments' (Giddens, 1991, 3). Reflexivity in this case refers to those types of social theory which, in the act of explaining the world, re-configure or alter aspects of reality. Reflexivity is thus both action and the production of knowledge and meaning, 'in the sense that terms introduced to describe social life routinely enter and transform it' (Giddens, 1991a, 20). Through the use of reflexive forms of knowledge, ideas about the social are never merely descriptive.

This means, in effect, that the act of seeking to understand the present prepares the ground for future developments; the use of knowledge is part of social evolution. Reflexivity is thus 'a central characteristic of modernity, accounting for the dynamism of modern social systems' (O'Brien, 1999, 8). In the hands of Scott Lash, 'reflexivity' is also applied to the condition of modernity, but modernity itself is divided into two tendencies. The first is associated with the logic of scientific rationality which characterises the Enlightenment. The second is 'reflexive modernity', in which individuals must use their 'reflexive judgement' in a variety of situations to work out rules of conduct and response (Lash, 1999, 3). This is necessary, according to Lash, because the guiding certainties of the Enlightenment period are no longer convincing.

The reflective/reflexive challenge is found also in Henri Lefebvre's 'Introduction to Modernity', in which he observes that 'by modernity ... we understand the beginnings of a reflective process, a more-or-less advanced attempt at critique and autocritique, a bid for knowledge' (Lefebvre, *op. cit.*). The difference between Lefebvre's statement and the position taken by Giddens, is that Giddens' reflexivity describes 'the outcomes of social action without reference to the conscious intentions of acting subjects' (O'Brien, 1999, 24). This should come as no surprise; modern societies are complex structures which appear to evolve in ways which seem beyond human control, while the study of human action demonstrates how often unexpected consequences can grow from apparently straightforward decisions.

Modernity and time

Osborne recognises the movement from a conception of the present which is merely 'a simple addition in a linear sequence of chronological time' to a 'qualitative transcendence of the past' which then becomes 'a reorientation towards the future' (Osborne, 1995, 10). Despite the need to distinguish between simple references to *the contemporary* and modernity as a social project, it is still true that the *idea* of modernity 'could be conceived only within the framework of a specific time awareness' (Calinescu, 1987, 13). This 'time awareness' is further described as 'that of *historical time*, linear and irreversible, flowing irresistibly onwards' (*op cit.*).

In other words, the existence of a social formation which displays any kind of 'forward' impetus or capacity for change, depends on a conception of time which *can allow the idea of development to take place*. Thus, a model of time that is, for example, reversible or cyclical, will fail to provide the necessary conditions for the type of advance which is characteristic of modernity.

If the idea that time is capable of renewal seems outlandish, it may be worth recalling that this is exactly what is implied in Newtonian physics. Time, in Newton's system, is conceived as an invariable quantity, suggesting that all events are capable of returning to their original state; in effect, time becomes reversible. Cyclical models of time, by contrast, may be suggested by certain aspects of ordinary experience. Human life, expended within the familiar domain of natural events like the changing seasons, appears to assume predictable 'rhythms', leading to the notion that time itself recurs. However, this impression is countered by other aspects of experience, which teach us that time is not capable of recurrence or renewal. In Barbara Adam's words 'through entropy, aging, and growth we may grasp time as irreversible and directional' (Adam, 1990, 169). This 'irreversibility' is certainly a factor in the commonplace creation of distinctions between 'now' and 'then', but also, as we have seen, a vital feature of any society that professes attachment to the idea of linear progress. In a discussion of Simmel's work on culture, Harootunian points out that modern life, 'driven by money and exchange', has 'destroyed all natural periodicities', because culture ensures the availability of all necessities throughout the year (Harootunian, 2000, 77). Individuals are then faced with a situation in which corporate power, partly responsible for this state of affairs, has to draw public attention to natural events like the seasons, doing so in order to encourage a differentiated form of consumption which universal 'availability' itself has made redundant.[14]

Now, although it is fairly easy to identify the outstanding evidence of contemporary progress (advances in transport and communication, for example), it remains the case that development within an industrial/post industrial society, seems attainable only through the sacrifice or degradation of other aspects of existence. Giddens, for example, speaks of 'the risks of ecological catastrophe' as 'an inevitable part of our contemporary experience' (Giddens, 1991, 4). Barbara Adam, in 'Timescapes of Modernity', goes further, arguing that environmental hazards are the inescapable outcome not only of large-scale production, but of the '24-hour society' and even democratic politics (Adam, 1998).

Marcuse, in his analysis of progress, argued in favour of a 'non-repressive' principle, one which could revolutionise the conditions of life faced by those who still constitute the majority of society; the working classes. He envisaged an existence devoted to enjoyment, rather than the struggle to survive. It is interesting to note that, to attain this goal, he advocated an end to the 'contentless transcendence' of modernity, and a return to a 'cyclical' notion of time, mentioned above and associated with Nietzche's 'perpetuity of pleasure' (in Habermas, 1980). It is remarkable that a critical social theorist of Marcuse's standing, should posit a form of pleasurable, but endless 'recurrence' as the chief aim of human liberation. It may suggest not only the end of alienation but, in proposing improvement without an orientation to the future, offers a startling departure from the challenging experiences of modernity, however illusory these may prove to be. Lash argues a similar case, when he insists that there is danger in a modernity which is 'too future-oriented, too forgetful ... of myth and origins' (Lash, 1999, 5).

Modernity as a project

The condition of modernity is, according to many commentators, supposed still to prevail in the present, whatever other tendencies or developments have begun to emerge. It is useful to note, however, that when the concept of modernity has been

---

14 In September 2001, for example, Marks and Spencer invited its customers to be 'Amazed by Autumn', referring to the seasonal introduction of 'classic clothing', 'multi-buys', a new fashion brand for women, low-priced 'children's basics' and extended opening hours.

removed from its use as a simple epochal marker, is has the ability to demonstrate marked differences, not only to earlier periods of development, but to less developed *contemporary* projects which do not share its objectives; this suggests both that the 'modern' is more than just a period of history, and that it is possible for other social formations to exist alongside modernity itself.

The idea that there are alternative perspectives on the meaning and status of the modern formation (observed at the beginning of this chapter), is evident in the variety of terms used to delineate the current formation. Terms such as 'late modernity', 'high modernity' (used sometimes of the Enlightenment), 'postmodernity' and even 'restricted liberal modernity' (Wagner's preference) are applied to contemporary modes of life. Habermas has suggested that modernity is an 'incomplete project' (in Brooker, 1992), while Norris notes Habermas' particular hostility to deconstruction as one symptom of the collapse of cardinal distinctions once made between different genres of writing and discourse (Norris, 2000, 49).

To identify a project as 'unfinished' may be conceived as a call to complete it, or might alternatively be interpreted as coming very close to asserting its failure (together with the consequent suspicion that in either case there cannot be a successor called the 'postmodern'). All the particular designations of modernity, however, grow from a cluster of ideas about its status as a *significant* social condition. Simply for practical reasons, therefore, some authors defend the continued use of the term as the primary means of 'orientation' from which to conduct debates about the social.

Goran Therborn (in 'European Modernity and Beyond', 1995), certainly takes this line, pointing out that modernity 'actually exists as a frequent topic of discourse' and therefore 'to deny or ignore it is simply to cut oneself off from much ongoing debate in a number of areas' (Therborn, 1995, 3). Such an argument is technically correct, though perhaps not the most effective which could be presented, in the sense that any number of ideas can be 'frequent topics of discourse' and might very well contain a substantial proportion of nonsense.

It also appears that, beyond the appeal to practical common sense, Therborn genuinely believes in modernity as a project, going on to declare that 'modernity ends when words like progress, advance, development, emancipation, liberation, growth, accumulation, enlightenment, embetterment, avant-garde, lose their attraction and their function as guides to social action' (*ibid.*, 4). Leaving aside the integrity of a word like 'embetterment', this list is worth considering for a moment, precisely because many commentators would dispute the worth of some of its contents. Therborn at least presents familiar concepts, each of which could mark the starting-point for a discussion on the nature of contemporary experience. However, the act of presenting these terms within the same sentence causes some degree of conceptual muddle.

They do not signify identical qualities, of course, but they are supposed to suggest broadly positive developments. The problem can be exemplified in the different meaning of terms such as 'emancipation' and 'accumulation'. These are two quite different social aims. The first is usually applied to the act of giving or attaining freedom to an oppressed group (Laclau calls it 'the elimination of power';

1996, 1) while the second indicates the amassing or collection of wealth. Other terms are ambiguous; the concept of 'growth', for example, does not necessarily generate unqualified approval. It is now possible to speak of 'limits to growth' (after Hirsch's study[15]), 'sustainable growth', and so on, as a way of recognising environmental degradation and other urgent questions.[16]

Although Therborn's declared intention is to present all those aspects of modernity that act as a motivating force and which continue to produce quantifiable results (demonstrating their relevance as social motors rather than necessarily their moral status), he does appear to value the attributes of modernity above rival conceptions. Modernity, according to this author, 'looks at the future, hopes for it, plans for it', while postmodernity has apparently 'lost or thrown away any sense of time direction' (*ibid.*, 4). Therborn stands, therefore, on the side of the modern project, though he notes its 'contradictions, dilemmas, tensions, conflicts', and tries to identify 'routes to and through modernity' (*ibid.*, 5). The notion of the modern period as one marked by contradiction, mentioned earlier and exemplified in the nature of Therborn's list, certainly demands further explanation.

Contradiction, capitalism and identity

Another way of making the operation of contradiction within modernity apparent, is to note the ways in which social roles and human identities are shaped by the forces of contemporary society and culture. Berman attempts to capture the sense of social fragmentation which has accompanied the supposedly unifying power of industrialisation and political centralisation, noting that 'modern environments and experiences cut across all boundaries of geography and ethnicity, of class and nationality, of religion and ideology; in this sense, modernity can be said to unite all mankind ... but it is a paradoxical unity ... it pours us all into a maelstrom of perpetual disintegration and renewal, of struggle and contradiction, of ambiguity and anguish' (1985, 15). Here, Berman recognises the instability of a social force whose apparent success in one sphere (the creation of near universal modes of existence) leads to exceptional distress in another (caused by the provisional status of personal identity). This particular contradiction is actually 'felt' by human subjects, and seems to be produced by the socioeconomic sphere as an inevitable by-product.

Giddens, in his work on this subject, argues that *doubt* has become 'a pervasive feature of modern critical reason', a feature which 'permeates everyday life' (Giddens, 1991, 2). He goes on to indicate that one consequence of this doubt is that within 'our present-day world the self ... has to be reflexively made' yet this task has to be 'accomplished amid a puzzling diversity of options and possibilities' (*ibid.*). According to Giddens, the 'reflexive project of the self', consists of sustaining 'coherent, yet continuously revised, biographical narratives' (*ibid.*, 5). Within the

---

15 Hirsch, F, ' Social limits to growth', 1977.

16 See Backstrand's work on transboundary air pollution for a social-constructionist view of environmental discourses and policies.

context of modernity, the 'notion of lifestyle takes on a particular significance' (*ibid.*).

Wagner attributes similar importance to the creation of self within the context of modernity, describing a situation in which 'it is becoming less possible for individuals or groups of human beings to escape the reach of modern institutions' (1994, xiii). Thus the 'transformation of the human self during modernity' is a process of both 'liberation and disciplinisation' (*ibid.*, xiv). Lash points to the condition of life within 'contemporary risk societies', in which 'living with risk, living with ambivalence is forced upon us' (Lash, 1999, 3).

A similar example of modernity's apparent inconsistencies is set out by Calinescu. Drawing on the work of Daniel Bell, he describes a situation where 'today's 'pop hedonism', cult of instant joy, fun morality', stands in stark contrast to the Protestant work ethic associated with the rise of capitalism. In describing the 'generalised confusion between self-realization and simple self-gratification', Calinescu distinguishes between the modern era and 'capitalism as a system' (Calinescu, 7). The confusion he identifies has its origin, he believes, in capitalism rather than in 'the culture of modernism' (*ibid.*).

According to this author, capitalism 'could develop only by encouraging consumption, social mobility, and status seeking' (*ibid.*). Yet this aim contradicted the original 'moral' basis of the capitalist system, the belief in Christian obligation and hard work.

For his part, Bell identifies 'an extraordinary contradiction within the social structure itself ... on the one hand the business corporation wants an individual to work hard, pursue a career, accept delayed gratification ... to be, in the crudest sense, an organisation man ... and yet, in its products and its advertisements, the corporation promotes pleasure, instant joy, relaxing and letting go' (in Calinescu, *op. cit.*). This formulation of Bell's is a little crude, in the sense that the power manifested in consumer culture is such that it can overcome these contradictions, at least at the level of address. He inadvertently recognises this when, still wondering at the 'extraordinary' contradiction within the social structure, he notes that 'one is to be 'straight' by day and a 'swinger' by night' (Calinescu, 7). By speaking to different aspects of individual need, by choosing an appropriate context in which to deliver particular messages, and by referring to ideas which aid the process of self-identification, the corporate voice is able to reflect both the necessity of labour and the impulse to escape.

This, essentially, is the resolution of the problem, in the sense that the sphere of enjoyment can be separated from the sphere of work – becoming a 'swinger' (Bell's term) is an act through which one demonstrates one's freedom, or ability to make a temporary detour; a diversion partly facilitated through forms of address and spheres of action constructed by corporate bodies. While the capitalist system has shown itself adept at presenting culture on a mass scale, it is also the case that it has demonstrated an inability to 'equalise' relations between different social groups; in fact, its actual practice is increasingly to offer different messages, products and forms of conduct to different social and class groups. Segmentation and psychographic profiling are the tools used to govern the citizen's imaginary relationship to the social world (Price, 1998).

Some authors have gone further, to trace 'the crisis in identity' to the *global* formation of modern experience, an influence which seems to have altered the relationship between individuals and the points of reference they once used, in traditional societies, to establish their moral and spatial location. Friedman, for example, is one writer who takes this position. In his opinion, 'national identities' have been weakened as the power of 'global modernity' has increased, resulting in the 'dissolution of ... citizenship' as understood within the context of 'a territorially defined and state-governed society' (Friedman, 1994, 86). This form of identity has supposedly been replaced by alternatives based on 'primordial' loyalties, ethnicity, 'race', local community, language and other culturally concrete forms' (*ibid.*). At this stage, it is worth pointing out that other commentators see in this development a particular danger. This is the tendency to suppose that 'contemporary neo-tribalism' (in Schlesinger's words) is no more than the disordered compilation of off-the-shelf identities, whereas it may actually represent an attempt to reconstruct forms of belonging through ethnic forms of nationality (Schlesinger, in Sreberny-Mohammadi, 1997, 69/70). Thus the 'grand narratives' of nation and belonging may be resurrected from within apparently 'post-modern' discourses.

Modernity, contradiction and capitalism

A notable feature of many attempts to describe the modern condition, or of discourses about modernity, is the departure made from more sober forms of academic language. From Marx's description of the bewildering change brought about by the dynamic of capitalist production ('all that is solid melts into air, all that is holy is profaned'; Marx, in Berman, 1982), to Berman's apocalyptic declaration that to be modern is to live in an environment which promises 'adventure, power, joy, growth, transformation' but which simultaneously 'threatens to destroy everything we have, everything we know, everything we are' (Berman, 1982, 15), the voices heard rarely sound dispassionate.

Indeed, dramatic metaphors and poetic turns of phrase are often employed in an attempt to convey the sheer complexity of the modern experience, the magnitude of those forces which contribute to its character, and the shifting nature of the phenomenon thus described. The high-flown style and intellectual passion associated with writing on this subject emerges from the need to find a way of representing a complex social formation, but reflects also the fact that individual authors are composing dispatches from within the maelstrom itself.

At first sight, modernity appears as a powerful, unified phenomenon, by virtue of its dynamism and wide-ranging social impact. Yet despite the idea that the modern project is a manifestation of focused effort and reflexive will, it does indeed appear to be riven with certain types of paradox. One has already been mentioned; the way in which greater individual opportunity is set against increasingly catastrophic forms of global risk, which act to threaten both the individual and the society as a whole (it is this awareness that companies like bp trade upon in their attempt to create a 'receptive' consumer[17]).

Another conspicuous feature of the literature on modernity, is that each act of description seems to prefigure many of the issues and concerns which are now associated with *postmodern* attitudes. It is as though the transformative power of modernity threatens to exhaust traditional forms of description and to demand extraordinary measures. As a consequence, themes associated with postmodernity, such as the end of history, the ambiguity of meaning, and the failure of 'grand' or even coherent narrative, appear at first sight to confirm the dangerous trajectory of modern existence. As a fragmented response to this condition, postmodernity may from one perspective represent a crisis in explanation and a failure of nerve. Yet, the fact that it is able to identify the various features of a contradictory system, suggest the possibility that such elements *taken together* might provide a coherent frame of reference. In this sense, postmodernity functions as a critical reflection on modernity and its last redoubt of defence. Or, put another way, once 'the 'modern' becomes 'tradition', the 'postmodern' can play the modern' with the result that postmodernity 'must be the name for a new modernity' (Osborne, 1995, 4). It is then possible to detect the decay of this process, as authors identify the onset of 'philosophy after postmodernism' (which Crowther used as his title for a book which appeared in 2003).

The notion of paradox or 'contradiction' within modernity, while it can refer to opposite or opposing statements, forces or ideas, may also suggest confusion and inconsistency, particularly internal inconsistency within a statement or position, or in this case, within a social structure. Care needs to be taken, however, when subscribing to the idea that the problems of modernity can be ascribed simply to the existence of a state of 'contradiction'. There is, indeed, a logic to the kind of conflict or contradiction which arises in the contemporary social world. In other words, contradiction here is not chaos, but rather the consequence of the growth of the multiplicity of forces which shape modernity. An example may be found in the socioeconomic system so closely associated with the development of contemporary society – capitalism.

The capitalist system

Although some authors, like Dennis Wrong, believe that the concept was a retrospective development, the creation of a 'system' where none had existed, and that 'Karl Marx never used the term, usually describing the social order ... as "bourgeois society"'(Wrong, 1998, 3), it remains a useful description. Capitalism, far from being in Wrong's words 'nothing but an economic system which has the palpable advantage but also the ideological disadvantage of actually existing' (*ibid.*),

---

17 See Chapter 4.

is as noted above 'socioeconomic', an economic system which creates both classes and social relations and maintains the separation of production from consumption (a feature essential to an understanding of media and communication forms within modernity).

If 'capitalism' was not Marx's preferred term, he at least argued that 'capitalist production moves in contradictions' (in Freedman, 1961, 169). Once again, it is important to ask how exactly the nature of such contradiction manifests itself. In simple terms, one could say that the very strengths of capitalism contain the seeds of an eventual weakness, the centralisation of production and the falling rate of profit storing up trouble in social and political form. In the theory of capitalist production as explained by Marx, economic power becomes concentrated in fewer and fewer hands, so that 'along with the constantly diminishing number of the magnates of capital ... grows the mass of misery, oppression, slavery, degradation, exploitation; but with this too grows the revolt of the working-class, a class always increasing in numbers, and disciplined, united, organised by the very mechanism of the process of capitalist production itself' (Marx, 1954, 715).

The capitalist economy creates an industrial proletariat which it can exploit, but in so doing ensures that an organised class can eventually pose a challenge to the rule of the bourgeoisie. The transition to socialism is thought inevitable not because of an automatic movement from one system to another, but in Dodd's words, because of 'a conjunction between structural contradictions and the conscious activity, or praxis, of the working class' (Dodd, 1999, 19). It is the outcome of a logical contradiction, the distinction made above, rather than an inexplicable or unexpected consequence. 'Capitalist production', according to Marx, collects human beings 'in great centres, and causing an ever-increasing preponderance of town population ... concentrates the historical motive power of society' (Marx, 1954, 474). To the extent that the forces of production strengthen the development of society towards, eventually, a socialist or cooperative model, they can be characterised in a positive manner; in this sense, Marx is an advocate of modernity.

Indeed, his attitude to the rise of capitalist forms of organisation makes a positive evaluation of modernity and its associated systems: 'in the sphere of agriculture, modern industry has a more revolutionary effect than elsewhere ... the irrational, old-fashioned methods of agriculture are replaced by scientific ones' (*ibid.*). Science here stands for rationality. As Giddens rightly observes, the 'progenitors of modern science and philosophy', including Marx, believed that they were attempting to produce 'securely founded knowledge of the social and natural worlds' (Giddens, 1991, 21). However, the sense of certainty thus achieved becomes an illusion, in that (as noted above) the reflexivity of modernity 'actually undermines the certainty of knowledge, even in the core domains of natural science' (*ibid.*).

The challenge mounted by labour to capital, and thus the development of a more just society, did not develop in the way Marx imagined. He saw that capitalist social relations eventually become a hindrance to the further development of production, but also supposed that the crises experienced in the system threatened the whole basis of bourgeois society, when he and Engels wrote that 'the productive forces at the disposal of society no longer further the development of the conditions of bourgeois property; on the contrary, they have become too powerful for these conditions' (Marx and Engels, 1967, 86). The shortcomings of the Marxist vision lie, according to Dodd, not exclusively within flawed analyses of phenomena such as the labour theory of value, but in a larger difficulty; the attempt to draw together 'a theoretical argument regarding the political economy of capitalism', with 'a normative argument regarding the position and political potential of the working class' (Dodd, 1999, 19).

Of course, the occurrence of contradiction within modernity can be variously interpreted, in certain cases as a 'dialectical form of change' (Therborn, 1995, 21). This is perhaps a more useful perspective because it helps to highlight the processes of development. The dialectic, as a method of enquiry which (from the Greek 'to converse') pursues truth through the clashes and oppositions of formal argument, forms a central analytical tool in the work of Marx. More particularly, in the concept of 'dialectical materialism', the contradiction located in argument could also be found within the social order itself. The material world is conceived as dynamic and subject to change, forcing individuals and societies to adapt to new circumstances. It is exactly at times of general crisis that the dialectic is supposed to be played out across whole societies. One form of crisis which illustrates the formation of modernity in the most dramatic manner, is that of internal civil conflict, a clash of forces which brings the social, economic and ideological aspects of modern existence into sharp focus; another is the onset of international crises and wars.

Conflict and modernity

Therborn argues that the European route to modernity is civil war, in the sense of 'conflicts ... for and against a particular social or cultural order within a given population' (Therborn, 1995, 21). This kind of struggle is he believes, qualitatively different from the straightforward 'evolution' of societies or the imposition of change from above. Therborn's definition of civil war also escapes the superficial assumption that it is defined primarily by physical conflict; it becomes instead an expression of deep-seated social and political antagonisms.

An example of a full-blown ideological struggle is found within the English civil war of the 1640s, in which certain typical features of modernity can be discovered in a social formation usually regarded (probably because it is 'pre-industrial' and its controversies are sometimes couched within religious discourses), as too underdeveloped to qualify as modern. Yet in this period certain themes and characteristics appear which seem, when compared with those restricted bourgeois developments of the eighteenth century celebrated by Habermas, exceptionally vibrant and democratic. Outram describes 'the experience of social elites' (Outram, 1995, 27) during the Enlightenment, but finds the controversy over other classes' intellectual development too difficult to resolve. Yet the dissemination of radical ideas in the seventeenth century (sometimes expressed, admittedly, through myths such as the 'Norman yoke'), seems to have been achieved throughout the social order. Many intimations of modernity, both intellectual and structural, are evident in the sixteenth century, including the growth in a new urban population; that of London may have increased eight-fold between 1500 and 1650 (Hill, 1975, 40).

Hall, from remarks cited above,[18] may be enlisted to support the case for granting the Civil War period the status of 'early modernity'; yet the philosophical and scientific ground for such a development had been established much earlier, from the sixteenth century onward (Dear, 2001). The reflexive character of the period is also a notable attainment, in which a new world was imagined or 'drawn into' the present. The 'secular' development of knowledge may be observed in both the assumption by ordinary people of functions originally reserved for the clergy, and in the rise of state power, which provided a new locus of authority and influence. In the latter case, this is made apparent in the decision made in 1588 to extend military training to the whole population.[19]

Subsequently, the forces unleashed by the war ensured that the whole notion of a social order founded on the exercise of established authority, was itself called into question. The reconstitution of the social and political landscape may be exemplified by the creation of the New Model Army, which brought together a cohesive military force composed essentially of 'the common people in uniform' (Hill, 1975, 25).

The contradiction here is found in the attempt to shore up hierarchical government by recruiting support from amongst those whose entire outlook ultimately posed a threat to its stability; this was Parliament's dilemma when it turned to the lower orders for support in its struggle against royal prerogative. The Scottish poet Drummond argued that the gentry, by encouraging revolt, had disrupted the long accepted hierarchy of subordination (Hill, 1975, 24). Simonds D'Ewes, a Parliamentarian, declared that 'we know not what advantage the meaner sort also may take to divide the spoils of the rich and noble among them' (*ibid.*, 23). These fears were exacerbated by the displacement of rural populations which had become 'the victims of enclosure'; it meant that areas of London became in Hill's opinion, the refuge for 'masterless men' (*ibid.*, 20).

Returning to the question of secular thought, one of the salient features of modernity is the supposed change in the conception of self vis-a-vis 'established' modes of orientation, such as secular authority and religion. During the English civil war, the existence of radical sects (and doctrines like Familism and Anabaptism), strengthened the belief that there was no need to use priests as intermediaries between God and the individual, and that a direct relationship could be established. The consequences of such an idea were pictured at the time; Bishop Cooper complained that the common people had 'conceived an heathenish contempt of religion and a

---

18 Hall places the rise of modernity with the 'rapid and extensive social and economic development which followed the decline of feudalism' (Hall, 1992, 1).

19 The 'necessity' of such a measure from the state's perspective can be set against the concern expressed at the time that, once trained, servants would become unsettled and unwilling to return to their masters.

disdainful loathing of the ministers thereof' (*ibid.*, 28). Furthermore, if the idea of unmediated communication with God was combined with the conviction that human beings were made in his image, it was a short step to the belief that human subjects were themselves divine.

Amongst the political radicals, the conviction grew that force of arms was not only morally defensible, but had been sanctioned by the Almighty; as 'The Souldiers Catechisme' of 1644 argued, 'seeing God hath put the sword of reformation into the soldiers' hand, I think it is not amiss that they should cancel and demolish those monuments of superstition and idolatry' especially as 'the magistrate and the minister that should have done it formerly neglected it' (*ibid.*, 30). The civil war was conceived as the harbinger of cataclysmic events. Winstanley, one of the period's most radical thinkers, observed in 1649 that 'the rich generally are enemies to true freedom' (*ibid.*, 38), while John Warr, another radical pamphleteer of the period, pre-figured eighteenth century declarations of political rights in 'The Privileges of the People', writing that 'all forms of government [are] seated in the people' (Warr, 1992, 82). In an address of 1649 to the disillusioned soldiery, Walwyn declared that it was 'not a mere mercenary army ... but were called forth ... to the defence of your own and the people's just Rights and Liberties' (in Morton, 1975, 231). In terms of democratic conception, therefore, this period represents an important precursor to a more developed modernity, as well as a model of equality still to be attained.

The American Civil War and the First World War

Looking beyond the English context, contradictory demands take an acute form during the American civil war, which at first appearance reveals exactly the kind of opposition between categories described by Therborn. 'Reason, enlightenment, emancipation, progress, development, achievement, change, modernity' on the one hand and 'heritage, birth, past experience, tradition' on the other (Therborn, 1995, 22). The first set of attributes would seem to belong to the North and the second to the South; this rather simplified perspective would suggest, in the words of Bensel that 'the American Civil War was a part of the process by which the 'modernising' North integrated the 'pre-modern' South into the national political and economic system' (Bensel, 1990, 5).

However, the picture is perhaps a little more complicated, in that some of the typical features of modern social organisation can be found most dramatically in the southern states which, forced to mobilise some eighty per cent of its white male citizenry of military age (Gallagher, 1997), turned sooner to conscription and the exercise of central state authority than did the more economically powerful North; this can be attributed more to 'the battlefield challenge presented by the enemy than by the domestic consequences of economic development' (Bensel, 1990, 6).[20] As

20 The southern economy was, however, founded upon slavery; in many rhetorical declarations, the war was fought to preserve southern 'institutions', of which slavery was the lynch-pin. Stephen Dodson Ramseur, who became a Confederate soldier in the war between

the conflict developed, so did unforeseen contradictions between the basis of the Confederate social order and the means needed to defend it; slaveholders in the south were hard put to ensure that their slaves did not escape to Union lines, where they were often declared 'contraband' of war and put to work for the Union cause.[21]

Turning for a moment from those writers whose professional function is to provide an overview of, or explanation for, the existence of modernity, we may find alternative but equally valid ways of investigating human responses to the modern configuration. Barbara Adam notes that 'the social world is explained in terms of either how it is, how it is changing, or how it ought to be ... with few exceptions, social theorists conceptualise as single parts in isolation what bears on our lives simultaneously' (Adam, 1990, 3-4).

It is possible to discover a sense of this simultaneous effect when studying those 'qualitative' accounts of experience (found in novels, autobiographies, diaries, verse and so on) which present themselves as personal responses to particular circumstances. This does not mean that these writers are unaware of the modern condition, or the attitudes and discourses associated with it. It might, however, become clear that such material provides a vivid description of modernity, supplementing the more abstract accounts created by social theorists. Besides Therborn's reference to civil war and modernity (see above) it is clear that any traumatic event produced by contemporary forces can create circumstances which dramatise the reformation of identity within the modern social order.

For example, the impact of what has been called 'mechanised' or industrialised conflict can be seen in the memoirs of a number of writers. Among the English authors who produced accounts of the First War, Edmund Blunden displays an enduring commitment to certain values associated with the 'old' (pre-war) world. Blunden's prose reveals a set of aesthetic values drawn from Edwardian romanticism, expressed through references to the felicities of a rural existence. This provides a frame of interpretation, useful for establishing the difference between the old social order (represented as a coherent moral universe) and a new, irrational and frightening state of affairs – a 'world' war.

---

the states, pronounced slavery 'the very source of our existence, the *greatest blessing* for both master and slave, that could have been bestowed on us' (Gallagher, 1997, 97).

21 In this situation, various solutions were sought. In Duplin County, North Carolina, local slaveholders had formed a patrol guard of twenty local men (with a pack of hounds) to stop defections. When members of this patrol were drafted into the Confederate army, one slaveholder by the name of Jere Pearsall wrote to Jefferson Davies to complain; 'they have been of *great* service in preventing escapes of Slaves, & also preventing desertions &c' and went on to write that 'I have just heard, that the said company has been disbanded, and the members of the Company conscripted' (in Berlin, *et al.*, 1997, 143). The army denied Pearsall's request to reinstate the patrol. The contradiction is here between the whole logic of Southern society, fighting to preserve slavery, and the immediate need for men to fight for this purpose, whose absence at one (local) point and movement to another (for the purposes of national concentration) allowed the basis of that society to melt away.

In more than one passage Blunden draws attention to mechanised warfare which Giddens links to the rise of a 'world military order' (1991, 24). In the following extract, he records his reaction to an unfamiliar way of life:

> the past few months have been a new world ... the bowed heads of working parties and reliefs moving up by 'trenches' framed of sacking and brushwood; the bullets leaping angrily from charred rafters shining in greenish flare-light; an old pump and a tiled floor in the moon; bedsteads and broken mattresses hanging over cracked and scarred walls; Germans seen as momentary shadows among wire hedges ... (Blunden, 1928/1982, 84).

The experiences identified here are out of the ordinary, yet the remnants of the civilisation which war disrupts (the broken artefacts in ruined houses), supply references that continue to exert meaning within unfamiliar conditions of existence. Blunden uses the town of Givenchy as an example of the once stable peacetime environment, the 'relics of a yesterday whose genial light seemed at once scarcely gone and gone for ages, relics whose luckless situation almost denied them the imagined piety of contemplation and pity' (Blunden, 77). In the following excerpt, Blunden witnesses a bombardment, setting it within an almost arcadian frame:

> on the blue and lulling mist of evening, proper to the nightingale, the sheepbell and falling waters, the strangest phenomena of fire inflicted themselves ... the red sparks of German trench mortars described their seeming-slow arcs, shrapnel shell clanged in crimson, burning, momentary cloudlets, smoke billowed into a tidal wave, and the powdery glare of many a signal light showed the rolling folds (*ibid.*, 26).

The artillery bombardment here is evidence of a new order of events, a world of destruction pre-figured in the trench warfare which characterised the later part of America's civil conflict half a century before. It is described in a lyrical manner which, perversely, transforms the event into spectacle. Authors like Blunden, Graves ('Goodbye to All That', 1929) and Sassoon ('Memoirs of an Infantry Officer') represent, at first sight, a gentlemanly consensus in which the First war becomes essentially elegiac.

Closer inspection of an author like Graves, however, reveals someone who appears to represent modernity in both form and content. His attitude to the French villages threatened by war, in contrast to Blunden's, is entirely business-like, speaking for instance of 'Morlancourt, a country village still untouched by shell-fire (later it got knocked to pieces; the Australians and the Germans captured and recaptured it from each other several times)' (Graves, 1929/1960, 159). There is little in the way of regret, and no attempt to create nostalgia. The two autobiographies appeared within a year of each other; Blunden's in 1928 and Graves' in 1929. What distinguishes the 'voices' of these two men, who shared much in common but whose attitudes to the effects of war appear to be significantly different? Part of the answer lies in Graves' awareness of changes in social attitudes. He writes from a perspective which could almost be described as another age, but in the process considerably misrepresented his original outlook. In his biography of the author, Richard Perceval Graves notes that 'by mid-1929 Robert Graves' attitude towards Christianity consisted chiefly of a certain cool cynicism; and in 'Good-bye to All That' this cynicism is projected on to his past life in a manner which very much distorts the truth ... Graves says little about the strong religious feelings inspired in him by the Great War' (Graves, 1990, 104). In addition, the letters he wrote home were subsequently altered to support his later attitude to the conflict.[22] Graves' work sold 20,000 copies in its first five days of publication, capturing the mood of disillusion which had become, in retrospect, applied to the war.[23]

Modernity and meaning

From what has been seen so far, modernity's most notable characteristics may be found not only in cultural, economic, social and political developments, but in the *meanings* attributed to such events, meanings which are circulated by a number of 'issue proponents', to which the media belong and over which they, to some degree, exercise judgement (Dearing and Rogers, 1996, 2). An understanding of modernity is created through the reflexive interpretation of the conditions of existence; the trajectory of industrialised capitalist economies thus makes a particular kind of sense in the context of public attachment to political, social and scientific 'rationality', and the apparent movement towards democratic rather than autocratic forms of government. The point is that the modernist project overall is never quite 'achieved'; the *uneven development* of capitalism, challenges to current notions of rationality (expressed through interest in the postmodern and deconstruction), and the changing status of civil liberty, all suggest that the condition of modernity is not a single thing or an accomplished event.

The rise of one kind of capitalism, for example, does not preclude movement towards another; Therborn describes, for example, Europe's 'unique moulding as an *industrial class society*' which evolved from 'an agrarian society to an industrial and then to a service society' (Therborn, 1995, 68). One of the barriers to a sophisticated understanding of modernity lies in the tendency to simplify social reality 'until we have reduced it to choices of single or paired aspects' (Adam, 1990, 4). One example will demonstrate the dangers of creating simple oppositions. Milward describes 'an assumption which underlies most ... writing about the European Community ... that it is in antithesis to the nation-state' (Milward, 1992). An opposition between the idea of 'community' and 'integration' on the one hand, and the continued existence of sovereign nations on the other, has coloured political discourse to such an extent that alternative accounts of this aspect of European modernity has been stifled. Milward makes the argument that, far from standing in opposition, the actual 'evolution of the

---

22 Sassoon and Blunden, studying an advance copy of the biography for review, found what they considered to be inaccuracies on 250 out of 448 pages.

23 Such was the strength of this feeling that Charles Sorley, whose 'Subaltern's War' of 1926 was quite open about his initial enthusiasm for battle, came under attack for the supposed militarism of its outlook.

European Community since 1945 has been an integral part of the reassertion of the nation-state as an organisational concept' and that 'without the process of integration the west European nation-state might well not have retained the allegiance and support of its citizens in the way that it has' (*ibid.*, 3).

O'Brien *et al.* sound an important note of caution, when they argue that the 'typical' experiences we are supposed to accept as 'modern' in fact relate only to certain social groups, to the extent that theories of modernity are often no more than ideas about *western* social formations. The problems of a certain kind of knowledge could then be seen as follows; a 'Westernised', limited, partial or selective modernity becomes 'constitutive of the very world it is said to represent' (O'Brien, 1999, 4). Wagner also supports this perspective, drawing attention to the rather unquestioning application of the phrase 'modern society' to 'the social formations of the Northwestern quarter of the world' (Wagner, 1994, 3). The end result is a less than effective model of global systems and an impoverished view of human existence. A narrow concept of modernity thus prevents an effective intervention in what O'Brien calls 'the mediation of social change' (O'Brien, 1999, 5).

Modernity, power and social control

The study of contemporary life and culture is based on the assumption that certain fundamental questions demand an answer; one of the most important grows from the long established conviction that all social systems are maintained through relations of power. Sociologists work to understand how, and in whose interests, modern societies are maintained. The range of opinion on this issue can vary from positions which assert the existence of a dominant class, whose activities in the economic and ideological spheres supposedly ensure absolute conformity from all subordinate groups, to the conviction that the exercise of influence has become so diffuse that no particular social group may be said to direct another.

The point of this section is first to note that media and cultural studies have inherited the question of power and control from sociology; clearly, the media and related bodies (public relations firms, for example) stand among those institutions which appear at first sight to exercise influence over public opinion and the direction of public policy. Such influence may be detected in both structural terms (media institutions are corporate bodies and have some access to the centres of political power) and in the broader political sense; they are organisations that fulfil an essential role in the circulation of public meanings. The concept of power and the idea of social control are thus important aspects of the present enquiry.

Hindess, in 'Discourses of Power', distinguishes between two conceptions of the term 'power'. The first conception is of 'a simple, quantitative capacity' (Hindess, 1996, 137). Power is therefore conceived here as 'a generalized capacity or essence of effectiveness which is bestowed on individuals and collectivities by virtue of the resources which they happen to possess' (*ibid.*). If the term power is taken to mean in the first instance the possession of the *capacity* to do or produce something then a useful example, explored more fully in Chapter 1, might be the 'power' of speech. Power then becomes the individual ability to perform, so that we might expect some differences between the standard attained by individuals. Power however, of whatever kind, is only ultimately meaningful when it is used to attain goals (it is 'concerned with the bringing about of consequences', according to Philip in Kuper, 1985, 635). However, once capacity-as-power is attributed and proven in use, it does not always need to be actively exercised. Power may still exist where it is 'at rest'.

Thus the next stage is the question of power as influence. Weber made the observation that power is the probability that one actor within a social relationship will be in a position to carry out his or her own will despite the resistance of other individuals. Here, we have moved from the notion of 'power to' to the concept of 'power over.' This suggests not simply the possession and use of ability, but the idea that there is some resistance to be overcome.

Using again the example of speech, 'power to' achieve something has a close relationship to 'power over'; coherent speech requires the mastery of language, but effective, goal-directed speech is an attempt to master some aspect of the environment, or to influence other individuals. Speech use is therefore a form of behaviour or action (producing the term 'speech act'), which anticipates some degree of resistance. As such the speech act can be variously interpreted; some writers see it as essentially innocent, or at least co-operative, while others characterise it as largely strategic or competitive. Philip advances the view that, where behaviour is understood as tactical or strategic, 'agents become literally game-players or actors' and the end result is 'a highly reductive account of social structures and institutions' (in Kuper and Kuper, 1985, 637). Going a little further, it should be noted that speech actions or behaviours are never free from the taint of manipulation, or the struggle for position and advantage; but most experienced participants understand that this is the case, and often co-operate in monitoring the development of those informal rules which govern public conduct.

There is no such thing as utterly selfless co-operation, an idealistic tendency associated at the societal level with Habermas' conception of the public sphere (see below) and in linguistics with Grice (see 'Studies in the Ways of Words', 1975). It is better to recognise the strategic element, as does Wrong when he writes that 'people exercise mutual influence and control over one another's conduct in all social interactions – in fact, that is what we mean by social interaction' (Wrong, 1979). Here, the existence of strategy does not produce a reductive account of human relations.[24]

One way of illuminating the question of utterance-as-strategy is to examine the link between speech and discourse. Where utterance, as it usually does, intends to achieve a particular goal, a speaker will select what he or she regards as an effective argument, which is likely to include a set of references to the meaning of the

---

24 Wrong is supported by the linguist Firth (1951; in Coulthard 'Introduction to Discourse Analysis'), who said that language is 'a way of behaving and making others behave'. In this sense, the power of speech may be simultaneously co-operative and strategic.

situation or event the speaker intends to affect. In doing so, the speaker must choose from a range of plausible statements. In every case where the speaker succeeds in making sense to an audience, there will exist to some degree 'typical', habitual or institutionalised forms of speech, designed to be effective within a particular context. A coherent discourse may well be made up of ideas and arguments taken from a variety of sources, because no discourse is ever entirely pure (see below). A discourse is thus always thematic in nature and variable in performance or delivery.

Not only must the conditions which surround the form of expression be favourable, the groups or individuals involved in the project itself must be recognised as having the right to speak. When examples of successful influence are studied, it is often apparent that there is some pre-existing acknowledgement of established authority. This stands in stark contrast to the direct form of coercion outlined by Lukes who stated that power can be the direct manipulation of others; 'A exercises power over B, when A affects B in a manner contrary to B's interests' (Lukes, 1974). He also recognised that this type of power can occur when B is unaware that his or her interests are being undermined.[25] Where, however, the speakers and/or the address are regarded as legitimate, then this may involve 'mobilising commitments or activating obligations' (Philip, in Kuper and Kuper, 1985, 638). This is reminiscent of Hindess' second conception of the idea of power, where capacity is 'brought into an equivocal relationship with that of power as a right' (Hindess, 137). This results from 'obligation of ... subjects to obey', so that the holder of such power 'appears to have both the capacity and the right to call on their obedience' (*ibid.*). In the modern period, according to Hindess, 'that obligation has commonly been ... based more or less directly on the consent of the subjects in question' (*ibid.*). This issue is an essential aspect of address and also helps to explain the way modern societies are ordered and controlled.

'If societies can be said to exist, what now binds them together?' ask two authors in a study of contemporary power (Bergalli and Sumner, 1997, 1). Social control as a theory posits the deliberate regulation and management of an entire society;[26] arguments over the nature and effectiveness of social control are thus a feature of the growth within modernity, of a number of practices. These include critical social theory, social engineering by state agencies, the rise of corporate power, and the growth of bureaucratic speech or discourse. Sociologists writing about social control in the first quarter of the twentieth century 'were concerned about the dizzying effects of rapid change, increased mobility and transport, the new technologies of mass communications ... the violence of contemporary culture ... and the apparent lack of an overweening moral force to guide people ...' (Bergali and Sumner, 1997,

---

25 Tetzlaff argues that 'left theories of communication/media/language/aesthetics ... have almost always conceived of social power as operating through unification, centring, the repression of contradiction' (Tetzlaff, 1991, 10).

26 In 'Modernity and Self-Identity', Giddens draws attention to three other dimensions to control. He calls the first *surveillance* which is 'the supervisory control of subject populations' (Giddens, 15); the second is *control* of the means of violence; the third is the media.

2). Social control can be, therefore, a project, in the sense that it is 'concerned with that domination which is intended and which fulfils a function in the life of the society' (Ross, 1901, in Kuper and Kuper, 1985, 765). The rather uncomfortable place of the concept within sociology can be explained by consciousness of its history as a directive function of bureaucracy. In addition, the tradition associated with Talcott Parsons, who explained social control as 'those processes ... which tend to counteract ... deviant tendencies' (Parsons, 1951, in Kuper and Kuper, 1985, 765), actually narrowed the field of enquiry and, with the collapse of the notion of 'deviance' itself, threatened the whole usefulness of the term. Sumner maintains, however, that the concept has 'always tended to focus on the integration of social systems' and to 'neglect the negative forces or contradictions which push towards conflict' (Bergali and Sumner, 1997, 4).

Conflict within modernity is apparent within the range of texts which appear within both commercial and political spheres. The notion of 'competing capitals' has been employed to describe the opposition of some cultural products and their attendant messages to older, production-based paradigms of social order. Frank notes that in America in the 1990's, 'every product ... was presented as a cherished accoutrement of rebellion', as a consequence of consumerist discourses which emphasise 'pleasure and gratification' rather than social conformity (Frank, 2001, 24[27]). Miller and Lawrence[28] (in Miller, 2001, 490) argue that the 'triumph' of globalised economics and culture is effected through 'neoliberalism's mantra of individual freedom', and thus also draw attention to the question of 'cultural citizenship' within the context of commercial practices; this question forms part of the study of corporate address which follows in Chapter 4.

---

27 Frank, 'The Conquest of Cool', in *Red Pepper*, September 2001, 24-25.
28 Miller and Lawrence, 'Globalisation and Culture', in Miller, 2001, 490.

Chapter 4

Advertising and Corporate Address

Introduction: commercial address

Texts, as the first three chapters attempted to demonstrate, circulate within the context of a social system which enables the promotion of particular genres of address. The primary focus of this book, the directive or unitary mode of address, may be linked to those purposes which appear as forms of political or commercial persuasion. Yet texts are composed within the conjuncture of modernity, an era represented by what Friedman calls 'a disintegrative-reintegrative social process', in which individuals are taken from their 'traditional' location and placed within a 'more abstract set ... of relations' (Friedman, 1994, 27).

As a purely historical observation, this is of limited use, in that human subjects are bound to find themselves 'born into' the midst of contemporary society and its attendant values. Yet its value lies in the principle of 'reintegration' itself, if this idea can be conceived as an ongoing or reflexive process, used within advertising and other forms of commercial communication, to *realign individual 'consumers'* with the various values which, at any one time, produce financial and semiotic value. When Baudrillard, for example, contemplates the question of social control and declares that there is a contradiction between the 'great egalitarian and democratic principles' Western society promotes, and its actual commercial practices expressed as a system of differences within a 'code of signs' (Baudrillard, 1998, 19) then it is possible to recognise the outline of the greater context in which all texts operate. Described by Jaworski and Coupland, this is the existence of 'global as well as local discourse practices', relevant to both 'their production and reception' (Jaworski and Coupland, 1999, 7).

With regard to the practices of modernity, commercial address can be understood as a typification of contemporary discourses, in the sense that advertising and other similar texts represent an essential element of what Friedman calls the 'specificity' of 'commercial capitalist systems' (Friedman, 1994, 27). That is to say, such texts embody both cultural and financial imperatives, yet in the act of representing the qualities or attributes of goods must retain a high degree of flexibility. Leiss and his co-authors note that the characteristics of goods 'are distributed and redistributed across previously distinct categories of needs, experiences, and objects' (Leiss, *et al.*, 1990, 69). The process of reception, on the other hand, may be linked to the constitution and reconfiguration of identities; when the characteristics of goods change as a matter of principle, then 'the needs through which individuals relate to them must also be in a state of permanent fluidity' (Leiss, *et al.*, 1990, 68).

There seems little doubt that these modes of address create a certain anxiety, or that behavioural nuances are shaped by the necessities of consumption. There is, however, some divergence between an audience's 'creative appropriation' of the 'linguistic product' and the original intention of the message itself (Bourdieu, 1991, 38). Rather than to merely note differences between intention and reception, or point to the principle of 'aberrant' decoding,[1] my suggestion is to concentrate on the production of messages as 'composites' of discourse, forced by *the imperative of coherence* to employ references within the common order of experience. While it is the case that differential access to power is embodied within public communication, it is doubtful that 'successful ideological effects', can be achieved simply by 'exploiting the possibilities' of polysemic meaning within the 'legitimate' or dominant language (Bourdieu, 1991, 39). This is because the existence of multiple positions and points of identification may achieve resonance *at the expense* of unitary or 'ideological' cohesion.

The problem facing all those who compose messages is indeed the contradiction between the attempt to create response in an audience and the need to achieve consistency in the messages themselves. This position is quite different to the mechanical conception expressed by Stevenson, in which 'oppositional views leak through ... and messages are contradicted' (Stevenson, 1995, 29), and closer to the idea of the 'articulation' of discursive elements and the consequent realignment of meanings, advanced by Laclau and Mouffe (in Chouliaraki and Fairclough, 1999, 121).

One aspect of this issue is the construction of identity within modern social formations, and the role taken by texts in this process. Friedman notes that 'external' forms of identity appear as social practice or as 'symbols' employed by a population (Friedman, 1994, 28). This may be related to the way in which texts offer materials for the reflexive composition of identity; in a critique of Giddens, Anthias speaks of 'reflexive projects of the self', in which individuals are imagined to become the 'essentialised figure' of high modernity, identified quite dangerously in her opinion, with 'western social forms' (in O'Brien *et al.*, 1999, 156). Stevenson also refers to contemporary social formations and the construction of identity, arguing that 'global flows of information decentre the subject' (Stevenson, 1995, 29).

'Brand-led' interventions

This chapter takes as its primary focus[2] therefore, those modes of 'brand-led' intervention in contemporary culture made by major trans-national corporations[3] and advertisers, which attempt to re-configure notions of citizenship, human rights,

---

1   A term coined by Umberto Eco in 1960, to indicate the possible dissonance between creative reference and interpretation.

2   Yet the essentially political nature of this process will also demand some reference to party-political utterance.

3   Examples are taken from Nike, IBM, BP, Shell and other sources.

inter-group relations and by extension, social and cultural identities. The use of advertising and more particularly branding as a promotional tool for products and organisations has been well-documented (Davidson, 1992; Hart and Murphy, 1998), and its employment as a means of creating 'global presence' through object and image-reference[4] has become a cause celebre (Klein, 2000). More attention needs to be devoted to the conceptual project which underlies corporate enthusiasm for lauding the value of public relationships.[5]

This part of the argument will begin therefore by characterising the dominant mode of address in lifestyle and corporate advertising, as 'promotional discourse' (Wernick, 1991, 18), within the larger field of what the Introduction has already described as 'strategic' communication (Habermas, 1984, 85; Fairclough, 1989, 198). Promotional discourse is understood, therefore, as a mode of intervention in public life, which is not primarily concerned with 'selling goods', but rather with generating publicity for a cause or perspective[6] and which is often advanced through more obviously 'material' acts, such as charitable works, sponsorship, and public donations (see Timms, 2004). Corporate advertising, presented by its supporters as information, equitable social exchange or public accountability, is in effect I would argue 'reputation management' (Simms 2000, 1), devoted to maintaining an aura of progressive modernity.

Apart from the analysis of television commercials and other advertising material, this chapter also examines corporate mission statements, together with a study of the ways in which web-sites[7] are employed to present controversial or contested subject matter to a variety of 'imagined' audiences.[8]

---

4   An example of object/image reference may be found in a recent advertisement used by Nike, in which the primary frame of meaning is not linguistic but depends upon a design composed of images of the *material object* – in this case, photographs of Nike shoes which are used to create the familiar 'swoosh' sign itself.

5   At this point, the recurrent use of the term 'corporate' should also be acknowledged; currently fashionable, it suggests a critique of monopoly capital, yet in some contexts appears to offer an assessment of scale only, rather than a critical analysis of capitalism *per se* (the character of which becomes subsumed in the more general reference).

6   Wernick gives this definition: 'a promotional message is a complex of significations which at once represents (moves in place of), advocates (moves on behalf of), and anticipates (moves ahead of) the circulating entity or entities to which it refers' (1991, 182).

7   In the case of the web-site as a 'new media' form, the subordinate purpose of the enquiry will be to reinforce the validity of a theory of address which recognises the contextual circumstances in which it appears.

8   Audiences as constructed from 'the vantage-point of institutions' (Ang, 1991). This would suggest further exploration into issues of democracy and technology within contemporary social formations. See Axford and Huggins, 2001, for a study of new media and politics. For this part of the study, some thirty web-sites, produced by various advocates (including major corporations, consultancy firms, state or trans-state organisations, single-issue campaigns, hackers' groups and anarchist collectives), were analysed. Representative samples (from a pharmaceutical company, an environmental campaign, a consultancy firm, a major trans-national, and an anarchist group) are discussed.

Discourse and the representation of social groups

While it is appears that companies like Nike[9] have made their products into a badge
of distinction, demonstrating how branded goods enable corporations to move
more easily through already permeable social frontiers, there are dangers inherent
in heavy dependence on the power of the 'brand image' (Wilmshurst, 1985, 135;
Brierley, 1995, 42). When, for example, a heavily branded product acquires negative
connotations, these can re-infect the centre itself; or conversely, where the company
is thought to represent retrogressive values or practices, all aspects of activity, from
the core to the periphery, may come to appear sinister.[10] In such cases, the logo and
other signifiers become a symbolic millstone, requiring either expensive re-branding
or a commitment to re-invigorating the range of products. In 2000, for example,
British Petroleum underwent a conversion to Green imagery in advertisements that
declared it had gone 'beyond petroleum'[11] (see case study, below).

This chapter's primary concern is not, however, with the semiology of the
image nor with what Dant calls the social value of objects (Dant, 1999), but with
strategic discourses and interventions, suggesting a focus on particular examples
of such address, the marketing theories from which they emerge, and their place
within the semiotic dynamic of late modernity. An emphasis on discourse in this
case should not be taken to imply a neglect of non-linguistic symbolic systems, but
to indicate instead a decision to consider them as elements within a larger system of
signification.

References to texts as examples of 'multi-modal' discourse, drawing attention
to 'the absolute interrelation of discourse and its mode of appearance' (Kress and
van Leeuwen, 2001, 24) are thus regarded as a progressive but rather premature
development.[12] Therefore, the chief frame of reference here will remain a more basic
concept of discourse, in the belief that it remains the most appropriate description of
a significant field of social and critical enquiry, and that its association with linguistic
modes of communication has been successfully widened to encompass all types of
public communication.

The chief analytic purpose of this chapter, is therefore to identify particular
discursive tactics as they are revealed in the modes of address associated with the
phenomenon of advertising and corporate communication, particularly as these
attempt to give life to concepts such as global connectedness and citizenship.
As indicated before, address as it is used in the course of this book refers to the
construction of a message which attempts to call into being some aspect of a

---

9   For a discussion of 'image reference' see (Price, 2003).

10 See Mottram's warnings about the problem of 'monolithic structures' which centralise
the meanings of the brand (Mottram, in Hart and Murphy, 1998, 65).

11 McDonalds, in comparison, also faced with negative publicity, decided to reconstitute
its product, creating simulations of global cuisine in a standardised form.

12 For a similar appraisal of contemporary textual formations, to that expressed by Kress
and van Leeuwen, see my argument in Chapter 1 that 'texts as types of expression must
assume or become the technical means of their own accomplishment'.

recipient's subjectivity, involving the use of propositions created with a model of an individual's social and cultural predilections in mind. The enquiry will be pursued therefore with reference to both subjectivity and notions of a public sphere in which identities are enacted and contested.

The process of address: 'global' identities

The characterisation of audience or, in commercial terms, the creation of a 'target market', depends on the imagined composition of a social group which, while its component parts may exist in 'sociological' terms prior to the referential and propositional action of text, is brought into alignment through specific instances of address. 'Segmentation', the deliberate imposition of general characteristics on a given populace, is used to imagine 'what types of people inhabit the social world' but for the larger purpose of directing modes of address to consumers across the globe (Price, 1998, 146). Indeed, reference to issues such as the globalisation of culture and the creation of economic interdependence, has itself become a celebrated commercial theme, often based on appeals to notions of universal community.

It is the conviction of the present work that such a development has occurred as a result of structural changes in capitalist organisation, as conglomerates came to re-align their practices to meet the demands of a 'global' marketplace, and promotional services use modes of address thought particularly suitable to such conditions. These developments are matched by and enhanced within the 'internationalisation of the advertising and public relations worlds' (*ibid.*).

An awareness of such change appears within the appeals made by specialist companies, which offer services to help orientate business to the concept of greater and more successful transnational trade. In the transcription which follows, an advertisement for the agency 'World Writers' addresses an audience of advertisers, describing itself as:

> the single-office global advertising agency set up in 1989 to service corporations seeking to market their brands in the global marketplace[13]

This company attempts to reconfigure their clients' understanding of the global marketplace through a series of trade advertisements which play on the laboured refutation of stereotypes. In one example, a photograph of an elderly Sikh man in an orange turban is presented with the question 'ABC1?', a reference to the use of classification by social class which is intended to signal how wildly inappropriate such devices are in identifying this individual and the market he may represent. The text below it reads as follows:[14]

---

13 Campaign, March 17 2000.
14 Printed in Campaign, March 3rd 2000.

Utterly British or Uttar Pradesh? Either way, his official language is English, but if you're trying to sell him something, that doesn't help much. The real problem is culture. It's too subtle, too deep and too bound up with personal identity to nail down. If you don't understand it, you can walk blindly past the opportunities and into the pitfalls, without even knowing.

An identical strategy is found in another advertisement from the same company, in which a picture of a man whose features are disguised by a white headdress, is printed with the statement 'Early adopter', followed by this text:[15]

He's got DVD, an ISP and a mobile even smaller than yours. He's well-heeled, well-travelled, and he speaks three languages, none of which is English. You know all this because your research company told you. What you don't know is how you're going to change his mind about a new laptop.

The point of such an assault on stereotypical preconception owes much to but is not identical with the 'one-world' rhetoric of companies like Benetton, and shares its function as a 'corporate' rather than product-based announcement. It is however dissimilar in one important respect; it uses technology and physical/social mobility to represent the sophistication which supposedly attaches to the world of enterprise. In essence, it is the discursive treatment of change within 'late modernity', which forms part of the reflexive conditions under which 'ideological' positions are both composed and critically interrogated, by corporate and academic sources alike.

An example of the type of discourse which constructs a conceptual framework within which other related interventions (advertisements, corporate statements, television commercials) can be made, is often found in financial magazines. These are devoted both to descriptions of economic conditions and to representations of the world which might help to favour free-market models. Anthony B. Perkins, a feature writer for a U.S. journal[16] demonstrates awareness of the onset of certain 'globalised' conditions, yet also helps to formalise a particular way of describing and understanding the process, when he writes that '... we now live in a world ... where Brazilian peasants, Indonesian entrepreneurs, Chinese villagers, and Silicon Valley technocrats can operate in a single global village' (Perkins, 2000, 27). Such remarks are the consequence of a certain way *of imagining social relations*[17] and resemble similar descriptions which appear in commercial form. The 'attitude' or perspective displayed here emerges also in contemporary advertising, as though a process of intertextual reference produces variations on a theme. As Bakhtin argued, 'any utterance, in addition to its own theme, always responds ... to others' utterances that precede it' (Bakhtin, in Allen, 2000, 21).

---

15 Printed in Campaign, March 17 2000.
16 'Red Herring' (no. 86, 2000, 27).
17 Discussed in more detail below.

MSN's 'butterfly' television commercial,[18] for instance, which advertises the power and convenience of Microsoft's search engine, features a series of representations of males and females which represent various forms of identity, including different nationalities, age-groups, occupations and interests. The butterfly symbol moves with ease between various locations and attendant human figures, beginning with an oriental schoolgirl, before moving on to a traditional English 'gentleman', a South American carnival dancer, a ballerina, a sumo wrestler, a 'lollipop' man or crossing-guard, and finally a young couple, each visited by the butterfly.

These individuals, whose appearance is composed in quite stereotypical and thus easily recognisable ways, are set within incongruous locations, thus allowing the intervention of the voiceover which indicates that the web is 'a world full of opportunities' but which may also prompt in its users a sense that they may 'feel out of place'.[19] The spaces in which the characters find themselves are, in turn, a sheep-farm in what seems to be the Australian outback, the edge of a swimming pool in a sunny (American?) setting, an English coastline, an art gallery, an outcrop of rocks, a museum display of stuffed polar bears in an Arctic scene, and an ornate cathedral or ballroom. Each 'place' and person in the frame is associated with the web's supposed creation of electronic contact regardless of ethnicity and national boundaries.[20]

It appears also that a form of 'technophobia' is assumed in an untutored audience, constructed by the advertisement's use of the first person, and the representation of MSN as a safe and easy base for exploration, or as the commercial explains, a 'home' (an echo of both an everyday term and a technical designation). Social location, the conjunction of physical and moral attributes (Harre and Gillett, 1994) and situational place are thus conflated, producing an oddly static view of (social) mobility in a realm which supposedly provides endless opportunities for transition.

Privatised identities

It is worth noting that such conservative modes of representation remain in line with a tradition established in 1980's television commercials, produced to enable the sale of public utilities. The first of these, in 1982, was the privatisation of British Telecom, which was effected partly through the use of a seven and-a-half-million pound advertising campaign, followed in 1986 by the sale of British Gas, assisted by a twenty-eight million pound media launch[21] (Saunders and Harris, 1994, 15/16).

In these examples, individuals are shown 'in situ' in terms of both place and identity; representations of class, ethnic, and gender groups are not intended to

---

18 MSN television commercial, broadcast Christmas, 2000.

19 MSN television commercial, 2000; excerpts transcribed by the author.

20 The creation of *community*, a more laudable aim, requires established interaction between participants.

21 The use of a character called 'Sid', who never appeared on-screen, represented 'one of the millions of ordinary middle-aged or elderly working-class people at whom this share issue was explicitly being targeted' (Saunders and Harris, 1994, 16).

suggest equality (individual locations remain immutable), but rather assert the equality of access to shares and thus to the benefits of de-regulated capitalism. The complex interaction between concepts of 'public' and 'private' interest, explored further below, is noted by Saunders and Harris when they describe how 'privatisation seemed to have had the paradoxical effect of removing enterprises from the public domain of politics while at the same time publicising and politicising their affairs to a greater extent' (Saunders and Harris, 1994, 70). Indeed, the whole issue of address made by private institutions within the public domain illustrates the range of transitions which are made between the two realms of action (see below).

Yet at the moment the question remains the consistency of representation whenever specialised issues (technological or financial, in this case) are presented to a supposedly inexpert public audience.

A salient feature of contemporary commercial discourses, particularly television advertisements, is the way in which subjectivity is illustrated through a series of individual positions which emphasise difference and 'unique' attributes, yet which also remain tied to stereotypical images of social groups; these are 'connected' by the theme of positive cross-cultural interaction and the representation of 'global' opportunity and group commonality, but only within certain bounds, governed by an over-arching social narrative devoted to the maintenance of 'colourful' difference and the guiding authority of private capital.

Perkins, writing in this vein, advocates the positive attributes of economic globalisation; episodes of mass migration for example, demonstrate the principle that 'open markets equal economic growth', evidenced by 'the flow of political and economic refugees from Cuba and Mexico to the United States' (Perkins, 2000, 27). This position is clearly at variance with authors like Martin and Schumann who describe such extreme forms of economic liberalism as 'the law of the wolves' (Martin and Schumann, 1997), while writers like Stallabrass portray globalised culture as the engine of disaster (Stallabrass, 1996). For present purposes, one significant feature of the social and cultural fragmentation analysed by David Tetzlaff (1991) and identified again by Bloomfield and Bianchini (in Stevenson, 2001), is the creation of a so-called 'cultural pluralism' which Stevenson believes to be more 'the product of the free mobility of goods and peoples than legally formulated rights and obligations' (Stevenson, 2001, 7).

Flexibility, globalisation and politics

As a corollary to promotional behaviours, which consistently attribute moral purposes to economic activities (Shell's 2005 commercial on wind-power is an example), capitalist hierarchies help circulate a series of myths about the development of a 'globalised' network economy. One private consultancy, the Australian Centre for Innovation and International Competitiveness, offers 'a unique scenario-based creation of preferred futures' (AIICC website 1999); in effect, advice about how companies should manoeuvre to present current actions in the light of idealised goals.

A closely related instance is the rhetorical promotion of an 'information society'; this term is, according to Miege, not so much a description of an existing state as 'a programme of action' designed to convince spectators that they inhabit a post-industrial order (Miege, in Calabrese and Sparks 2004, 91). The reproduction of popular articles such as Kelly's 'Twelve Principles of the Network Economy' (1997) reveal some of the rhetorical claims forming the mind-set of this managerial elite; once in place, these assertions about the 'new' economy and the 'sudden disintegration of established domains' (Kelly 1997) provide the background assumptions upon which new narratives can be built. BT, in a recent TV advertisement (2005), also draws attention to a 'digital network economy', where 'business is done' but which seems to defeat the logic of global inter-connection by using imagery taken from perceptions of a *British* base for trade in goods and information.

There is, however, a good strategic reason for this use of the nation as a strong reference-point. Appeals to national interest seek to present economic change as an opportunity, and represent a well-established feature of political discussions of globalisation. In much the same way as corporate promotion, political parties create the impression that technological modernity is an irresistible force. As Johnson and Steinburg argue, politics becomes a device for 'transmitting transnational requirements to national agents' (Johnson and Steinburg, 2004, 236). In other words, references to globalisation become a rhetorical device, an alibi which allows those in positions of authority to position themselves as the managers of the process, again with reference to a vision of the future.

Blair presented precisely this form of rhetorical question at the 2005 Labour party conference, when he asked 'how do we secure the future for our party and our country?' and hoped that Labour would be the organisation that made Britain 'at ease with globalisation' (Blair, Labour Conference 27.09.05). This theme appeared again in the Labour leader's depiction of globalised economic relations:

> I hear people say we have to stop and debate globalisation. You might as well debate whether autumn should follow summer. They're not debating it in China and India. They are seizing its possibilities, in a way that will transform their lives and ours. Yes, both nations still have millions living in poverty. But they are on the move. Or look at Vietnam or Thailand ... All these nations have labour costs a fraction of ours (Tony Blair, Labour Conference, 27th September 2005).

Such statements reinforce the perception that Labour's agenda of 'neo-liberal economic reform' is based on 'the presumed requirements of a global economy' (Clarke and Newman, in Steinburg and Johnson, 2004, 53). At certain points in the discourse, uncomfortable realities appear, only in order to be dismissed; the perception that economic success does not require full employment ('millions living in poverty') is rendered free of serious consequence, when Blair uses the idea of progress to divert attention from the existence of the disaster he had mentioned. Millions may live in poverty, but at least these competitors are 'on the move'.

Within the logic of the proposition, 'new' economic structures *necessarily* require the acquisition of new skills and a 'flexible' attitude to the working lives of individuals (Miege, *op cit*). In the context of capitalist social relations, in which there is strong antipathy to the notion of regulation, any call for flexibility may be regarded as an edict in the guise of an emancipatory practice. Critics of 'flexible change' note that its apparent hostility to bureaucracy actually reveals an attempt 'to reinvent institutions decisively and irrevocably, so that the present becomes discontinuous with the past' (Sennett, 1998, 48).

Some go further, drawing attention to the misleading character of terms which have actually become naturalised. In his work on the concept of 'the market', Aldridge argues that there is a case for seeing 'the so-called market system' as 'an ideological device for cloaking the grotesque inequalities of capitalism in a fog of illusion' (Aldridge, 2005, 7).

Rhetoric and flexibility

A set of propositions about the growth of a technological condition is presented as a desirable trajectory and even, in some cases, an immutable fact. There is no doubt that some elements of the business community promote the concept of flexibility as a specific characteristic of the 'digital' age. BT, to take one example, insists that 'customers and citizens have become more sophisticated and more demanding'.[22] The activities of these 'customers and citizens', however, are not presented as anything other than commercial. BT notes that 'they want to interact and buy products and services on a 24/7 basis using a multitude of channels' (*ibid*). The attribution of desires to the consumer includes, as indicated above, reference to flexibility; 'they want to work in a flexible environment, but they also expect this flexible approach to be secure and safe' (*ibid*).

It is however the perceived existence of a receptive international audience (the peasants and entrepreneurs referred to in Perkins' article), combined with a supposedly weakened nation-state, which allows corporate power to assume responsibilities which once appeared to be the duty of the state. Such acts of public address, beginning in earnest during the First World War,[23] eventually entailed the production of posters, public information films such as health and safety warnings, and state-sponsored investment schemes. Public exhortations, once the preserve of state bodies or charitable institutions, have become increasingly marked by their private character. So, for example, the Chief Executive of re-branded corporations like BG (British Gas) can declare that 'companies like BG are taking on many of the responsibilities previously confined to governments and the public sector' (Varney, 1999, 2).

---

22 'Doing business in the digital networked economy', BT 2005.
23 See for example Turner, 1952, 177; Jowett and O'Donnell, 1986, 63.

This tendency may, indeed, be somewhat exaggerated in the new 'literature' of globalisation (Heertz, 2001), and thus subject to attempts to rectify such assumptions (Pilger, 2001[24]). It is important to ask, however, what allows authors like Heertz to identify the actions of certain transnational companies like BP as increasingly 'progressive' (Heertz, 2001).

Such progressive appearances cannot be maintained without the *compression* of disparate references and concepts into *the same representational space*. The process of compression, in which contradictions are squeezed out by appeals to general and usually emotive qualities, are apparent in commercial forms of address; music, imagery, rhetorical flourishes and simple appeals are preferred to the process of argumentation. In the case of advertising narrative, this requires the manipulation of the image to demonstrate the power of technology and the networked web-based economy; a recent TV advertisement for a retail outlet refers to 'digital' customers buying on-line and shows them walking through the solid walls of the computer store itself. With regard to political speeches and policy statements, the same principle applies, except the possible range of concepts is controlled through the use of rhetorical technique.

At this point, it is worth noting that rhetoric, so often described as 'empty', plays an important role in the production of individuals' understanding of their relationship to the real. Through the generation of simple, recognisable references to actual conditions of life, those in authority (whether commercial or political), are able to establish what might be described as the 'terms and conditions' for further understanding.[25]

One of the main techniques of rhetorical address, besides repetition, is the exclusion of references which may upset the perspective being advanced by the source. Fairclough, in his discussion of the rhetorical strategies of New Labour, notes the deliberate elision of references to uncomfortable factors such as the existence of rapacious multinational companies, which 'are not directly represented as social actors' in Tony Blair's speeches (Fairclough, 2001 23).[26]

In Blair's rhetoric, reform and marketisation cannot be held apart; the existence of democracy is dependent on the penetration of society by the market. Or, put another way, the imposition of markets supposedly guarantees the export of democracy. One 'order of discourse' in particular has provided the frame for new ways of representing commercial motives as universally beneficial. This is the concept of *corporate citizenship*.

---

24 Pilger's argument is that the state still wields considerable power; *New Statesman*, 6th August 2000.

25 This is not to argue that representation 'creates' a world beyond the social. A realist perspective on the generation of meaning would argue that *the use and exchange of symbols* is a material action with definite outcomes.

26 In an analysis of 53 speeches made by Tony Blair over a period of two years, Fairclough notes that the term reform (code for neo-liberal deregulation) occurs most often when an *external* body or organisation is said to require some response (Fairclough, 2000, 19).

Corporate citizenship and public values

'Corporate citizenship', a notion which motivates various forms of 'multi-modal' discourse[27] in web-pages, magazine articles, advertisements and commercials, is first and foremost a description by companies of their own position *vis a vis* the society they inhabit, and by extension an orientation towards values not usually associated with the private sector. The Global Business Responsibility Resource Center, an on-line corporate consultant, defines corporate citizenship as follows; 'business decision-making linked to ethical values, compliance with legal requirements, and respect for people, communities and the environment'[28] (GBRRC, 2000, 1).

A strong and relatively early advocate of corporate citizenship was the United States Department of Labour. In 1996 (in the context of a decrease in the state's declared responsibilities) the Department announced that 'corporate citizenship is about treating employees as important assets to be developed and as partners on the road to profitability'[29] (United States Department of Labour, 1996, 1). In both the excerpts reproduced above, the concept represents a notion of social responsibility and partnership; the place of labour within capitalism is thus recognised as 'important', yet it remains in essence an economic asset to be developed. As the Department itself advised; 'investments in employees are at least as important and profitable as investments in plant and equipment' (*ibid.*).

Such beliefs are constructed through discursive consistency. The Corporate Citizenship Company, an on-line consultancy group, offered for example a 'six step process' for clients wishing to build 'an intellectually defensible, managerially robust and cost-effective social responsibilities reporting system' (CCC, 16.8.2000). The first step is 'the identification of the specific values and principles to which the company is committed' (*ibid.*). One group which uses the internet to address a business audience, 'Business for Social Responsibility' (see above), offers guidance for the production of a typical socially-conscious report, providing headings for leadership examples, mission statements, and sample policies. It presents this service in terms which utilise the particular capabilities of the internet as a technology:

> To create a report containing all of the information listed to the left, click the ALL button, then click on the CREATE REPORT button below (BSR, 2000).

While this suggests the automation of a process which should preferably require some thought, BSR is also anxious to describe the kind of good practice which should be copied by companies wishing to update their moral credentials, arguing that:

---

27 'Multimodal' discourse is the term used by Kress and van Leeuwen (2001) to describe the combined mode of address (image, design, sound, language, etc.) from which contemporary media texts may be composed.

28 'Introduction to Corporate Responsibility', 2000, 1.

29 U.S. Department of Labor on Corporate Citizenship, 5 September 1996.

The mission or vision of a socially responsible business frequently references a purpose beyond 'making a profit' or 'being the best', and specifies that it will engage in ethical businesses practices, and seek to create value for a variety of stakeholders, including shareholders/owners, employees, customers, vendors, communities and the natural environment (BSR, 2000).

The objective described here, to 'seek to create value for a variety of stakeholders' may be understood as a definite proposition, yet it is too general to provide an insight into how the process may work, or what differences in outcome may be attained. 'Value' in general is supposedly created for all, but the various types of value are not described, nor is the question of the relative access to power or influence of each stakeholder investigated; owners and customers may receive quite different forms and degrees of benefit.

Yet however generalised such propositions may seem, consultancy groups provide, in effect, templates for the production of a 'liberal' business discourse for the attainment of two purposes; that of internal discipline (in which employees are supposed to 'sing from the same sheet', as noted by Cameron, 2000[30]) and in order to present a coherent position which can be subjected to external scrutiny.[31] CCC and BSR,[32] however, offer an opportunity to produce a coherent 'point of view' which is able to anticipate and respond to criticism, 'a corporate mantra' (Price, 2003) with which to prepare an ideologically consistent intervention in the public realm. This kind of development has led to the construction of new definitions of corporate conduct.

Corporate transformation? bp and Shell

The declared alterations in bp's behaviour,[33] exemplified in 'image' or brand change, are embodied in discourse, yet require care in their production as they are more than 'positional'; that is to say, statements of intent made within this context are regarded as binding, and capable of being judged against actions or 'performance'. In 1999, the company revealed what it called 'the triple bottom line', the idea that 'to judge a business by its financial performance alone is not enough, and that it should be judged by its Financial Performance, Environmental Performance and Social Performance' (bp website, 1999). Social performance is set out in the following terms:

> our *behaviour*, that is, whether we live up to the values expressed in our company's business policies; our *impact* on people, and our overall *contribution* to society (*ibid. italics* in the original).

---

30 See the section below, 'Carbon Footprints and capitalism'.

31 Much of this (including ideas about 'benchmarking') will be familiar to those who encounter regulated speech events within education (see for example Wernick, 1991, 158; Fairclough, 1995a, 91; Cameron, 2000, 17).

32 The Corporate Citizenship Company and Business for Social Responsibility.

33 From the re-branding exercise which began in 1999.

There has been a distinct tendency, in both private institutions and public life, to regard reputation management as primarily driven by 'spin' and deception, generally speaking the operative capability to represent, largely through language, any event in a favourable light (Jones, 1999; Cameron, 2000). This does not quite explain the mode of operation here, however, within a frame which seems to acknowledge the exhaustion of older, more confident interpretations of modernity and the paradigm of unimpeded progress. Here, declarative language is supposedly to be tested against material achievements.

These utterances represent strategies, and certainly produce 'social narratives' about responsibility; indeed, they use measurable or quantifiable outcomes as the 'technical' or empirical evidence for such stories.[34] Bp, for instance, advertised its Environmental and Social Review as 'comprehensive, open, and independently verified' (BP press advertisement, July 2001). Shell produced a report for the year 2000 entitled 'People, planet and profits', which adhered to 'transparency and openness' by printing critical remarks received from public sources. These included comments on many aspects of the company's business:[35]

> I am afraid that Shell's commitment to human rights comes too late. Blood will always, always be on your hands and no Business Principles will ever change that (Shell, 2000).[36]

It is, however, the underlying purpose of Shell's apparent even-handedness which must be regarded as the decisive factor in the construction of public accountability. Self-criticism does not imply that structural change is to follow; companies are unlikely to jettison shareholders in order to become co-operatives. In this case, the strategy is designed to show an openness and to achieve resonance through a winning candour, but the appearance of such material within the generic context of corporate address confirms its status as a strategic intervention.[37]

The creation of the present work is that more 'extended' examples of discourse (those which attempt to construct more complex propositions and narratives) reveal the strains of attempting to produce 'ideological' rather than merely grammatical cohesion. In the first place, the way in which cases are presented, and the 'frame'

---

34 The difference between traditional 'management speak', in which actions are codified in such a way as to control or discipline their impact in the social world, and theories of corporate responsibility, are evident in the explicit statements made by, for example, groups like 'Business for Social Responsibility' which recommends that firms embrace a 'commitment to close the gap between what the company says it stands for and the reality of its actual performance'. Empirical data can be altered, however; see below.

35 The practice of using genuine public statements emerged from the fashion for 'focus group' work in both commercial and political research, in which on occasion, statements made by members of the public would be employed directly within the course of an advertisement or party political message (Price, 1998, 162; see also previous chapters).

36 'People, planet and profits; a summary of the Shell report', 2001.

37 A coherent argument against Shell's position is not printed.

in which they are constructed, may reveal underlying purposes. For example, Shell's argument in a series of 'environmentally aware' corporate advertisements is introduced through statements and rhetorical questions which set the parameters for the propositions which follow:[38]

> The issue of global warming has given rise to heated debate. Is the burning of fossil fuels and increased concentration of carbon dioxide in the air a serious threat or just a lot of hot air?[39]

The question (the second sentence) forms an anaphoric reference to the opening statement, while the first sentence ('the issue of global warming') is endophoric, indicating the existence of perspectives on the issue which circulate within a wider social context. The reference to 'warming' provides a punning resonance transferred through 'heated' and 'hot air', suggesting the ordinary inflections of everyday conversation.

Yet the notion of global warming, rather than an undisputed fact which demands action, becomes a matter of debate in which there are considerable uncertainties. Taken together, these statements call to mind a commonly-held value, that there are 'two sides to every question'. Although this principle informs everyday interaction, forming one part of what Semin and Gergen call 'dialogue consensus' (Semin and Gergen, 1990, 234), its deployment as a frame for a promotional announcement is less appropriate, and therefore essentially rhetorical.

The intention appears to be to create an impression of even-handedness, a conversational gambit to allow the production of an 'answer' that suits the purposes of the company. This suggests that the whole presentation which follows is to be based on fair everyday judgement, but in so doing distorts the broader context within which the issue is constructed.[40] The material which provides a reply to this question seems, however, perfectly definite in its stance:

> Shell believes that action needs to be taken now. We are delivering on our commitment to reduce greenhouse gas emissions from our operations. We're working to increase the provision of cleaner burning natural gas and encouraging the use of lower-carbon fuels for homes and transport. It's all part of our commitment to sustainable development, balancing economic progress with environmental care and social responsibility. Solutions to the future won't come easily, particularly in today's business climate, but you can't find them if you don't keep looking.[41]

In analysing this passage, some of the ideas previously presented by the company as somewhat questionable, have now attained the status of fact; 'greenhouse gas emissions' are harmful by-products of the industrial process. This, together with the reference to 'sustainable development', demonstrates how business has come to

---

38 See Appendix.
39 'Cloud the Issue or Clear the Air?', Shell advertisement, 2000- 2001.
40 For a social constructionist view of environmental discourse, see Backstrand, 2001.
41 'Cloud the Issue or Clear the Air?', Shell advertisement, 2000- 2001.

adopt specific terms used by environmental groups.[42] The reason for the employment of such references by corporations, is both practical (these are established phrases indicating recognised debates[43]) and 'ideological' (Shell must try to inflect such terms in such a way as to make them useful within its own frame of argument). The larger context is an awareness of a crisis in the world's environment. In other words, private companies work within the known context of public debate yet attempt to re-contextualise particular concepts in order to articulate new propositions.

The re-combination and re-contextualisation of terms helps to compose frames of reference which are, in turn, able to promote values which ultimately appear opposed to environmentalism. Similarly, Green movements also seem to provide evidence of such convergence in reference; the question is, whether this represents a divergence in proposition and eventually in meaning.[44] If the corporate sector, pressure groups, and political parties use the same references and propositions, then it would appear that they may be addressing the same issues; nonetheless, they appear to be doing so for different purposes.[45] The discourse of 'social responsibility' employed by Shell is linked to a dynamic sense of positive intervention, in which a similarly direct appeal to the consumer is made.

A number of challenges will therefore present themselves in the course of research into this field: what are the uses and limitations of the concept citizenship itself, with regard to the promotional discourses employed by commercial institutions; what kind of analytical tools are best suited to the interpretation of corporate and advertising messages and texts; and inevitably what theoretical perspectives are suggested by the methods of analysis chosen? It is this issue – the relationship between textual interpretation and theory – which requires an immediate response.

Intention and global reference

Any study which interrogates forms of address suggests in the first instance some reference to the symbolic realm in general, but would also probably consider, as mentioned above, those theories of language and communication which posit a 'strategic' mode of intervention, a practice which supposedly infects the public sphere (Habermas, 1989; Habermas, in Outhwaite, 1994). Promotional discourse

---

42 For example, the United States Green Party, in its 2000 platform (ratified at its National Convention in June of that year), stated that 'Greens support sustainable development and social and economic justice across the globe' (U.S. Green Party, 2000).

43 They are essentially 'exophoric' in that they make references to established external events (see chapter 1, 1.11).

44 The American Green party declared that 'we support ... social responsibility in all businesses, whether privately or publicly owned' (U.S. Green Party, 2000).

45 Indeed, the growth of 'ecological' publicity was noted by Tilson in an article on the ability of the nuclear industry to re-generate its image and identity through a variety of methods, including the use of direct address intended to by-pass the external 'gatekeepers' which normally mediate corporate messages (Tilson, 1993, 429).

(see above) would seem an appropriate description of the kind of address made by trans-national companies, considering that such discourse is 'set free from the immediacies of buying and selling to develop a life of its own' (Wernick, 1991, *ibid.*).

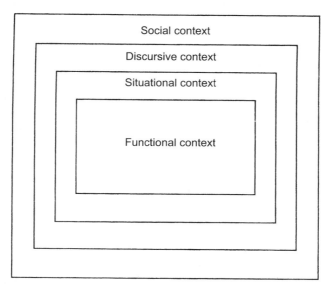

Illustration 3: Four Levels of Context
Source: Price, S., 1997.

Evidence may certainly be found for the existence of corporate intervention in public life; some television commercials, for example, are in reality an exercise in public relations.[46] While brand consultants like Murphy assert that branding 'consists of imposing one's will on the consumer' (Hart and Murphy, 1998, 2),[47] Simms, writing in a business magazine,[48] argues rather more subtly that the whole purpose of branding consists essentially of 'reputation management' (Simms, 2000, 1). Similarly, Warwick Business School's conception of corporate citizenship is of 'managing uncertainty' (Andriof, 1998, 1). If it is possible, then, to produce a general model of intentional corporate address which has the goal of reputation management,

---

46 The bp commercial of November 200, which describes the company's achievements in reducing car pollution but makes no explicit attempt to sell a product, is a case in point; see below for a transcript.

47 This should not however imply that the methods employed in publicity campaigns are necessarily successful, for reasons which relate to the mechanics of address (explored in previous chapters; but see also below).

48 'Enterprise IG', Haymarket Publishing Ltd., 2000.

account should be taken of the functional, situational, discursive and social context (Price, 1997) in which public utterances based on these values, are made.

Current principles for analysis have referred to the relationship between intention as a general approach, and actual *expression*, bearing in mind the general difficulty of trying to promote ideas and values in any circumstances over which an advocate has less than perfect control: which includes practically every situation that could be imagined. One argument might be to draw attention to an obvious distinction between belief and the process of its expression (Price, 1993/98; van Dijk, 1998). Yet this may seem to suggest a rather simplified process, in which something resembling an unsullied belief is translated into an effective expressive action.

There are certainly intentions at work in the material studied in this chapter, in the form of instrumental goals; in the case of advertisements, general purposes may be easier to identify than the existence of specific beliefs, particularly as advertisers are led by what one practitioner called 'the leading edge of value change' (Strauss, in Price, 1998, 162).[49] Yet, in following social and political trends, some reflection of public values must inevitably ensue; in simple terms, the message must 'create meaningful associations' (de Mooij, 2001, 38).

This is why it is possible for commercial organisations to embrace the language of political radicalism and to provide meanings in new forms; the radicalism is not entirely lost, because it must refer to the original context to make sense, but is circulated in a muted form.[50] In other cases, in what Goldman calls 'legitimation ads' (*ibid.*), it is possible to identify a dramatisation of values which the private sector has come to describe as 'good corporate citizenship'.

This may be characterised in turn as *attempts to control* the social and cultural environment in which a company operates, as a response not just to the threat of economic failure, environmental degradation and increasing political disruption, but in some cases to the very real possibility of a catastrophic erosion of the social base which provides many companies with potential employees, consumers and shareholders.[51] Martin and Schumann, for instance, accuse countries which once benefited from 'turbo-capitalism', of now 'eating up the social substance of their cohesion even faster than they destroy the environment' (Martin and Schumann, 1997, 9).[52]

---

49 Goldman, from a Marxist perspective, is a little blunter in his appraisal of this process: 'corporations ... seek popular legitimacy by joining cherished values and social relations to their corporate images' (Goldman, 1992, 85).

50 See for example the NatWest student leaflet in the Appendix, 'Your freedom needn't be a struggle', August 2001.

51 Goldman identifies an earlier parallel to this theory of erosion, when he notes that in the case of the family, 'corporate capitalist development' freed people to 'pursue more individualised life courses' (Goldman, 1992, 87).

52 The International Monetary Fund also expressed concern about 'growing outcries from civil society' (IMF, 2000, 1) while the decision by the Asian Development Bank to devote 40% of its assets to the alleviation of poverty, was a belated response to the financial crisis

Dissatisfaction with corporate performance has led to the proliferation of statements which address public concerns. British Petroleum declared itself to be 'on the side of human rights', Nike apologised for offending one of its 'most valued' consumer groups with its 'chainsaw' advertisement (October 2000)[53] and a McDonald's executive declared that Coca-Cola is nutritious because it is 'providing water, and I think that is part of a balanced diet' (Green, 1995).[54]

Such declarations may be used as evidence of moral sincerity, but a more cynical interpretation of what many companies present as their social duty can be found within the pages of financial newspapers and the small print of corporate reports, which characterise such statements as belated attempts at recuperation. Philip Stephens in the Financial Times, for example, argued that the purpose of 'global financial security' is not driven by 'misguided notions of international philanthropy' but serves instead the prosperity of the United States (Stephens, 2001).[55] Conflict between the powerful and the subordinate is discovered in many sources; in the case of advertising, discussed above, the trace of conflict may be discovered within the texts themselves.[56] However, clear poles of difference may sometimes be found in openly opposing positions, competing discourses which in recent years have employed the same means of communication to engage in public disputation; the example given in this chapter is that of the 'world wide web'.

Competing discourses on the web

It has already been suggested that, within commercial address, internet technology and use has become a metaphor for a particular manifestation of modernity (see the discussion of the MSN advertisement, above). The notion of *competing* discourses emerges from the fact that the web contains various points of view which compete for attention.[57] When a message is constructed, it is created from a number of

---

of 1997, in which 'millions have lost their jobs and cannot find work' (Chino in Thornhill, 2001).

53 'When one of Nike's most valued consumer groups raises its voice against an ad that we have aired, we listen. Our intent was to strike a chord with women and girls in a positive way, and obviously it had the opposite impact on a number of people, particularly women who have been victims of violence. For that we offer a sincere apology'.

54 David Green, senior vice-president of marketing, January 1995.

55 Financial Times, 5 January, 2001. Indeed, the relationship between international finance, corporate power and the poorest countries can be portrayed in quite stark terms. In 1993 for example, net disbursements by the World Bank totalled some 7 billion dollars; but the borrowing countries paid out 6.8 billion in contracts to trans-national corporations.

56 See Fowles' argument that advertisements present a perfect and 'polished ... surface to the reader' but the surface perfection hides all the conflicts which go to make up the finished product (Fowles, 1996, 77).

57 Discourse in this instance simply means the expression of an identifiable position on a particular issue, a point of view distinguished from other perspectives, rather than some precise manifestation of 'dominant' or 'subordinate' ideology.

symbolic resources. Taking language as an example, it has become apparent that it contains a host of pre-existing structures (grammars, categories, rhetorical formulas) and fashions of expression that, together with ideas, opinions and beliefs provide a resource for the advocate. It is not however a pure source; the prospect for reproducing unadulterated meanings, suited to a single purpose, are somewhat uncertain.

Above all, any point of view must be tempered by what it is and is not possible to say about events (what makes sense and what seems reasonable in any context). This, combined with ideas or explanations which have gained public currency, create what Fairclough calls the 'discursive practices of a community' (Fairclough, 1995b, 55). In turn, these practices make up the discursive context of address on the web, or indeed within other media form in which propositions are shaped and delivered. From an advocate's perspective, then, whatever general characteristics audiences possess, it must be assumed that individuals have no necessary commitment to the positions offered, requiring some *staged introduction* to the perspective advanced.

These sites display, therefore, an orientation to the 'psychology' of their public, and allied to this demonstrate knowledge of web users' behaviour. The content and structure of web-sites anticipates this aspect of reception, providing a theatre of attraction within what Goldhaber calls an 'attention economy' (Goldhaber, 1997). A major structuring effect in this case is thus provided by the very range of behaviours and practices deployed by individuals as they 'surf' the web.

In this respect, Ang's view of audience as 'an abstraction' constructed from an institutional vantage-point, in which it is more 'a repertoire of practices and experiences' than a stable entity (Ang, 1991, 170), is also suited to the conceptualisation of web users. Ang's typification of audience as a repertoire of habitual acts acknowledges the shifting nature of its arrangement, but still allows it to exist as a concrete element within a wider social reality (Price, 1997).

Although internet traffic as a whole may be de-centred and difficult to predict, it is not entirely transitory or random. Behaviour within and between web-sites may be seen as the active pursuit of goals within *a series of spatially and thematically ordered transitions*, marked by periods of engagement and recapitulation. This process can be seen in the typical movement of the individual between new sites, home pages, and links, encountering opportunities for response (making purchases, sending messages, contributing to blogs).

The web therefore encourages habitual, structured use in which subjectivity does not 'disappear' but is composed through the acceptance, rejection or toleration of specific forms of address. In providing more than linguistic formations, web-sites have much in common with established genres, including newspapers, magazines and advertisements, all of which use their generic form (including design and image) as a means of 'speaking' to audiences. More significant in the case of these sites, however, is their appearance, in Barnet's productive phrase, as 'a way of *spatialising* ideas into discrete units' (Barnet, 2000, 76).

The way in which *hypertext* is constructed, and the movement between links and sites characteristic of web use, has led some commentators to the conclusion that such phenomena express creative freedom, breaking down barriers between 'writers' and 'readers' and even eroding subjectivity itself (Landlow, 1992). From these observations, theorists of 'hypermedia' have argued that hypertext confirms poststructuralist theories of non-linearity, and that it represents an opposition to the 'logocentric' tradition of Western thought (see Barnet's insightful analysis, 2000).

This chapter takes a different perspective, suited both to its focus on comparative analysis of the discourses used in and between individual sites, and to its espousal of a more realist hermeneutics. From this perspective, then, discourse is embodied within a number of expressive forms, which include aspects of design, imagery and the spatial sequencing of ideas. These may all be described as 'non-linguistic' semiotic systems (Jaworski and Coupland, 1999, 7) or what Kress and van Leeuwen call 'multi-modal' texts (Kress and van Leeuwen, 2001). Examples of discourse as language use, however, may be found by examining units of meaning, from individual terms, to more complex propositions (statements or assertions moderated by foreknowledge of the public context in which they are employed).

Analysing web-sites

Sites are made up of different types of material, not all explicitly designed for the web. A significant amount is reproduced or adapted from other sources (reminiscent of Bruck's dictum that agencies re-circulate discourses taken from other sources).[58] Where specific terms appear, there is often an interesting opposition of use between business organisations and critics of the commercial sphere. British Petroleum, for example, on its 'Human Rights' page, speaks of the need to 'manage the uncertainties of democracy', while an anarchist site (www.spunk.org) mentions the 'democracy of Capital', which requires absolute freedom for the capitalist to exploit labour power. Another U.S. source,[59] argues that 'the dollar rules over democracy'.

Sites, whatever their allegiance, make discursive interventions in public debate. Within its 'Social Responsibilities' link, and beneath its corporate logo, Boots carries the following public declaration, which contains a number of propositions:

> We're committed to maintaining and enhancing our reputation as a well managed, ethical and socially responsible company. We believe that the relationship between the company, its staff and the wider community provides the firm foundation on which commercial success can be built and sustained.

---

58 An initial method of gauging the variety of discourse use within web-sites, is to make a search across a sample of material for key terms, logging the contexts in which they appear. For example, the application of six terms – Citizen, Corporate, Democracy, Justice, People, and Workers – to a number of sites, produced some useful results, though this chapter has space to report only a few instances.

The term 'worker' is another interesting case where quite different uses occur.

When Bill Gates mentions the word, he reconfigures the term by referring to 'knowledge workers' (Gates, COMDEX speech, 2000), while www.spunk.org describes 'wage-workers'. McDonald's by comparison has a 'People Promise' and a 'People Vision'.

59 Located at www.radio4all.org.

It is hardly surprising that the primary goal of a company is the 'commercial success' that is mentioned in the final sentence of this passage. The argument, however, that this can be achieved through a series of relationships between 'the company, its staff and the wider community' is characteristic of discourses of responsibility and service most tellingly expressed through the doctrine of corporate citizenship as defined above.

Corporate citizenship is in one sense yet another form of 'branded' address, in which the whole organisation comes to represent certain prescribed values. In characterising its social role, however, a company must also describe the features of the environment it inhabits, and the people it addresses.

From this it is possible to argue that the exercise of corporate citizenship is not intended merely to adjust the outlook of individual companies, but to create a disciplined form of address based on a set of clear precepts; it is a mode of intervention through language, sponsorship and social investment which creates 'subjects' who must ultimately conform to its notion of leadership. While Cameron observes that branding is 'extended to the verbal and other behaviour of employees' in an attempt to present a consistent image or 'style' to the customer (Cameron, 2000, 101), the concern of the present chapter is with the external promotion of values through address, seen in the wider context of the corporate regimentation of language, described by Czerniawska as 'a new tool by which to influence collective culture' (Czerniawska, 1998, 26).

Organised opponents of particular companies, in the light of corporate adherence to responsibility, must decide on the most effective approach when attacking their chosen targets. A particular critic of Boots (see above) is Friends of the Earth. Its web-site carries a re-design of the Boots logo, altering it to 'Pollutes', which can be downloaded as a screensaver. Tampering with part of a corporate image is a familiar tactic within such campaigns, and is a particular feature of the Adbusters site.[60]

In terms of linguistic address, however, FoE replicates the language of a consumer group: 'we questioned top retailers and makers of all kinds of products we use every day ...'. This even sounds like the typical opening gambit of an advertiser. The page continues as follows:

> Boots, the highly trusted health-care store, turns out to be particularly bad when it comes to addressing the urgent issue of potentially health-threatening chemicals in the products it sells.

FoE then appeals to the individual consumer to take action: 'what you can do: tell Boots to come clean'.[61]

---

60 At www.adbusters.com.

61 This is followed by an e-mail which can be sent to Boots' customer service: 'Dear Boots, I am shocked to hear that, through the products you sell, you are exposing me to chemicals which build up in my body ... Please let me know what you are doing to address my concerns'.

As this example shows, web-based campaigns are not necessarily innovative. The actions requested are mundane: the downloading of a screensaver and the sending of prepared e-mail. The language employed is unimaginative and concerned only with the individual consumer. Discourse thus appears to be the product of 'contextual intention' (Price, 1996, 99), a purpose shaped by the sense that, in order to succeed, messages should attempt to reproduce the values of those addressed. In choosing to speak in the voice of the consumer watch-dog, however, Friends of the Earth fails to offer a more radical proposition to its public.

Diversity, anarchy and community

At this point, the question of tactics and their relationship to political orientation provides a good opportunity to investigate the frames of reference created by dedicated opponents of corporate power. Indeed, one conception of discourse characterises its production as a matter of opposition between competing poles of opinion (Howarth, 2000, 114). The study of web pages dedicated to the promotion of anarchism was prompted by the explicit judgement expressed in many negative descriptions of anarchy as an 'extreme' social conception, and by extension of anarchism as a political creed.

In addition, the characterisation of anarchist practices means that it is very difficult to 'assimilate' into configurations of mainstream culture. Anarchy is employed in the sense of political, social or cultural disorder; Dahlberg, for example, in his essay on Minnesota's online democracy, compares the forum 'Minnesota Politics Discuss' unfavourably to 'other more *anarchic* cyberspaces' (my emphasis in Dahlberg, 2001). However, before this term is conflated with chaos or confusion, it is worth recalling its attendant complexities.

The Ancient Greek root of 'arche' gives the sense of an origin (the beginning of something) or an originator (someone who 'leads off' a song or poem). This produces by extension the notion of social or cultural leadership. 'An-arche' is therefore the lack of a leader (Grene and Lattimore, 1959). In Homer, it is the absence of a military commander or chief (Iliad II, 691-717).

In modern usage, however, anarchy as an undesirable state or condition is balanced against the persistent trace of a less negative evaluation: the simple absence of any form of government and thus, in the opinion of anarchists themselves, authoritarian imposition.

Their typical defence may be represented by Malatesta, who once argued that, because most conceptions of social organisation demanded authority of one sort or another, the idea of anarchy would indeed seem alarming; 'since it was thought that government was necessary and that without government there could only be disorder and confusion, it was natural and logical that anarchy, which means absence of government, should sound like absence of order' (infoshop.org). However, as anarchy is not an established state of affairs, contemporary anarchist tactics can actually include the vigorous promotion of disorder. Propositions, as argued above, may be purposeful statements, yet they are made in anticipation of general scrutiny. The suspicion that one's pronouncements are also being examined by a repressive state, can therefore produce some rather disingenuous linguistic tactics.

One anarchist site, infoshop.org, begins by using the first person singular, describing itself as 'your online anarchist community'. Under the adapted logo of the game Monopoly it posts a description of 'Mayday in the U.K.' together with a rationale for the 'anti-capitalist actions' it advertises. The visual reference to Monopoly once again demonstrates the force of Bruck's observation that sources are re-used in media forms, and that 'the discursive material' used by this particular issue proponent 'is not [its] own' (Bruck, in Wasco and Mosco, 1992, 142).

In plain terms, this familiar game becomes a useful and comical 'cultural reference' (Eco, 1960), the meaning of which is turned from the principle of accumulation to the pursuit of property destruction. Within this modified address, it is possible to detect the use of certain rhetorical devices, such as the 'inclusive we' (Atkinson, 1984). The piece moves from describing 'our times' to an evaluation of 'our labour power', marking a shift from a universal, inclusive reference to a more particular representation of those who live by selling their ability to labour; 'in real life one single commodity generates all profits – our labour power' (infoshop. org; 2001). Such shifts can represent the deployment of particular rhetorical tactics; Billig, for example, demonstrates how the use of 'we' during a family argument over royal privilege, can change from a reference to 'we the working people' to a more general designation of 'we the nation' (Billig, 1991, 187), marking a movement from a radical proposition to a less focussed depiction of social conflict (the opposite tendency to the one observed above).

The effect of the wide-ranging proposition contained in 'our labour power' is to transfer the general to the particular, carrying the force of an agreed notion about the character of modern times (an era inhabited by all), to a construction of class-based identity which, if analysed, includes everyone in the working population whose primary income is generated by selling their labour.

This configures a 'working' class of quite considerable magnitude, but keeps faith with contemporary anarchism's devotion to tenets it considers others to have abandoned. The paragraph continues, 'since labour power cannot be separated from people, we are literally bought and sold in the market place'. A similar observation is found in Williamson, with regard to advertising and to the effect that; 'advertisements are selling us something else besides consumer goods; in providing us with a structure in which we, and those goods, are interchangeable, they are selling us ourselves' (1978, 13).[62]

The site discussed here also offers its readers a variety of contacts and activities, carrying a notice from the International Network of Night Workers which calls for 'a night of property destruction on May Day Eve'; yet infoshop.org presents this notice, not on its own behalf, but apparently in response to the request of another

---

62 The next part of her comment is not very often cited; 'and we need those selves.' This suggests again that advertising fulfils a role in the composition of subjectivity.

group. This 'contribution' even appears in a different font to that used for the rest of the page. Taken as a whole, however, this page and its associated links (allowing movement through a defined 'space' devoted to argument and exhortation) suggest a form of co-ordination which calls to mind the creation of electronic communities envisioned by Rheingold (1994).

Re-vitalisation of a public sphere?

The anarchist web-site studied above may demonstrate, in some respects, certain features suited to the re-vitalisation of the public sphere (although web-sites, considering their often rhetorical character, are not ideal spaces for such developments). Some features of a progressive, collective field of action do exist; Rheingold, for example, looks for evidence of 'communitarian places on-line' (1994, 115), enabling the creation of a 'shared consciousness' (*ibid.*, 245). The activity and commitment of infoshop.org, and its interest in making interventions in the social and political environment beyond the world of 'cyberspace', distinguishes it from other forms of political action which are confined to the net itself.

However, despite some resemblance to online community, infoshop.org and indeed any web-site considered alone, would fail to satisfy the more stringent conditions of those who base their conception of the public sphere on Habermas' model of 'an ideal speech situation' in which 'only the force of the better argument prevails' (Outhwaite, 1994, 40). Certain 'validity claims' found in Habermas' work are clearly violated in this form of largely 'uni-directional' address. There is not for example 'the possibility of an unconstrained dialogue to which all speakers have equal access' (*ibid.*), rather the setting forth of a position with limited opportunities for response. Seen, nevertheless, within the *wider context* of the web as a whole, such material can be understood as a contribution to one position from which some form of debate is conducted. In other words, this site is a forum within a wider sphere, one. which is itself contested by opposing forces. It is worth noting that the anarchist site is in no doubt as to the identity of its enemy; a phenomenon called 'capitalism' is attacked, rather than 'corporate power' (a more liberal definition which can be used to make smaller capitalist enterprises seem more progressive).[63]

---

63 The clash of competing discourses on the web often appears in graphic form. The decision by some political organisations to use free host sites leads to an interesting juxtaposition of messages. The Anarchist Black Cross Federation, for instance, dedicated to the support of anti-imperialist political prisoners, carries biographies of imprisoned revolutionaries (like Marilyn Buck and Tom Manning, the latter a Vietnam veteran) beneath advertising banners for 'First Auction', a retail outlet for online bargain-hunters.

Beyond capitalism? Corporate discourses on-line

Fears that the internet itself is becoming dominated by commerce may be found in a number of sources; for instance, Dahlberg argues that, although 'state censorship and surveillance' poses a danger, 'a possibly greater threat to public online discursive spaces is the increasing commercialisation and privatisation of cyberspace' (Dahlberg, 2001). There are two components to this undoubted growth in corporate strength; the enlargement of its commercial influence over internet content, and the concomitant increase in corporate discourse (Weisburg, in Andersen and Strate, 2000).

The Chief Executives of global corporations like bp, for example, now post their principles and re-print company articles on the web. The reasons for this activity are that 'consumers have adopted a more critical stance on the way business operates' and as a consequence 'companies have found themselves ... under greater public scrutiny' (Barrett, 1998).[64]

Facing a more combative opposition[65] and adverse media attention, corporations have realised, in the words of Chris Gibson-Smith, that 'the successful company of the 21st century will be one that can manage its social and environmental performance as effectively as its business one' (Barrett, 1998). In the case of BP, the question is posed thus; 'how do [companies] continue making profits without sacrificing their principles, and the principles of their employees and customers?' (Barrett, *ibid.*).

It is this last section of the question which is most relevant to the issues raised in this chapter. The principles of the corporation (in bp's phrase 'a company's core values') can only be expressed publicly (in this case, in a web-site) by producing statements or propositions which attest to values and beliefs. Indeed as seen above, Business for Social Responsibility provides a template for the production of a typical report, offering headings for mission statements and other material. It is the contention of the present work that statements about a company's responsibilities to 'a broad range of stakeholders, including employees, customers, communities and the environment' (BSR; *ibid.*) is a form of ideological preparation for the clash of ideas exemplified in the case of anarchist opposition (above).

Advertising, rhetoric and public address

Contemporary definitions of corporate citizenship can be found on various web-sites, including as seen above 'business decision-making linked to ethical values' (Business for Social Responsibility, 2000). The theory here is that increased social cohesion, product awareness and profitability can be generated by 'ethical'

---

64 Barrett, C 'BP: Human Rights' in *Shield*, 1998.

65 Business for Social Responsibility recognises what it calls 'a growing ability and sophistication of activist groups to target corporations' which appear through actions such as 'public demonstrations, shareholder resolutions, and even "denial of service" attacks on company websites' (BSR, *ibid.*).

behaviour.[66] The concept of 'social responsibility' used by Boots and many other companies, must be understood within the context of a larger system of ideas. It seems apparent that some of the 'beliefs' which motivate companies, including those which lead them to adopt models of social responsibility, will not be expressed in their original form; a correlation between improved financial performance and socially responsible business practices, discovered in a 1998 study made by a professor at McMaster University in the U.S., confirming an academic survey made in 1995, provides a useful example (Business for Social Responsibility, 2000, 2).[67] If corporate citizenship helps not just to maintain but to increase market share and profitability, this will probably not achieve prominence within public versions of its discourse. Such aims, in sociological terms, need to be operationalised before they are presented to a target audience.

In general, the goal or aim itself is conceived and essentially moderated by an awareness of the context in which an author is able to imagine varieties of action in the first place; in other words, there are obviously certain constraints at work. Any company or advertiser must ask what is possible in terms of public expression. The corporation must deploy its symbolic resources therefore within available public discourses (Price, 1998). For the sake of further illustration, one may consider the case of a company which wishes to demonstrate a commitment to more responsible uses of fossil fuels. If language is descriptive, it is also evaluative; or, to use the words of Dillon, 'linguistic accounts of phenomena are not simply descriptions, but descriptions for a purpose' (Dillon, 1995, 170). Here for example is a transcript made from a television transmission of November 2000, ostensibly a commercial but in fact an example of public relations. British Petroleum presented the image of a world made up of swirling green leaves, and used a male voiceover on the soundtrack:

Can we still drive our cars and have cleaner air? – we think so ... today, BP is improving air quality in fifty major cities around the world and across the UK – by introducing cleaner-burning petrol and diesel fuels – it's not an end to the problem, but the solution has to start somewhere – BP *soundtrack*: tweet tweet'

If this is treated as a symbolic manifestation of an underlying purpose, then we can see among other devices traditional techniques of rhetoric. The commercial is introduced by a rhetorical question (the answer to which will be provided by the communication source itself). This is followed by a number of assertions, again

---

66 BSR, for example, noted that 'a number of studies have suggested a large and growing market for the products and services of companies perceived to be socially responsible' (*ibid.*).

67 Tescos, the British supermarket chain, gained 'significant sales increases' (Grayson, 1999, 4) through its Computers for Schools promotion, described as a 'cause related marketing campaign' (*ibid.*).

characteristic of the techniques of rhetoric[68] outlined by writers like Atkinson (1984), and in a more positive sense by the American academic Thomas Farrell (1993).

This intervention does *not* however constitute a pure or ideologically stable achievement, not just because the statement may be made to disguise practices which contradict the values it expresses (the old idea that ideology works through an apparent surface which hides the true relations of power), but because 'the discursive material it works with is not its own' (Bruck, in Wasko and Mosco, 1992, 142). Indeed, in Farrell's opinion rhetoric itself is 'a practised imperfection' which offers an 'improvised framework of language community' (Farrell, 1993, 1).

Therefore, following an old maxim taken from the study of pragmatics (exemplified by the work of Paul Grice), in order to make an impact or even any sense at all, every statement must exemplify the *principle of relevance* (Grice, 1989, 27). The example of address given above cannot imitate traditional forms of public speech like allocution, where a formal address is made by someone in a position of authority to his or her followers (Price, 1997), exactly because its authority is not securely constituted.

Corporate address must therefore obey certain dialogic principles, perhaps even demonstrating a muted tendency to conversationalisation, but certainly at least exemplifying an awareness of what Fairclough calls 'an opening up and democratization of social relations', which includes 'a new public prestige for 'ordinary' values and practices' (Fairclough, 1995, 11). It is also worth noting that the conclusion of the piece transcribed above ('it's not an end to the problem, but the solution has to start somewhere') bears a striking resemblance to the statement used by Shell; 'solutions to the future won't come easily ... but you can't find them if you don't keep looking' (see above).

---

68 The inclusive 'we' (see Atkinson, 1984) and the reference to 'our' cars, however amicable, elides the distinction between source and subject. Captains of industry, parents, consumers in general are all equally culpable, according to this line. The same idea crops up in right-wing assessments of environmental responsibility; in a reply to Rob Newman, who argued that a choice must be made between capitalism or sustainability (*Guardian*, 2nd February 2006), the Shadow Secretary of State for the environment, Peter Ainsworth wrote in an echo of bp's discursive strategy, that 'we simply will not succeed in cutting UK carbon emissions unless the business community, which has indeed been part of the problem – but so have we all – is part of the solution' (*Guardian*, 6th February 2006).

Illustration 4: Power Station and Emissions
Photograph courtesy of Sally Hossack

'Carbon footprints' and capitalism

In discursive terms, the bp advertisement is a reply to something, a refutation of something less 'reasonable' but not fully expressed in the text; an argument that private motor vehicles should not be used at all. I take this as evidence of *political realignment*, characterised by an expansion of environmental discourse but linked to an attempt to weaken the links between green beliefs and radical action.

Five years after the cleaner fuels commercial, the bp 'carbon footprint' campaign emerged at a time when many corporations continued to make *modest* claims, apparently aimed at *incremental* improvements in the fabric of social life. *Everyday statements*, often employed as trademarks, drew attention to the benign, progressive attitudes supposedly characteristic of contemporary business. One of bp's slogans was 'it's a start', while Tesco claimed that 'every little helps'. Sainsbury's was intent on 'making life taste better', while the Halifax insisted on 'giving you extra'.[69]

Such statements seem at first sight to fall far short of the high-flown rhetoric associated with traditional political discourse. Why, then, should these utterances be

---

69 Little wonder that Baudrillard claimed *freedom of choice is imposed* on the consumer. Yet, within the apparent generosity of the privatised world, a disciplinary edict remains. You will be 'over the moon' if you switch to a Halifax mortgage, but 'your home will be repossessed' if you fail to keep up repayments.

regarded as part of a 'rhetorical condition'? Rhetoric can be identified as a principle of communication where a set of techniques is used by authoritative sources to mobilise symbolic content for *instrumental* purposes.

In other words, rhetoric is employed to produce effects and does so within *a hierarchy of communicative power*. The source speaks, while the audience is expected to answer, if at all, within the terms already set. Commercial rhetoric (unlike its political counterpart), is not actually 'mediated' at all; it is an example of 'paid for' advocacy, which escapes any external interference.

The inherently political character of commercial representation is most clearly revealed, however, because there are often *no products in evidence*, or because commodities are subsumed by brands and have become an *alibi* for publicity.

'Small carbon footprints': reputation management and 'rationalization'

The carbon footprint campaign was possible only in a discursive context receptive to concerns about the environment, and a more general cultural shift in favour of public avowals of vaguely progressive social goals. The measurement of the 'carbon footprint', based on awareness of global warming and, in particular, the supposed role of carbon emissions *as a prime* contributor to climate change, is presented as the first *literal-metaphorical* step in the process of recognising individual-collective responsibility for environmental degradation.

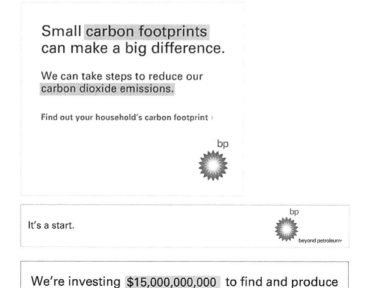

Illustration 5: bp Carbon Footprint Campaign

Take, for instance, the internet campaign (officially for a *product*, automotive fluids) which appeared on 11th November 2005. It reveals, at the linguistic level, several rhetorical features, common amongst those public interventions which amount to forms of advocacy. In the first place, there is the assertion: 'small carbon footprints' (restricted amounts of carbon emissions 'imprinted' on the planet) can 'make a big difference'. As a unit of meaning, irrespective of any external or exophoric evaluation, one might say that its *endophoric* structure at the level of the sentence produces a form of explicit significance (*a little x* can produce *a lot of y* where *y* is a desirable outcome).

Such statements have a pedigree, in particular those contemporary adages designed to make a contrast between an apparently negligible effort and a cumulative benefit; 'one small step for a man, one giant leap for mankind', is an example where the literal *step* represents a *metaphorical* advance. Such forms of address are current within dieting advertisements and other forms of self-help advice. The exophoric, external context is environmental awareness, expressed more clearly through the statement 'we can take steps to reduce our carbon dioxide emissions'. This links the concept of a 'footprint' with the notion of emissions and again suggests collective responsibility.[70]

The exercise is therefore predicated on some kind of *ideological settlement* within the broader consumer economy, based on the mutation of political positions and values. If one of the basic principles of address is imagining the subjective position of an audience, the evidence for how an audience is composed can be found in the finished text. If the analysts is at all interested in testing 'truth claims', then the bp campaign was an example of reputation management based on 'openness' and 'sincerity'. The *directive intention* was thus rationalized, disguising the motive of seeking increased publicity through an apparently positive intervention in public debate. The proof of this comes through bp's *description of purpose*, made not to 'the public', but to two core 'stakeholders', its workforce and its corporate customers.

Explanation and rationalization: 'It's time to turn the light on BP'

In its in-house magazine, under the title 'It's time to turn the light on BP' Leslie Viney explained that 'these ads are part of the company's biggest corporate reputational exercise since the introduction of the Helios logo and the launch of the "Beyond Petroleum" strapline in 2000' (Viney, BP Magazine, Issue 3, 2005). Viney cited Ian Adam, director of UK reputation and internal communications, who identified a 'two-pronged reputation campaign' aimed at 'opinion formers outside the organisation and at BP employees within it' (*ibid*). In other words, it is possible to trace the existence of a more private rationale, one which was not offered as part of the position promoted in the public sphere.

---

70 However, the use of 'we' is also however a rhetorical signal of authorial intent. It is not clear who the 'we' is in this case, but the range of reference may include: the author and his/her associates, the consumer/citizen, and the public in general.

Throughout bp's description of the process, it seems as though the company itself had conducted its own research. So, for example, bp claimed that the campaign followed 'a survey commissioned last year by bp with 1,000 influential people in businesses and non-governmental organisations' (*ibid*). A survey was certainly commissioned by bp but was actually conducted by a PR firm, Ogilvy Mather, which also handled the original re-branding at an estimated cost of £200m over two years (2000-2002).[71] The article went on to reveal a cause for concern as the loss of 'distinctiveness' against its competitors 'although BP was still among the top ranked companies in the world, top among oil companies, and top in being green' (*ibid*). The discursive context of bp's efforts was thus the contested ground it recognized within public debate. One senior executive noted that 'people see stories about petrol prices and profits, but ... the things that occupy our minds don't neccessarily get communicated' (Mather, P, *ibid*).[72] This signifies clear dissatisfaction with *mediated* coverage of the corporation's image, and explains its preference for forms of advocacy which are more difficult to interrupt.

Narrative and reality: three levels of description

Corporations seem to understand the connection between expressions of intent and the production of *acts* as independently-verifiable conditions. bp's director of global explained that 'we are very deliberate in making the *stories* we tell directly relevant to the countries where the campaigns are running' (Welch, D, *op cit*, *my emphasis*). Welch went on to assert that 'these are real stories where we're doing real things' (*ibid*). The existence of material initiatives cannot be denied, but the reason for the commission of 'real acts' is exactly their subsequent reproduction as useful narratives.[73]

Evidence of distinct purposes, expressed at three different 'levels' of description, should be set against this claim. The first level of explanation is that of *appearance*, the production of material for public consumption. The second, outlined above, is *rationalization*, the creation of a rationale directed at internal and external evaluators (the workforce and corporate partners), upon whom the company relies for its place

---

71 Which would equal somewhere in the range of $280m - $321m (as an average range based on those years' variable exchange rates). In 2001 bp invested $8.5 bn in oil and gas while its average annual investment in solar power was $33.3m. This amounts to some 0.4 percent of its 2001 petroleum expenditures. (Murphy, Cait 'Is BP Beyond Petroleum? Hardly' *Fortune*, September 30th, 2002).

72 'We are interested in environment, community ... about using energy in a more responsible way ... these are things we want to engage people in thinking about with us' (Mather, P, *ibid*).

73 Employees were approached in an attempt to reinforce this perspective. The bp report records that they were asked 'do you feel you understand and feel part of the company's values? have you been involved in dialogue'?

in the capitalist system. The third level is instrumental, presented by professional communicators as a form of *revelation* designed to impress prospective clients.

At this third level, the bp campaign becomes not an example of *sincerity* (the public appearance) or *strategy* (the private rationale), but a *case study* amongst others, all designed to illustrate the capabilities of Ogilvy. This company argued that the brand 'must actually surround the target audience'. This is reminiscent of Baudrillard's notion of 'ambience' (from the Latin, to go about or *ecompass*). In Baudrillard's view, this is a place of consumption which represents a spatial concentration of activity, the existence of which can be extended to a general principle – the ubiquitous appearance of commercial messages.

Ogilvy's position on bp's original transformation into an environmental advocate was explained as the need to establish 'a new visual identity and a new brand positioning', which defined the company as 'innovative, progressive, environmentally responsible' (Ogilvy website, February 2006). The organization does not *begin from* the view that the environment needs to be saved, but rather assesses any individual condition as a possible threat to the firms they represent. Ogilvy puts the question thus; 'which of these issues could cause significant damage to the client's reputation or business operations if not managed effectively?' (*ibid*). The purpose is not carbon reduction, but the creation of 'an effective issues management plan' which might 'provide guidance ... to influence the evolution of an issue' or 'possibly even make it go away' (*ibid*). In the end, bp did indeed try to make one salient issue disappear. It inverted the logic of its own *material-narrativity*, in which 'progressive' actions were prepared in order to secure publicity, by reducing its carbon emissions at the stroke of a pen and then producing the story of this apparent success. The spectacular decline it recorded in carbon output from 1,376 million tonnes in its 2005 sustainability report, to 606 million tonnes in a report from 2004, was achieved by 'counting only the CO_2 produced from the oil, oil products, chemicals and gas it produces itself, rather than all the oil and gas some of its operations buy in and sell on' (Seager and Bowers, *Guardian*, April 21st 2006).

Deregulation and address

Both state and private enterprise seek to extract value from the citizen-consumer. Purchases which contribute to the project of the self (see Fowles, 1996, 197) or to the 'household economy' are presented to the individual as an alternative to (even a *means of escape* from) the state's authoritarian demands which require the functional extraction of value.[74]

When I dealt in the Introduction with Gill's argument that the state 'does not seek to enter the moral realm' (Gill, 2003, 5), it was partly to emphasise the ways in which the private sector asserted 'its rights as a social actor' through the production of 'highly visible *moral performances*'. Although it is possible to exaggerate the

---

74 Taxation, payment of bills, completion of licences, and other formal necessities represent the supposed antithesis of free choice.

trajectory of the current period, the world has certainly moved beyond the 'relentless propaganda on behalf of goods in general' described by J.K. Galbraith in *The New Industrial State* (1967).

The larger corporate aim which Galbraith identified, the maintenance or expansion of market-position, requires a consistent intervention in consumer society but, exactly because the economy depends on encouraging a consumer mentality, it must entail an effort to influence public consciousness in general, even if it stops short of 'the total organisation' of everyday life (Baudrillard, 1998, 29).

The point here is that the material described above, together with a supposedly general increase in democratic exchange, can be understood (certainly in the British context) as the discursive evidence of the de-regulation of public bodies and the privatisation of public assets and the flotation of private companies on the stock exchange.[75] These developments, beginning in the 1980's, ran alongside a sharp fall in corporate taxes, and helped to increase private intervention in what were previously the concerns of the state.

In *Mythologies* (1984), Barthes insisted that 'capitalism is openly expressed', that it is an economic fact; its political representatives, Barthes considered, supposedly operate in disguise. He was right to argue that the dominant economic class is involved in a process of 'exnomination',[76] but it appears that the rhetorical condition of capitalist power demands its own subterfuge. This is the replacement of the term capitalism with the designation 'corporate'.[77] Capitalism becomes, in the meantime, a reference made by an outmoded left, or an activity for aspirational groups which were once excluded from the larger universe of established enterprise.[78] The multiple 'voices' assigned to the consumer, on the other hand, may be understood not as 'pluralising modes of democratic engagement' but as the 'ideological supplement' of corporate capitalism (Coles, on Zizek, in Tonder, L & Thomassen, L 2005, 69). In Coles opinion, once each post-modern identity is identified, It 'merely clamours ... for its own interests within the system' (*ibid*).

---

75 An early case was the flotation of the Abbey National in July 1989 (see Saunders and Harris, 1994, 17). The Midland Bank became the *HSBC*, and underwent a major re-branding exercise.

76 'The bourgeoisie is defined as the social class which does not want to be named' (Barthes, R Mythologies, 1984).

77 'Corporate' is an achieved state, defined as 'forming a body politic' (Concise Oxford dictionary, 1963); politic moves in sense from *sagacious* to scheming and crafty.

78 Note, for example, the arrival of 'capitalist chicks', one of whom celebrates 'competition ... the driving force in nature' and the 'new wave of young, multi-ethnic, dual-gendered, intelligent and generous capitalists' (Capitalist Chicks website, February 2006). The difficulty of interpreting the meaning of a 'dual' gender cannot be pursued here.

Publicity and the 'public sphere'

In one HSBC television commercial from the 1990's, the faces of consumer-citizens are shown in close-up, attentive but also seemingly troubled. A voice presents a series of questions, and begins by asking: 'Let's be honest. How many of us have no idea where all our money goes?' Questions may at first sight appear to be more democratic in character, because they may seem dialogic in nature (Hirschkop and Shepherd, 1989, 4). The 'public' in this case remains silent, however, responding instead by raising their hands. In other words, it is shown to agree with a set of questions which are essentially rhetorical and not part of reasoned discussion. The audience (both the one represented and the absent one which is actually addressed) is not treated democratically; its role is merely to accept the terms of the address.

Even within this limited example, it would seem that Habermas is correct in identifying the use of contemporary publicity, in which forms of media address cannot form part of 'rational moral and political discourse' (Habermas, in Bernstein, 1994, 81). Publicity seems to have lost its critical function in favour of 'staged display' (*ibid.*). The public sphere was meant in its original conception to be a place of equality and freedom, but (according to Outhwaite) 'in the realm of the mass media' this sphere has changed in meaning; publicity changed from being 'a function of public opinion', to 'an attribute of whatever attracts public opinion' (Outhwaite, 1994, 82). The HSBC advertisement is thus an example of staged rhetorical display. The words and phrases are presented in order to present limited commercial options. Information of a sort is offered, but only to create new custom for this particular bank:

> You can find a way of saving. ISA's mean more people can save tax-free. And who finds the thought of getting one a bit daunting?

Dyer also notes this tendency, when she describes the idea that 'rhetorical language ... carries the implication of extravagance and artifice, not to mention a lack of information' (Dyer, 1982, 152). Extravagance in this case can be seen in the technical support accorded to the narrative form, expressed within the expensive production values in which messages are embedded. Yet advertisements cannot exclude references to actually existing conditions if they are to achieve resonance with the public they address; in other words, as argued above, an audience must recognise the environment which is represented.

In Britain, the issue of health is an important aspect of debate within the public sphere. Some of the sources which contribute to the public articulation of concerns about the nation's health include statistics which demonstrate the length of time British employees spend at work[79] and the publication of hospital waiting lists by central government. These, together with apocryphal tales and personal experience, tend to create an awareness of a service in crisis; this forms the discursive background to the rise of privatised health care and its public representation. In the late nineteen-

---

79 See Toynbee and Walker, 2001, 113, for the work/life 'imbalance'.

eighties, for example, BUPA commissioned an advertisement (known as 'Scanner' by the advertiser responsible for its creation), which provided a narrative account of a mother's admission to hospital. This traded on public fears of ill-health, against an implied decline in the reliability of public services. Using a family as the dramatic centre of the event, the voiceover is heard as follows:[80]

> To be sure of private health care they became members of BUPA. This priority was brought home to them recently when Sue fell ill. She was treated in a BUPA hospital where her problem was diagnosed with a body scanner. You see, BUPA has priorities too. No one takes a profit. Anything left over from caring for its members today is reinvested for their future, like hospitals, health screening centres and the latest medical technology. Most people choosing private health care join BUPA. BUPA – Britain feels better for it.

Here, the ostensible narrative is the story of foresight, illness, and recovery. The larger 'social narrative' is one in which private health care has become a necessity, a 'priority' which sensible individuals recognise, the value of which is demonstrated through the illness which strikes Sue, and which could strike all; the difference being that those who are unprepared will suffer the consequences. The movement from general social need to the intervention of BUPA is achieved through a linguistic sleight-of-hand, a non-sequitur linking the diagnosis to the quasi-explanation 'you see, BUPA has priorities too'. An uncomfortable change of structure is evident in the transition from narrative mode to direct address. Finally, the nation as a whole supposedly benefits from this service. The commercial closes with a type of assertion familiar from political advertising; 'BUPA – Britain feels better for it'.

In the overall context of deregulation, Myers argues, there has been a retreat from 'socially responsible' forms of address, allowing private corporations to represent their services in place of state provision (Myers, 1999, 39). The scenario described here thus dramatises common fears and anxieties about the lack of state support and in general what Myers calls 'people's anxieties and anger' (*ibid.*). In the case of this television commercial, the consumer is supposed to identify with the victim, yet the advertiser is careful to avoid a more traumatic outcome; the representation of death would run counter to the purpose of the message.

In such examples it is possible to observe a microcosm of commercial domination, what Habermas calls the 'collapse of the public sphere' (Habermas, in Bernstein, 1994, 84). The scope of the public realm expands through mediated dramatisation of its concerns, yet its function as the location of meaningful dialogue 'has become progressively insignificant' (*ibid.*). In other words, while interventions proliferate, the range of their discourses become narrower, so that 'arguments are translated into symbols to which again one cannot respond by arguing but only by identifying with them' (Habermas, 1989 in Livingstone and Lunt, 1994, 20).

Thus this type of commercial appears at first sight to confirm Habermas' view that the media's aim is to influence individual opinion only so far as it provides a 'pseudo sphere' of passive spectatorship (Livingstone and Lunt, 1994, 19).

---

80 Transcript by the author.

However, there are other issues within the realm of discourse which require more careful consideration. Thompson, for example, advocates the idea that contemporary audiences have adopted new forms of 'power and awareness of rights' (Thompson, 1990, 115). As a consequence they may be perceived as still able to compose a public opinion that can continue to act as a critical influence in democratic debate. It is impossible, then, not to take account of the contribution made by media forms to the circulation of important public meanings, yet it is important to recognise the nature of the references and propositions which are made.

A rather more speculative viewpoint emerges from the work of Fowles, who argues that advertising has limited power in affecting or persuading an audience; his opinion is that advertisers are able merely to 'recondition the public's symbols' in the hope that consumers will interpret correctly the intended meaning (Fowles, 1996, 9). He insists that 'very few of these contrived symbols actually get appropriated by the public; most are deflected as meaningless and die unlamented deaths along the roadway of commerce' (Fowles, 1996, 9). The present work proposes instead that Fowles's statement here is disingenuous, intended to disguise a moral issue by showing that neglected messages are harmless. The point is not that the public will remain safe through ignorance or neglect, but actually concerns the use and re-circulation of those messages which are recognised and valued, and the ways in which a dialectical relationship between text and subjective position is achieved.

Chapter 5

Ideology, Commerce and Politics

The public sphere, ideology and analysis

Habermas' notion of 'the public sphere' (1989), has been described as a space or public arena where 'political opinion can be formed freely' (Shattuc, 1997, 93) and as a site governed by the 'public reason of private citizens' (Peters, 1993, 541). This conception of a place where free, rational exchange can be sustained provides one of the best known normative models for the exercise of interaction within contemporary mediated culture, and has become an intellectual rallying-point for the development of progressive discourses. The concept of the public sphere has become an essential element within the re-formulation of democratic culture, appearing in works on culture, citizenship, media and politics (Garnham, 1986; Dahlgren, 1995; Thompson, 1995; McGuigan, 1996).

It represents, not simply a movement from spatial to metaphorical reference, as Garber argues (in Isin, 2000, 257), but rather a synthesis of two concepts: space and democracy. Habermas' intervention stands, moreover, within an activist tradition. Bernstein characterises this as a project concerned with practical tasks as well as theory (Bernstein, 1985), while Outhwaite speaks of Habermas' 'practical concern' with the possibility of 'rational moral and political discourse' within modern societies (Outhwaite, 1994, 39). The active character of Habermas' philosophy may demonstrate its sensitivity to the Marxist inheritance, revealed for instance in 'The German Ideology' where Marx and Engels argue that 'the philosophers have only interpreted the world in various ways; the point is to change it' (Marx and Engels, 1974, 123).

From the standpoint of communication theory, however, the creation of a scenario in which 'public' and 'private' relationships are strictly delineated, and in which certain social forces are deemed more rational or progressive than others, may create difficulty in assessing the moral status of commercial messages, as seen above. While authors like Goldman insist that the process of producing and circulating 'commodity-sign values' is 'inseparable from processes of ideological reproduction' (Goldman, 1992, 9), one question asked in this chapter is whether or not persuasive communication necessarily undermines the maintenance of an independent public domain in the sense intended within certain interpretations of Habermas' work. More particularly, it investigates advertising, promotional and corporate texts in order to establish their role in the circulation of public meanings.

Texts here may be understood as those significant events or productions (from catch-phrases to developed narratives) which a culture or cultures makes notable and which always refer, whatever their origin, to lived experiences in the broadest sense.[1]

Thus the debate over the ideological character or otherwise of cultural texts and artefacts[2] and the related issue of their origin within a system of commodity production, remains an important subject, but must be addressed in the light of a vital supplementary question. This concerns the way in which texts achieve popular cultural value, or *value-effect*, which is to ask in essence why certain messages resonate in the way they do, and what mechanisms are used to re-circulate ideas which texts (in the terms of this book) 'propose' to audiences.[3] This aspect of the overall enquiry is not intended to signal a turn to reception studies, especially where this might be associated with models which subsume the issue of power under the sign of sub-cultural activity (Fiske, 1989). What follows below will attend instead to those arenas of social power identified by Habermas, within and between which social meanings emerge and circulate. The purpose of such a study is to investigate the general usefulness of the larger theories of publicness and communicative action, and their value as an alternative to the cause-effect model encountered in much social theory.

In beginning this process, it seems apparent that the nomenclature or system of terms used to describe the various structural 'locations', itself reveals the enduring sense of an ordered but essentially divided social system.[4] Habermas certainly recognises the ambiguity inherent in the categories he employs, noting that events are deemed 'public' when they are 'open to all', yet explaining in addition that the term 'need not refer to general accessibility' (Habermas, 1989, 1). The example given is the existence of 'public' buildings which, though not actually open to citizens, house state institutions and therefore represent 'public authority' (ibid.). A demarcation in this case can be made between officially-constituted bodies and a citizenry which periodically sanctions their function through the electoral process; the people are formally and physically separated from the seat of such power, which is nonetheless exercised in their name.

---

1 Thus, for example, the act of going to the cinema may be seen as a broader activity than mere passive reception, in line with Webster and Phelan's observation that it has always 'been viewed more as a social activity than as an occasion for seeing particular films ... it represents a continuation of the original 'audience', made up of those who went out to a public social event ... the occasion had a significance beyond that of any 'message' communicated or any individual gratification obtained' (Webster and Phelan, 1994, 89).

2 Found in the work of Adorno and many subsequent authors (see for example Zizek, 1994).

3 Texts are seen here as the 'vehicle' for propositions.

4 Initially, it should be noted that the division between public and private institutions is an empirically verifiable condition, but that the attribution of particular modes of communication to each (in essence, a belief in 'strategic' vs. 'communicative' actions) is rather more problematic.

Illustration 6: Parliament – The Seat of Power?
Photograph courtesy of Sally Hossack

Another example provided by Habermas, intended to demonstrate the function of public opinion as a critical source, proves equally as complex. The existence of the public as the carrier of informed opinion is, in his view, exactly what makes the 'public character' of events like court proceedings meaningful (*ibid.*, 2). Yet such occasions are characterised by forms of conduct and linguistic codes which can act as barriers to real public intervention and judgement. This may not affect the essential status of the institution, in so far as it remains in formal terms within the public sphere, and is therefore subject to scrutiny, accountability and so forth. However, as Bazerman points out, the law (with its 'status-seeking' professional class) and legal talk and texts, constitutes a 'specialised discursive system' which 'orders and regulates' many different spheres of existence (Bazerman, in Gunnarsson *et al.*, 1997, 43). From this it may be seen that those sectors identified as belonging to a public realm do not all contribute straightforwardly to the production of Habermas' essential prerequisite for democratic exchange; the ideal speech situation, in which it is possible in McGuigan's words for human beings to 'communicate with one another without necessarily exercising coercion or manipulation' (McGuigan, 1996, 177).

The discourses of the law belong, ultimately, to forms of expert knowledge and professional behaviours, in common with many other forms of directive or 'disciplinary' address (Foucault, 1975), including apparently 'innocent' modes of self-critical subjectivity.[5] Analysis cannot proceed, however, without considering that other location of institutional conduct, which critical theory opposes to the public sphere; the notion of a 'private' domain. This however, animates just as wide a range of related meanings. It is composed of both the realm of the personal (issues pertaining 'legitimately' to the individual) and of activity or business (commercial or other) conducted beyond public scrutiny.

It is interesting to note that Benhabib identifies three fields of experience belonging to the private sphere: the domain of moral and religious conscience; the intimate or personal sphere; and the free flow of commodity relations (Benhabib in O'Baoill, 2000). It seems then that a positive sense of justifiable seclusion or secrecy, or *rights of privacy*, applied to the individual and his or her personal conduct and belief, is extended to all forms of ownership and thence to the activities of private commercial organisations. The term 'private' has thus taken on what Mosco calls the 'burden' of including 'the most intimate of human experience *and* the market behaviour of the transnational business system' (Mosco, 1996, 164).

If the growth of privacy (in Turner's words 'a social principle for the division of cultural space'[6]) belongs to the onset of self-reflexive modernity,[7] then the contradiction which appears with the concomitant rise of industrial production is, as Turner describes it, based on the requirements of capitalism to create both *individualism* and *individuation* (in Kuper and Kuper, 1985, 646/647). That is to say, subjects must devote themselves to the consumption of commodities (stimulated by advertising), creating as a consequence a type of private hedonism, while at the same time they are treated by the state as 'standard' categories for the purposes of 'taxation, registration and surveillance' (*ibid.*).

'Functionalising' citizens

The latter constitute examples of what Habermas calls the 'functionalisation' of citizens for 'various public purposes' (Habermas, 1961, 34). 'Privatisation', on the other hand, which is presented in the present work as both the assimilation of public resources and an attempt to re-compose individual psyches, is directly relevant to these debates, as it represents the commercial absorption of fields of action which at least once preserved 'principles of universal access' irrespective of financial power (Mosco, 1996, 153).

Under present circumstances, the purpose of 'universal access' becomes the opportunity to promote products to new groups of consumers. One current argument is that, within what may be called for the moment 'privatised' discourse, i.e. that which stems from private sources and/or which is intended to 'privatise' subjects in

---

5   See for example Rimke's article on 'Governing citizens through self-help literature' (Rimke, in *Cultural Studies*, vol 14, no 1, 2000).

6   See Turner, in Kuper and Kuper, 1985, 647.

7   Evidenced, for example, in the eighteenth century by the growth of autobiography; Turner, in Kuper and Kuper, 1985, 646.

their consciousness (Habermas, *ibid.*), there can exist certain appeals which, because they must embody existing 'states of mind' (or particular audience values), may reproduce albeit within a commercial context, some progressive elements. This is certainly the argument advanced by Meijer, who makes a positive assessment of advertising's potential as a form of public communication (Meijer, 1998, 235). This approach, despite the possibility of any formal agreement which might be made with the underlying principle of address (in that the sender must 'model' the subjective position of its audiences), should recognise more clearly two important issues.

The first is the notion that a 'positive' approach to audiences by advertisers may be inevitable during a period in which there 'is a trend in selling consumer benefits rather than product attributes' (Leiss, *et al.*, 1990, 50). Second, the nature and purpose of advertising address is such that it uses social representations for a number of practical reasons, but in the case of the 'lifestyle'[8] and corporate formats[9] dealt with here attempts to do so within the context of an 'avant-garde' mode of address. It treats culture as a resource which, as Fowles notes, draws on its 'repository of symbolic material … in an attempt to fabricate new symbols with enlivened meanings' (Fowles, 1996, 9). In such cases, there is a marked tendency to employ quite unusual characterisations of individuals and of situations.[10] This tendency may be compared with the use of advertisements for more didactic purposes, in which the product (or more often) corporate image may be promoted in the light of particular treatments of social change, at times deliberately referring to political radicalism, such as the practices and discourses associated with 'new social movements' (Price, 1998, 163).

The rationale for the use of any strategy will remain tied however, to the requirements of all symbolic display, which entails a return on private commercial investment. References and representations are often reproduced where, as we saw above, they represent the 'leading edge of value change' (Strauss, in Price, 1998, 162) and are thus able through the power of association, to strengthen the symbolic capital and *referential power* of the company and/or agency concerned. Or, in simple terms, these texts refer to widely known ideas or events or more especially, as

---

8   Leiss describes lifestyle as the most complex of the four 'advertising formats', in which 'a more balanced relationship is established between the elemental codes of person, product and setting' (Leiss, 1990, 259).

9   Formats: the product-information format is a type of advertising where the product is at the centre of all other elements of the display, which point out and explain the virtues of the product. The product-image format gives the product special qualities it might not originally appear to have – a symbolic relationship is established between the product and some abstract qualities outside the day-to-day use of the product. The personalised format uses a direct relationship between the product and the human personality. In the lifestyle format, the viewer or reader is meant to associate the product, the people and the people's use of the product with a particular kind of 'consumption style'.

10   See for example the Furla adverts (2001), which produce the 'enlivened meaning' mentioned by Fowles by juxtaposing an image of a typical model's stance within the context of domestic chaos.

indicated above 'movements', which will prompt some form of audience recognition and response.

If the logic of this position is taken further, then it also provides a useful contribution to the debate over advertising and ideology (see below). That is to say, it is possible to recognise the 'non-ideological' character of capital, in so far as it appears to use any set of ideas which strike a chord in audiences. It is certainly quite 'liberal' in this respect, selecting whatever notions are most likely to achieve resonance. Yet within the cycle of reproduction it is the very fact that these ideas are framed within a wider economic relationship that makes them once again 'ideological', in the sense that they are purposive and therefore inscribed with power relations.[11]

Notice may be drawn in particular to the ways in which television commercials represent social groups as *diverse* and multiple but through the process of representation can present personal/social *development* as possible only with the aid of products, companies, services, investment plans, and so forth[12] (see below for a fuller exposition).

Ideological address produces however, an incomplete proposition, exactly because to be understood its purposes cannot dominate its mode of discourse or presentation; that is to say, it must operationalise its raw commercial purpose, presenting it in a narrative format, or in an ironical context, or perhaps expressing it in mythical terms. Thus, in Zizek's terms, the point of ideology is that it is not 'not necessarily "false" and can certainly be "true", or quite accurate, since what really matters is not the asserted content as such but *the way this content is related to the subjective position implied by its own process of enunciation*' (Zizek, 1994, 8). The process of analysis must therefore compare what is asserted to what interests seem to be represented within the process of communication.

The exact method of commercial and corporate 'presentation' must be seen therefore within the context of the political relations enshrined within capitalism, whether those relations are thought to be merely necessary (the way of things), a positive good, or a force for social fragmentation. There are certainly clear tensions between various attitudinal perspectives in the creation of each text (between for

---

11 Zizek notes this problem when he describes the movement between the ideological, the 'non-ideological' and an apparent return to the realm of ideology; 'Today, in late capitalism, when the expansion of the new mass media in principle, at least, enables ideology effectively to penetrate every pore of the social body, the weight of ideology as such is diminished ... the system, for the most part, bypasses ideology in its reproduction and relies on economic coercion, legal and state regulations, and so on [yet] the moment we take a closer look at these allegedly extra-ideological mechanisms that regulate social reproduction, we find ourselves knee-deep in the already mentioned obscure domain in which reality is indistinguishable from ideology' (Zizek, 1994).

12 Williamson thinks that advertisements can actually 'incorporate anything' in terms of ideas, and 'works in hollowing historical meaning' from the signs it uses (Williamson, 1982, 167).

example research data, creative insight, and client perspective[13]). In addition, it is also the case that there is a contradiction at work between the message and the product (see below).

However, in the cases cited by Meijer, the existence of progressive intent and positive representation (in this case of ethnicity), neglects to state that the composition of such a representation serves a purpose; it associates a social reality (the existence of multi-ethnicity) with capitalist *ventures*, rather than with any public or state-sponsored *politics*.

A further issue concerns the vexed question of the 'origins' of the consciousness which is addressed, in so far as one must admit the existence of pre-formed discourses which may emanate from previous instances of private intervention.[14] This suggests at the very least that the different spheres are not impermeable, and may even demonstrate reciprocal development. Despite the interventions of commentators like Meijer and Fowles, the dominant perspective remains the notion of a powerful appropriation of public discourses through mass media forms. One expression of this view is found in Ang, who writes that contemporary cultural production is 'adamantly intentional and resolutely non-interactive' (Ang, in Lury, 1993, 89).

This also entails a reading of audience which proposes its 'virtual inclusion' in the mechanics of consumerism (Lury, *ibid.*). Another example of this process is observed by Bobbio, in his references to a 'rhetorical presentation of old age', found on television; this consists of an 'attempt to ingratiate potential new consumers' into commercial discourses, so that the elderly appear happy to be in a world in which 'they can finally enjoy some particularly fortifying tonic or exceptionally attractive holiday' (Bobbio, 2001, 9). This book is in broad agreement with the concept of inclusion, as it appears above. However, it also asks *what exactly is being included* or enveloped within the address itself, suggesting that any coherent message will, in considering/constituting subject-positions, produce acts of communication which can never be unitary in content, though they may assume an imperfect unity of form in particular texts.[15]

The riposte, then, to the realist perspective could be that content is irrelevant, and that it is the overall process of mediation which situates or interpellates subjects. Writers like Baudrillard go further, to assert that media such as television present real events in an 'ecstatic' relation, in a series of stereotyped and unreal ways that allow 'their senseless and uninterrupted concatenation' (Baudrillard, 1990, 10).

---

13 See for example, Fowles, for the following schema: any advertisement represents a temporary armistice between the advertiser and its advertising agency. Any major advertising effort embodies an unresolved conflict between research information and creative execution. Within the advertisement or commercial, tension will exist between the product and the appeal An advertisement or commercial does not stand alone but enters into a number of intertextual relationships, which supply further dynamics to the message (1996, 78-79).

14 Zisek examines the concept of a 'society of the spectacle' in which the media 'structure our perception of reality in advance and render reality indistinguishable from the "aestheticized" image of it' (Zisek, 1994, 3).

15 See the discussion of the 'Network Q' advertisement in Chapter 1.

Habermas, however, perceives the media (as one source of public communication) as having 'ambivalent potential' (in Outhwaite, 1994, 105); because the mass media belong to 'generalised' communication forms, they break free from the 'provincial' spatio-temporality of older, more restricted contexts (*ibid.*).

Hence, they can reproduce elements of the public sphere itself. Other systems, in contrast, reproduce 'materially' rather than symbolically, and are functional, oriented to power and wealth (O'Baoill, 2000). This causes them to 'interfere in the process of the symbolic reproduction of daily life' (Rasmussen, 1990, in O'Baoill, *ibid.*). Over and above the question of mediation, the function of these other modes of privatised relations must not be forgotten; as Poulantzas argues, 'an enterprise is also an apparatus', reproducing 'political and ideological relations affecting the places of the social classes' (Poulantzas, 1974, 32).

In this sense, production of ideas is not the sole preserve of the 'ideological' sphere, just as not all within the processes of production is purely economic (*ibid.*); 'economic' relations, for example, are constituted as cultural and social practices. In the terms used within this book, it would thus be appropriate to argue that the economic is imbued with the power of representation, and the discursive with material force; or better still, following Mosco's line of reasoning, that both economy and communication are 'processes of exchange' which are multiply determined by 'shared social and cultural practices' (Mosco, 1996, 72).

Exchange, economics and address

Once a split between the economic/structural and the discursive/subjective is abandoned, discourse may be seen to embody material forces which *are enunciated in each act of expression*. All symbolic expression may then be understood as exemplifying action. Using Danet's remarks about language, it is possible to conceive that a major function of expression is to provide 'recipes for the constitution of new social relationships ... and for transformations of the status of individuals or groups' (Danet, in Gunnarsson *et al.*, 1997, 13). This rather general definition of the field would include other quite opposed functions, such as the achievement of positive democratic exchange, or the maintenance of unequal power-relations.

Wernick, in his study of promotional culture, draws attention to the link between industrial production of commodities, and the conceptions of action and value to which they must refer. He avers that the 'brand-imaging' of mass produced consumer goods 'links them symbolically to the whole world of social values' (Wernick, 1991, 22). This in itself does not constitute an attack upon the social role of advertising, as Wernick would appear to recognise when he offers a definition of ideology as 'that level of reality ... at which people orient meaningfully to their world' (*ibid.*, 23).

This statement, which severs the link between the ideological and any pejorative or 'dominant' inflection, is useful in so far as it avoids the otherwise automatic assumption that 'systems' of belief are necessarily distortions of empirically verifiable truths, or that they can be produced only by dominant groups. Yet the difficulty is that Wernick wishes to retain the conviction that values in general, where produced within a capitalist mode of production, remain 'socially conservative' (Wernick, 1991, 24).

This issue has been addressed by a number of commentators, with one tradition in particular assuming a correlation between commodification and negative ideological intent. Strinati, for example, describes cultural production as a process of standardisation which also 'serves to obscure the standardisation and manipulation of consciousness practised by the culture industry' (Strinati, 1991, 86-87).

Commodity production and social value

The process of commodity production, as it appears in Marx, turns on the theory of value. In describing the commodity, Marx cited the English empiricist philosopher Locke who argued that 'the natural worth of anything consists in its fitness to supply the necessities, or serve the conveniences of human life'; the measure therefore of value is human need and use and 'the utility of a thing makes it a use-value' (Marx, *Capital*, 44). He gives examples of commodities, such as 'iron, corn, or a diamond', and describes these as 'material' things possessing values which only become a reality through consumption (*ibid.*). These remarks reveal the dual nature of goods, as 'both objects of utility, and depositories of value' (Levin, 1996, 57). Pursuing this argument further, and following Marx's reasoning, it becomes apparent that individuals or groups in one locale or social space may require a commodity which can only be obtained elsewhere. As a result, another form of value comes into being, based upon the necessity of exchange. In one sense, this differentiates between necessity (what is immediately available) and desire (what might be obtained), suggesting a departure from the very simple view of need initially advanced. Sahlins contends that the problem originates with Marx's 'naturalisation' of use value, in the sense that he appears to neglect the issue of the social determination of need, adhering instead to a biological view of human wants (in Mosco, 1996, 141). Marx also describes how any given commodity can be exchanged for other commodities in different proportions.

In terms of exchange, therefore, economic worth can subsist in what the marketplace is prepared to accept as valuable. This marks the beginning of a form of alienation, in this case of people from the materials that sustain existence; an abstract market principle has replaced the straightforward notion of use alone. Levin calls this the 'alienated character of exchange relationships' (Levin, 1996, 59). The growth of the market may therefore be seen as a significant factor in the growth of collective oppression but, according to Marxist theory, what actually dominates individuals in a market economy, is not commodities as material objects 'but unacknowledged social relationships set up and resolved through commodity exchange' (Catephores, 134). Marx went on to speak of 'the language of commodities' and advanced the concept of the commodity as a 'social hieroglyph' (in Levin, 1996, 58); taken up by Baudrillard, this gives rise to a third order of value – sign value.

It is impossible to ignore the fact that certain private institutions seem to have assumed the chief responsibility for the production of public 'sign values' and of cultural production in general (see above). Large-scale companies seem, as argued above, to have taken advantage of a 'de-regulated' public environment. Corporate citizenship may have begun life in the mid-nineties as a label for the activity of companies, but may also come to refer to *the subjectivity of those who are addressed* in the drive to create receptive communities. Furthermore, when private capital talks of its 'responsibilities', it is clear that this concept is often bound together in political discourse with the concept of rights (Fairclough, 2000, 40). The corollary to corporate responsibility is therefore corporate rights.[16]

Corporate and large-scale address shows therefore an *instrumental* sensitivity towards the various audiences it both imagines and by the same token attempts to compose; those stakeholders, consumers, clients and ultimately citizens it describes and configures in the process of address. An increased willingness and urgency to address communities of consumers directly, without reference to the state, found in television commercials, policy statements, web-sites and magazine advertising, may reveal the ways in which corporate sign-value has become the substitute for a once more tangible relationship between public authority and the subject.

Indeed, as Heater argues, there is a real danger that the subject will remain 'consumers of products and services, not citizens in the proper sense'; he cites for example the 1991 Tory government's 'Citizen's Charter' which refers in a number of places to 'customer' and 'client' as if these were synonymous with 'citizen' (Heater, 1999, 10). One way of exploring this issue is to consider how subjects or citizens may address one another.

Definitions of citizenship

Over two hundred years ago, the title of citizen was a linguistic weapon, an address adopted by the French revolutionaries to enact what Derek Heater calls 'the symbolic reality of equality' (Heater, 1999, 1); aristocratic distinctions were thus abolished within public speech. In addressing one another as 'citizen', the French of 1789 engaged in a kind of performative utterance (Austin, 1962, 8). At the moment of expression, an act is performed, demonstrating simultaneously inclusive solidarity and a clear ideological distinction from the *ancien regime*; a democratic variant perhaps of Althusser's interpellation (Althusser, 1984, 48), keeping each social actor up to the mark.

However, in common with the idealised public realm imagined by Habermas (see above) caution must be exercised if such examples are thought to offer a

---

16 This connection was made explicit in the American town of Wellfleet, where a telecommunications company called Omnipoint cited a the Civil Rights Act of 1964 in its defence against a citizen's group which had attempted to prevent the building of a mobile 'phone mast. The company won the case; the people of Wellfleet had 'violated' the rights of the corporation (Boothroyd, 2000).

flawless model of public practice. This is especially the case when a study is made of the kinds of rights and responsibilities which were actually assigned to different groups of citizen in this period. As Hufton has pointed out, men and women were expected to meet quite distinct obligations; in the year III, when men were called upon to take oaths of loyalty and receive 'certificates de civisme', no such demands were made on women, who were seen instead as 'citizenesses' owing in Hufton's words 'first allegiance to the responsible citizen in the shape of husband or father' (in Kates, 1998, 315). At other times, women were offered the palliative of blind faith in the new order. Even those who express a strong belief in the material power of language would probably hesitate to defend the position taken in the 'Moniteur' by a revolutionary journalist, who imagined that any woman in childbirth could 'think of the constitution' and as a consequence 'feel no pain' (*ibid.*, 314).

This should remind the theorist that citizenship as a category is always bestowed, as Marshall said in 1964, on those who are seen in any era as 'full members of a community' (in Heater, 1999). Another obvious example may be found in the fifth-century Athenian polis, where citizens were native males who had reached the age of eighteen (Manville, 1990, 8). Women belonged to the polis or 'citizen body' only indirectly, through their relationship with a male relative who acted as their guardian or 'kyrios'. The concept of citizenship has nevertheless been revived in recent years, providing in the words of Bianchini 'an essential bridging concept ... between the individual and the community' (Bianchini, 1993, 79).

With the onset of more powerful global economic structures at the beginning of the 1990's (McChesney, in Andersen and Strate, 2000), it is possible however to identify increased efforts, made by corporate power and its academic allies, to intervene in the arena of the citizenship debate.

From the historical examples given above, it is possible to see quite plainly that 'citizen' could be used as a form of solidarity and as a way of representing consciousness of a *place* in a wider moral order. It is also important to notice however, that from the beginning a number of other social agents have always employed the term; public speakers, journalists, professional rhetoricians, politicians, legislators, and military leaders, whose role it was to make active interventions in the public sphere. Corporate forms of address stand within this tradition.

In the contemporary age, when in Heater's words citizenship has become 'a commonly held status throughout the world' and one which is virtually global in its extent (Heater, 1999, 140), the uses of certain forms of critical analysis may help to discover the ways in which people are positioned through address. This book argues therefore that there is a reciprocal relationship between linguistic categorisation, symbolic value and social practices.

Modes of analysis: public texts

Although some sources condemn advertising for encouraging consumption and, as a result, limiting the freedom of public discourse (Dahlgren, 1995, 22), such a stance does not help to construct a workable model of textual analysis. Advertising is clearly not the 'ideal speech situation' (Outhwaite, 1994, 40) and in some ways it could be 'systematically distorted communication' (*ibid.*), but it does appear, from what has been seen above, to circulate ideas and issues which are already part of public consciousness, thus maintaining some functions of the public sphere as described by Habermas.

The types of public discourse examined thus far encompass television advertisements, corporate interventions, and political speeches, all of which reveal a broadly political character (selling financial services, health care, or promoting ideas about public conduct and communication). Although they seem anxious in certain cases to exclude uncomfortable references to potentially disruptive issues, they do have another function. That is to say, they raise 'questions about where we draw boundaries between social worlds' (Myers, 1999, 38).

In other words, they encompass issues traditionally associated with state-public discourses, but in so doing genuinely reflect changes in power relations within the social system. Nevertheless, the role of critical enquiry is not merely to map or accept these changes, but to continue to adhere to the notion of the public sphere as 'a set of principles', which include 'democracy, equality, participation, and citizenship', all of which point to an alternative to 'the set of practices bound up with commodification' (Mosco, 1996, 168).

Established critical perspectives on advertising and commercial texts, often based on Marxist and feminist positions combined with post-Saussurean semiology (Barthes, 1977; Williamson, 1978; Dyer, 1982; Mattelart, 1991; Goldman, 1992; Bignell, 1997) provide, therefore, an interesting history of principled resistance to privatised discourses. Yet there are other traditions of analysis, emerging from the social semiotics of Hodge and Kress (1988), together with the occasional approach actually sympathetic to advertising, which provide an alternative to this tradition (Barker, 1989; Leiss *et al.*, 1990; Fairclough, 1992; Price, 1993/8; Fowles, 1996).

A generally negative position on commercial public address has long been the hallmark of published studies, long before semiology (see below) became a mainstream mode of analysis. Since the 1950's, the critics of advertising and commerce (Packard, 1957; Galbraith, 1958; Leymore, and others) have drawn attention to its supposedly negative effects on the consumer and on society in general. These have been variously thought to include 'brainwashing', the creation of desires that did not once exist, the promotion of acquisitive values, the growth in the timidity of programme-makers and newspaper proprietors who rely upon its revenue, and so forth. The 'psychological' paradigm, in which wartime contingencies first began to mould the attitude of governments to their subjects, is exemplified in Turner, who described how 'outright appeal ... to pride, to shame, to fear, to vengeance' appeared during the First World War and were subsequently exploited by the commercial sector (Turner, 1952, 177).

The use of direct address is noted by this author, who sets out the 'five questions to men who have not enlisted', including the query 'What will you answer when your children grow up, and say, "Father, why weren't you a soldier, too?"' (*ibid.*).

Techniques learned from mass persuasion were used to address a public which soon became used to mass exhortation.

The psychological aspect of address and marketing appears as a consistent theme in the conduct of textual analysis. Williamson, for example, argues quite simply that commodities have to be transformed into symbols which also carry a meaning for the consumer (Williamson, 1978, 11). Advertising agencies and other private bodies are thus positioned to 'manage' the relationship between an audience and the industry which produces these meaningful symbols. The moral issues which surround corporate address, thus centre on issues of material waste, commodification of human relations, and the estrangement of cultural forms from their 'natural' environment. Yet as other commentators note, the need for symbolism is 'one of the defining features of human nature' (Leiss, Kline and Jhally, 1985, 45), and that as a consequence there is 'nothing wrong in principle with advertising's participation in this universal process' (*ibid.*).

Williamson's argument is resolutely moral, attacking advertising because 'we are made to feel that we can rise or fall in society through what we are able to buy' (Williamson, 1978, 13). It is clear that the use of advertising texts in the creation of social status, relationships and identity lies at the centre of the issue. Manufactured goods, in Williamson's opinion, create classes of consumers and create an 'overlay on them' (*ibid.*). This overlay is ideology, understood here as the repressive effect of symbols, values, ideals and beliefs as well as the systems in which all of these are arranged. Baudrillard would appear to concur with this position when he asserts that when advertising speaks of a particular object, it 'potentially glorifies all of them' simulating what he calls 'a consumer totality' (Baudrillard, 1998, 125). Goldman goes so far to assert that 'the process of producing and circulating commodity-sign values' is 'inseparable from processes of ideological reproduction' (Goldman, 1992, 9).

Semiotics or semiology,[17] mentioned above, is the method of enquiry most closely connected with at least the visual analysis of advertisements, and one which has also come to be associated with enquiries into the 'ideological' status of the message. Its precepts depend upon the notion of signs (physical objects with associated mental concepts) which are capable of generating structures of meaning within a culture or society. Signs are inherently social, being circulated and interpreted in a variety of situations and contexts. The two major traditions of theorising within this field may be described as: the structuralist model, which draws attention to the relationship between the sign and its place in the overall structure of language or the symbolic,[18] and which distinguishes between temporal and spatial planes of language;[19] and the pragmatist approach which understands 'semiosis' (C.S. Peirce's term) as a continuous process of meaning-creation which allows human beings to make interpretations and to carry out actions.

---

17 From the Greek 'semeion', meaning sign.

18 It is structure, therefore, not the individual sign, which produces meaning.

19 Known within Saussurean semiotics as 'diachronic' and 'synchronic' (Price, 1996, 456).

Analytical approaches: semiology

Despite its strong linguistic orientation, semiology has been extended (notably by theorists like Barthes, 1977, and Fiske, 1982), into other fields, particularly that of image analysis and popular culture. The first acknowledgement of its limitations, however, may be found in the fact that it has not very often been applied to those communication systems which create meaning primarily through sound or intonation, presumably because they are not as easy to describe in formal terms.

A more significant criticism, within the remit of the present book, yet one which is related to the issue of the 'informal' creation of meaning above, applies in particular to the Saussurean tradition. This is its concentration upon the aspect of language known as 'langue', the abstract rules underlying speech and individual expression (the latter being called, in turn, 'parole' and supposedly infinite in its permutations). As van Leeuwen argues, this 'dominant' semiotic understanding allowed meaning to be ascribed as the use of 'a set of rules, a *code*' (van Leeuwen, 1999, 4).[20] Another effect of this preference was to neglect the 'social context of meaning-creation' (Price, 1998, 70). As Beneviste argues (in Cobley, 1996, 61), such idealist tendencies were exacerbated by Saussure's division of the sign itself into signifier (the object) and signified (the mental concept associated with the latter), without providing a third element which made sense of the first two – the thing in the world from which the sign as a whole obtains its meaning.

It is nonetheless the case that semiology became an important tool in the armoury of radical theorists, adhering to Saussure's description of it as 'the science of signs' (Saussure, 1960) and using it as an apparently objective mode of analysis. Leiss notes that, from the outset, semiologists 'concentrated on relationships among the parts of a message' (Leiss *et al.*, 1990, 198), while Dyer writes that advertisements 'create structures of meaning' which help to reinforce both 'consumer and social relationships' (Dyer, 1982, 116).

The task of the semiologist is therefore to work out what kind of relationships are being offered or created within commercial/political messages. A similarly structuralist observation is found in Williamson, who linked the human subject with the product in the famous declaration that 'advertisements are selling us something else besides consumer goods; in providing us with a structure in which we, and those goods, are interchangeable, they are selling us ourselves' (Williamson, 1978, 13).[21] In addition to its structural and 'scientific' pretensions, the Saussurean tradition is sometimes used in conjunction with notions of dominant ideology and its employment within a series of feints or disguises. Dyer, for example, claims that semiology is an appropriate method of analysis because it distinguishes between the 'outward manifestation' of texts, and the 'inner mechanisms' which produce meaning (Dyer, 1982, 116). Yet Dyer's own practice led her to emphasise the visual

---

20 van Leeuwen prefers to speak of 'semiotic resources' rather than codes (1999, 4).

21 The next part of her comment is not very often cited: 'And we need those selves' (Williamson, 1978, 13).

appearance of, for example, television commercials, without giving any account of linguistic or aural elements (Dyer, 1982, 131).[22] Radical 'deconstruction' of the ideological values supposedly carried within the commercial frame (Williamson, 1978; Dyer, 1982; Goldman, 1992) eventually gave way to more sober accounts of the power of analysis. Leiss, Kline and Jhally proposed a 'combined' semiological and content analysis approach, in order to bring together a 'rigorous and systematic' framework while retaining sensitivity to 'the multiple levels of meaning' (Leiss, *et al.*, 1990, 225). Nonetheless, in the view of these authors, semiology remains useful because it tries to answer a very basic question; 'how is meaning reconstituted both by advertisers and viewers of messages?' (*ibid.*, 200). Although semiological approaches depend on the use of 'internal' enquiry (what the various elements seem to mean in opposition/comparison) and 'external' or contextual factors, such as consumption and interpretation, Price argues that many semiologists concentrate on the former only, resulting in the idea that 'the meaning of the text then becomes a matter of their own individual explanation' (Price, 1998, 167).

Barker, another critic of the tradition, begins his analysis of the limits of semiology by noting that it emerged from the 'disappointed hopes' of the left, and that it was a 'way of investigating "culture" which fitted the needs of post-1968 radical suspicions'; furthermore, there was a search for 'the villains who were restraining workers, women, black people from radical action' (Barker, 1989, 132). According to this view, the media thus became a kind of scapegoat for those who felt that significant change had not occurred within society as a whole. For Barker, the crux of the matter is not that semiology is simply a theory 'dealing with how meanings are produced', it also 'contains a theory of influence' (*ibid.*, 152). It becomes 'systematic', to a degree to which it begins, in Barker's opinion, to express 'methodological commands' (*ibid.*). The first of these is that surface features must be treated as manifestations of an underlying structure; the second is that there is a 'unified system of differences' within each text (*ibid.*, 153); the third is that the system disguises its own origins as 'ideology' rather than the simple message or narrative it might appear to promote.

As Barker argues, it is impossible to know which surface features are ideological, and which act to disguise the existence of ideology. In addition, much semiological analysis tends towards the study of visual codes, which are themselves regarded as 'ambiguous' – in other words, there is already a variety of possible meanings in a culture in which images refer increasingly to each other, what Baudrillard calls reference 'from one sign to another' (Baudrillard, 1998, 125).

Once again, it should be apparent that the variant of discourse analysis utilised in this book marks a departure from more idealist conceptions of language use, but also opposes those tendencies which assume the necessary existence of a coherent ideological position within texts, one which supposedly attains its goals through

---

22 For example, Dyer describes the characters in a 'Comfort' commercial as 'lit from behind to emphasise softness and the scene exudes caring, warmth, mother love, etc.' (Dyer, 1982, 131).

subterfuge; both positions seem to be united in the work of Barthes. Discussing the long-established example of Barthes' response to the front cover of 'Paris-Match', which carried a photograph of a young African saluting the tricolor, Bignell employs a typical perspective, attributing the work of ideology to the use of a 'natural' disguise. He speaks of the dominant signification of the photograph as being 'the rightness and naturalness of France's colonial power', which an 'uncritical reader' would simply receive 'as an unremarkable and natural fact', while the semiologist is able to 'explain and unmask' the true meaning of the signs displayed (Bignell, 1997, 24).

This supposed process of deception, which accords a superior knowledge to the analyst, is a consistent theme in the literature of semiology. Williamson, engaged in the dissection of a Mateus Rose advertisement, declares that its 'general aura of nostalgia' proves to be 'nonsensical', owing to the fact that the person looking at the advertisement is not temporally differentiated from the people represented within the frame (Williamson, 1978, 159).

Yet this elision would seem to be a necessary element of any address which attempts to use nostalgia for commercial purposes, quite besides the enduring difference between the realm of the advertisement and the world of the viewer. This is not to argue that such forms of address do not use 'tactics' and implicatures, rather that the point of studying commercial and political material is to establish the *range* of representations which are offered to an audience, tracing the variety of reference within the larger context of discourse within contemporary social systems. This larger context is inevitably political.

Political address

Writing in 1964, American professor of political science Murray Edelman declared that politics was 'for most men most of the time ... a series of pictures in the mind, placed there by television news, newspapers, magazines and discussions' (Edelman, 1964, 5). Edelman's guileless reference to 'men' as a generic term for the electorate as a whole might offer an affront to contemporary sensibilities, were it not for the alternative reading available to students of ambiguity; the implication that male voters alone were the hapless victims of this spectacle.

It is, however, the model of reception outlined by Edelman which demands more particular attention. He argues that an audience can 'never quite touch' the political phenomenon it witnesses, yet is nonetheless deeply moved by its appearance (*ibid.*). This bears a close resemblance to standard theories of *presentation and effect* and demands further exposition.

In the realm of political science one clear antecedent is Lippmann's work on public opinion (1922), in which he argued that media forms 'shape the pictures in our heads of the world outside' (in Severin and Tankard, 1992, 225; Lenart, 1994, 4). Lippmann believed that, during the First World War, the American people had little real grasp of the political system, relying instead on ephemeral images of leaders and nations (Sproule, 1997, 38). This perspective describes a public dependent upon a form of 'mediation' which supposedly determines general perceptions of reality itself.

Such a depiction of media and its relationship to public knowledge appears in retrospect a prescient vision, not because it exactly reflects the actual configuration of power, but because it is the precursor of a now familiar conception of a 'postmodern' social order in which mass media forms not only intercede between audience and authority, but appear to govern social relationships.[23]

The 'appearance' of political messages

Other perspectives which invite comparison with Edelman's notion of pictorial 'transmission', include psychoanalytical explanations for the power of Cinema (Metz, 1982; Stam *et al.*, 1992), political conceptions which portray the entire social system as a commodified spectacle (Debord, 1977), and a version of stimulus-response or 'direct' effects theory (see Severin and Tankard, 1992, 247; Price, 1998, 390; Robins and Webster, 1999).[24] The concern of this chapter is not to construct a theory of 'outcomes' nor primarily to investigate audience behaviour, but rather to analyse how influence and meaning-creation are conceptualised; in effect, the ways in which theorists characterise the actual mechanics of public address and its implied reception.

The three traditions mentioned above, if taken together, offer a composite model which emphasises the *appearance* of political messages within a commodified system of meaning-production (a larger, society-wide 'spectacle'), and their unimpeded transmission to recipients. The question here is how exactly a message or display captures public attention, and through what mechanism it is then thought to achieve an effect. According to those theories which postulate strong outcomes, a mass audience is in receipt of a form of unitary address or, as described in at least the first part of Edelman's theory, a series of 'events' which manifest themselves as images.[25] In this scenario, politics itself is both 'a passing parade of abstract symbols' and yet also 'a benevolent or malevolent' power that sometimes approaches a state of omnipotence (Edelman, 1965, 5). The technique which is meant to reproduce such powerful influence is at first obscure, yet it is possible to discern the beginnings of an account. Edelman's explanation for the force exerted by political symbols or images is that they provide objects upon which 'strong anxieties and hopes' are placed (*ibid.*). Blumer, writing nearly two decades before, had already proposed

---

23 The further reaches of contemporary social theory move from domination to assimilation, by depicting a reality which is more than merely subsumed within the domain of the image; in Baudrillard's terms, the media 'have left their mediatised space to invest real life from the inside' (in Thomas, 2000, 198).

24 All these authors describe, rather than advocate, the principles of effects theory.

25 Boorstin (1962) speaks of 'pseudo-events' with regard to stage-managed occurrences in the public realm (see below).

the existence of a kind of 'emotional possession', in which individuals are 'likely
to be influenced by excited appeals ... appeals that play upon primitive impulses,
antipathies and traditional hatreds' (Blumer, 1946 in Robins and Webster, 1999,
133).[26] The model of effect which emerges in the notions introduced above, is
essentially quite abstract, standing within a tradition of linear rather than reciprocal
or interactive communication; it is one in which a source (pictorial-panoramic in
Edelman, linguistic-symbolic in Blumer) creates a response through an appeal to the
emotions, appearing to by-pass the guard of cognitive judgement, and suggesting an
adherence to sender-receiver models of message generation.[27] It is also important
to note that the emotional resonance created within the individual or group is
characterised as a *negative* force.

Research in the nineteen-thirties

Reference to powerful address and emotive response is not, however, confined to
the authors mentioned above. Research into the relative effectiveness of emotional
versus rational forms of communication had appeared in the United States during the
nineteen-thirties. In 1935, for example, during that year's local and state elections in
Pennsylvania, a field experiment was conducted which utilised two written appeals
to voters, one constructed as an emotional address, the other presented in more
rational terms (Hartmann, 1936).

The researcher was standing at this time as a Socialist candidate, thus rather
problematically combining the roles of politician and analyst. His analysis
of subsequent voting patterns, however, formed the basis for some tentative
conclusions about the greater success of the emotional appeal, described as 'a better
vote-getting instrument' than the rational approach (Hartmann, 1936, in Rosnow
and Robinson, 1967).[28] This author is certainly aware of the 'literary' tactics used
in the more successful address, describing how the 'sentimental open letter' uses
concrete imagery and reference to parental affection (*ibid.*, 145); an implicit belief in
psychological manipulation appears, but no theory of language or rhetoric emerges,
exactly because the two modes of address are categorised within the established
opposition between the rational and the emotional. The opening of the 'rational'
communication reads as follows:

---

26 Blumer's later work on elections is introduced in this chapter. The perception of
strongly held attitudes is characteristic of periods in which there are thought to be distinct
differences between political groups and marked competition between parties, suggesting in
turn a clear ideological divide . The first post-war election in Britain (by 1945 there had not
been a general election for ten years) is just such a case (Rosenbaum, 1997, 2/43).

27 See below for an assessment of the relative merits of these models.

28 Hartmann's leaflets carried only a rudimentary element of design, showing a cross
against 'Socialist' on part of a ballot paper; yet this does represent the 'visualisation' of the
action he desired.

You've heard of intelligence tests, haven't you? Well, we have a little examination right here which we are sure you will enjoy taking, even if you didn't care much for school when you were a youngster. The beauty of this test is that you can score it yourself without any teacher to tell you whether you have passed or failed.

This is how it works. First read each one of the seven statements printed below. If you *approve* of the idea as it stands, *underline* the word AGREE; if you *disapprove* of the idea, underline the word DISAGREE. Simple, isn't it? All right, then. Get your pencil ready. All set? Go!'

The writer seems fairly insightful in his use of the psychology of persuasion. The initial question, as a form of direct address, is intended to provoke curiosity, with the rest of the introduction promising both simplicity and novelty. Despite the author's characterisation of this as a 'rational' form of communication, it uses techniques and references, but more crucially a *form*, familiar from advertising practice; it attempts to overcome the 'impersonality' Kotler identified as a major drawback to commercial address (in Wilmshurst, 1985, 56). This is not to argue that advertising is 'irrational', merely to observe that political formats also deploy basic notions such as 'arousal or reinforcement of interest' set down as essential prerequisites for successful commercial campaigns (*ibid.*, 208). Once again, the text 'points away' from itself to indicate a lifeworld of experience, experience which in this case may not have proved conducive to the exercise the Socialist Party offers to its target audience (we have a little examination right here which we are sure you will enjoy taking, even if you didn't care much for school when you were a youngster). The kind of statements which follow may be represented by the first two on the list:

1. We would have much cheaper electric light and power if this industry were owned and operated by the various governmental units for the benefit of all the people.
AGREE--DISAGREE
2. No gifted boy or girl should be denied the advantages of higher education just because his [sic] parents lack the money to send him to college.
AGREE--DISAGREE'

The leaflet remains a good example of a text which employs both external and internal reference to orientate the reader towards the beliefs set out. It also represents an instance of an implicit narrative created by a set of statements which the respondent must actively sanction, rather than a complete story in an explicit form. It emerges thus from an 'abstract value system' (Chapter 1); the statements are generated from a position and themselves suggest in turn the systematic belief which gives them form.

The 'emotional' composition, on the other hand, is characterised by rational argument and again refers to an imagined recipient's subjectivity. They are however, much more explicitly narrative in form, systematic statements which tend towards a conclusion based upon a chain of cause-effect relationships. The second leaflet assumes the form of a letter and is dated 'Allentown, Pennsylvania, 1935':

Dear Mother and Father.

We youngsters are not in the habit of giving much thought to serious things. You have often told us so and we admit it. But while we like to play football and have a good time dancing and cause you a lot of amusement with our 'puppy loves', we sometimes think long and hard. You ought to know what many of us young folks are quietly saying to ourselves.

Our future as American citizens in 1940 looks dark. We want jobs – and good jobs, too – so that we can help in the useful work of the world. But we know that many of our brightest high school and college graduates find it absolutely impossible to get any kind of employment ...

We want to continue our education, but we haven't the heart to ask you to make that sacrifice. With Dad working only part-time on little pay and Mother trying to make last year's coat and dress look in season, we feel we ought to pitch in and help keep the family's neck above water. But we can't. The world as it is now run has no use for us.

Perhaps attention to a thematic rather than sequential interpretative framework will reveal certain elements which the author uses in both leaflets. For example, the theme of education and the 'gifted' or 'brightest' graduates would not sit uneasily amongst the discourses of more right-wing political groups (New Labour, for example), while the reference to the different pre-occupations of the Father and Mother as outlined above, may sound rather patronising and sexist.

This type of research derived some of its urgency from the emergence of totalitarian regimes engaged in the large-scale dissemination of propaganda; Hitler's recommendation for creating public address, for example, was squarely based on the construction of emotional appeals (Jowett and O'Donnell, 1986, 138), while the existence of home-grown American demagogues like Charles Coughlin, the 'radio priest', convinced researchers that the principles of negative persuasion could be transferred from the European dimension (Severin and Tankard, 1992, 92).[29]

Dictatorship and address

When Wirth, in an article of 1948, announced that modern societies depended upon mass channels of communication, and went on to express the fear that mass media might become centralised and perhaps appropriated by dictatorial regimes to 'orchestrate the sensibilities of rootless, volatile populations detached from traditional sources of orientation' (in Robins and Webster, 1999, 132), he rehearses themes which had already become familiar. These are the operation of malign centres

---

29 Coughlin devoted his energies in the mid-thirties to attacks on inequality and powerful vested interests, delivered through a forty-station radio network which reached some thirty million U.S. citizens; later in the decade, as he became isolated from and hostile to Roosevelt's New Deal, his diatribes became explicitly fascist in nature, containing qualified praise for Hitler and Mussolini.

of power, and a public which, because it is removed from long established modes of existence, becomes highly susceptible to manipulation.[30]

In many accounts of public persuasion, address appears therefore as a powerful force, especially where it is connected to or can draw forth a certain intensity of feeling, so often characterised as primitive or irrational. In the United States, the creation of specialist research bodies, political bureaux, and academic centres devoted to the elucidation of persuasive methods, became a pronounced feature of this period.

The establishment in 1937 of the Institute for Propaganda Analysis is a case in point. Beginning work under its first director Hadley Cantril, its early output consisted of bulletins, largely written by the educational publicist Clyde Miller. This individual, a major driving force in the early days of the Institute, set out the 'seven devices' attributed to propagandists. Although this list helped to draw attention to the Institute's work, its simplistic approach, together with the rather general nature of Miller's writing, worked against the IPA's attempt to attain a more secure academic reputation (Sproule, 1997, 136).

Later material included Lee and Lee's 'The Fine Art of Propaganda' (1939) which, based on work done by Miller, set out a typification of techniques used in mass address. The volume found its supporting empirical evidence in the form of Coughlin's inflammatory radio speeches (Severin and Tankard, 1992, 93; Sproule, 1997, 145).[31] The IPA's work reveals an interest in linguistic formations, but in its simplification of rhetorical technique, falls far short of a coherent theory of discursive influence.

For example, the concept of 'name-calling', which appears at the top of Miller's original list, reveals no more than the vague notion that abusive terms may stimulate hate or fear (Sproule, 1997, 135). There is no insight here into how exactly negative categorisation may appear within the larger structures of descriptive language; more recent work on this issue finds that powerful social categories appear not just as negative labels, but as a means of inhibiting 'multiple classification' (Semin and Fiedler, 1992, 29). The consequences of this may be to limit the ability of individuals to produce or interpret more developed or complex accounts of social actions and events. An awareness of 'language manipulation' during this period is demonstrated by Mueller, who compiled a list of Language Regulations (later called 'Daily Directives') issued by the German Nazi party's press office; Mueller described these as acting to impair 'the flexibility of language' through a 'freezing of the contents of symbols and an excessive use of nouns and the passive mode' (Mueller, 1973, 30). The directives included the following items:

---

30 Leiss *et al.*, for example, speak of the 'dawn of the new social self' as individuals are uprooted from traditional modes of life and transplanted to cities (Leiss *et al*, 1990), engendering a new mode of social existence. See also Marchand, 'Advertising the American Dream', 1986.

31 An analysis of rhetorical models appears below.

April 14, 1934. For obvious reasons, the National Socialist concept of blood and soil cannot be used in the propaganda designated for colonial areas ...

January 14, 1937. The concept 'race' cannot be used for advertising. It is not permissible to use the term to promote a new hat style or an automobile engine ...

September 1, 1939. The word 'war' has to be avoided in all news coverage and editorials. Germany is repulsing a Polish attack ...

October 16, 1941. There should be no more references to Soviet or Soviet Russian soldiers. At most they can be called Soviet army members [*Sovietamisten*] or just simply Bolsheviks, beasts, or animals.

The purpose of such restriction on reference is exactly to prepare the ground for propositions which serve the fascist interest; for example, the denial of 'war' seen above allows the fiction of Germany's response to 'a Polish attack' to be mobilised without contradiction. Mueller's analysis of the Nazi order of discourse shows insight into the 'diffuseness of its symbols, its mystical, technical, and archaic character' which in his opinion eludes rational enquiry (Mueller, 1973, 33).

This may begin to sketch out an 'operational' theory of discourse, in which terms, through controlled reference and proposition, produce specific compositions of attitude; it also may prepare the ground for later conceptualisations of regulated discourse, such as that offered by Fairclough, who describes the 'technologicalization' of expression as directly related to 'class and state interests' (Fairclough, 1995, 93).

By comparison, Miller's analysis seems weak; another instance of the superficial quality of his descriptions (*op. cit.*), is found in 'glittering generalities', the second item of propaganda he identifies. This advances the quite reasonable idea that the propagandist may refer to respected institutions or beliefs, transferring their 'authority' to his or her own more doubtful propositions (Sproule, 1997, 135).

Once again, the process through which this is meant to be attained, does not emerge with much clarity. While in broad political terms, the Institute for Propaganda Analysis demonstrates an allegiance to a reflexive and democratic standpoint, working within a tradition which attempts to resist the growing ability of powerful social forces to propose a unitary world-view, it is unable to provide convincing accounts of either cognitive or emotional persuasion.

Edelman's conception, my starting point in this chapter, offers in addition to its visual metaphors, a pronounced example of how the idea of 'domination' can be dramatised within critical theory,[32] and seems to provide continuity with the position advanced by the Frankfurt School.[33] For Adorno and his associates the acquiescence of the subordinate was engineered through the commodification of culture, so that the dependency of individuals and classes is, in McQuail's words, attributable to 'the definition of images and terms of debate common to the system as a whole' (1987, 65). In the view of Adorno and Horkheimer, the culture industry 'perpetually cheats

---

32 See for example Agger's analysis of domination as a theme or discourse, in 'Discourses of Domination', 1992.

33 This perspective in turn helped to provide an intellectual template for post-structuralist writers like Baudrillard; see below.

its consumers of what it perpetually promises', offering ultimately only the promise of pleasure, which is 'actually all the spectacle consists of' (Adorno and Horkheimer, 1944). In this case, there is not even the prospect of emotional fulfilment.[34]

Symbols and metaphors of effect

Based upon the descriptions produced by all such 'early' commentators, there appear to be two conceptions of address running through their work: a metaphor which posits the assertion of influence through forms of *pictorial* symbolism, manufactured in a sphere removed from the everyday,[35] and the composition of linguistic messages particularly suited to the animation of group/individual subjectivity. Each mode is credited therefore with the power to generate emotional responses. Once again, this is a common proposition within other theories of media influence, including Packard's reference to 'triggers of action' (pictures and words) in advertising (Packard, 1957, 27) and ideas about the image-based impact of media representations of violence found in many state-sponsored studies and within academic enquiry in general (Gerbner and Gross, 1976a; McQuail, 1987, 195; Price, 1998, 392).

Of the two propositions, the more dramatic paradigm is the affective image, display or spectacle. One reason for the importance accorded to the image is quite simply the supposed predominance of vision and of visual culture (Price, 1996, 120), which also provides substantial metaphorical resources for literature, public speech, argument and 'contemporary literary and cultural theory' (Erickson and Hulse, 2000, 1). It is also worth noting that, with the development of Cinema as an institution, the ability to project and distribute large-scale 'presentations' for mass consumption (what Gunning calls the 'harnessing of visibility' (in Elsaesser, 1990, 56)), seemed to provide an essential pre-requisite for the development of mass political exhibition.

Early assessments of cinematic effect (though within the context of fictional presentation) include Griffiths' defence of the explicitly racist narrative of 'Birth of a Nation' (1915), in which he argued that the medium was capable of grand effects, advancing the extraordinary argument that in the cinema, 'you will actually see what happened' and that film-makers were able to 'show the actual occurrence' (Sorlin, 1980, ix).

In this case, no difference is admitted between events in the past and their re-staging for the camera. The mimetic character and faithfully realistic nature of film and photography is still a salient proposition, found in Kracauer and Barthes (Price, 1998, 205/289). In later periods, cinematic address was more directly linked to propagandistic intent. Benjamin for example, convinced that 'capitalistic exploitation' of film denied the individual's right to self-reproduction, argued that

---

34 This model of deferred gratification, is sometimes expressed as a mirage-like promise, though at others it appears in a more basic form ('the diner sees only the menu', *ibid*), providing an interesting precedent for ideas about the deferral of meaning (see below).

35 A media which stands 'outside' the real appears again in Baudrillard (1998, 125).

'the film industry is trying hard to spur the interest of the masses' through 'illusion-promoting spectacles and dubious speculations' (in Thomas, 2000, 74).

Theories of visual effect depend, however, upon the notion of displays framed within a certain institutional and technological context, especially where this occurs within temporal and spatial constraints and entails a 'captive' audience. These produce in turn audience responses which seem to transcend everyday 'time-space' experiences. The most psychologically effective contemporary instance is therefore supposedly the cinematic experience, within which audiences are subjected to an intense organisation of temporal experience (Elsaesser, in Bennett *et al.*, 1981, 271) and which had a significant effect on the way time and space were imagined (May and Thrift, 2001, 11).

There is, according to this perspective, a dynamic relationship between audience and presentation. Elsaesser argues that 'a film not only immerses and absorbs an audience into *its* world ... the spectator immerses the film into *his* (psychic) world, brought to the threshold of consciousness by the energy emanating from the viewing situation itself' (*op. cit.*). This state of assimilation, in which the cultural artefact animates the identity of the viewer, envisages a strong psychic element, including notions of 'transformation and discharge' in the spectator (Elsaesser, in Bennett *et al.*, 1981, 271). Fuery describes a similar process when he writes of cinematic seduction of 'the spectator's gaze by the film, and the seduction of the film by the gaze' (Fuery, 2000, 170).

Besides Fuery's unconvincing notion of an artefact which is capable of being enticed into reciprocal exchange with a human being, and the descriptions of unspecified psychic effects, the vital point from the perspective of this book, lies in Elsaesser's remark identifying 'the energy emanating from the viewing situation itself' (*op. cit.*). It is context therefore ('situational context', in the terms of the present work[36]) rather than content, which invigorates the individual audience member.[37] Narrative representation, for example, which social psychologists advance as 'a way of making sense of the world' (Murray, in Shotter and Gergen, 1999, 176), makes no appearance in this conception.

Edelman also appears to believe in the psychic power of political address. While it is possible to argue that symbols may retain a dynamic ability to reach into the 'lifeworld' (Lebenswelt) of an audience, generating dramatic consequences, the question here is the balance achieved between context (the energy or 'field of force' which Elsaesser finds in the specific viewing situation of the cinema) and the content of the message. Just as early cinema, when deliberately employed in a highly charged context for instrumental purposes (Jowett and O'Donnell, 1986, 73), was thought to

---

36 This book distinguishes between situational and social context, rather than eliding the difference between the two as is sometimes done in mainstream linguistics (Georgakopoulou and Goutsos, 1997, 18).

37 Context is advanced here exactly because it constitutes a recognition that language cannot be 'abstracted from society and culture' (Georgakopoulou and Goutsos, 1997, 17).

produce marked outcomes in its audience,[38] so writers attempting to come to terms with the advent of mediated politics, offer analyses which emphasise the power of the electronic image.

Yet, the social location of reception, certainly in the case of television viewing, is not necessarily as highly charged as that experienced within the 'enclosed' spatial-temporal conditions of Cinema. The principle here is that films, programmes, election broadcasts and mediated speeches, may all 'establish social orders' (Fuery, 2000, 109), but the functional, situational and discursive location of consumption must be set out before grand assertions are produced.[39]

Referential symbols

At this point, a more precise delineation of Edelman's model of symbolic power may be useful. From his original description of visual display, he turns to the relationship between two categories of symbol – 'referential' and 'condensation'. According to this theory, the first element is a way of referring to 'the objective elements in objects or situations' (Edelman, 1964, 6). 'Referential' symbols are produced through social consensus and thus become stable categories of meaning; they include, for example, 'industrial accident statistics and cost figures' (Edelman, 1964, 6). It is possible, however, to imagine many other types of symbol which could, through general agreement, attain this 'first order' status. Indeed, these examples (assuming a quasi-empirical status as quantitative data) would only constitute reliable evidence within a larger frame of social knowledge; contemporary social theory treats 'hard facts' like this with extreme caution.

These symbols do however suggest some resemblance to Barthes' denotative sign, or Ogden and Richards' equivalent, the 'referent', the 'thing to which the sign refers' (O'Sullivan *et al.*, 1994, 262).

Meaning and 'linguistic cues'

In recognition, perhaps, of the tendency of all first-order signs to become more highly inflected second-order systems through the process of use and association (to become in Barthes' term, 'connotative'), or because the notion of a class of symbols confined to one basic level of meaning remains unconvincing,[40] Edelman hedges his theoretical bets and notes how the referential may also be employed as a mode of

---

38 The specific example refers to a film shown during the Spanish-American War, in which an image of the flag of Spain, torn down and replaced with the Stars and Stripes, is meant to have produced nationalistic fervour.

39 Taken from 'levels of context' in Price, 1997.

40 Price argues that 'the two orders of signification ... happen almost simultaneously in the human mind' (1998, 71).

'condensation'.[41] These symbols, according to the explanation offered, 'evoke the emotions associated with the situation' (Edelman, 1964, 6).

Once again, the end product of the communication event is an emotional response. Edelman, confident about the role of language in the production of meaning, argues that 'people who share the same role learn to respond in common fashion to particular signs' (Edelman, 1964, 115). Meaning and response are in this view 'a function of group interest or mutual role-taking' (*ibid.*).

This may sound like a more progressive, 'social' view of communication but, according to this line of reasoning, certain groups will receive language (phrases, key terms, etc.) as 'a sequence of Pavlovian cues rather than an instrument for reasoning' (*ibid.*, 116); the cues become the focus for 'releases of energy' out of all proportion to the form of the terms themselves (*ibid.*, 116-7). As before, this effect is not subject to intellectual processing, but here even by-passes the emotions; it is simply physiological, an automatic *group* reaction to a stimulus.

Such a perspective appears to belong squarely to those approaches which assume the success of carefully directed unitary messages. Robins and Webster make a criticism of exactly this view, in their attack upon Lasswell. In their opinion, he tends towards 'the persuasive use of communications channels to engineer public opinion and consent' (Robins and Webster, 1999, 132). They locate this within a general approach which 'applies a psychological model to the study of propaganda' and argue that it transposes 'a behaviourist stimulus-response framework onto the sender-receiver model' of communication (*ibid.*, 132/133).[42]

Edelman stands then within a tradition which offers little evidence for its insistence on the production of direct effects. Despite these tendencies, however, there remains the suggestion of a more productive model within Edelman's work. In proposing the existence of linguistic cues he demonstrates some advance on looser theories of rhetorical intervention associated with earlier commentators like Miller (see above). Reference to cues (words like 'communism', 'tyranny', and the 'general welfare'), recognises the performative force of key terms within political discourse.[43] Edelman uses Lasswell's theory of 'key signs', symbols or images which are meant to provide 'a unifying experience' and transcend social divisions (Edelman, 1964, 128). Price, describing newspaper discourses in the 1997 British General Election campaign, proposes a similar model of linguistic categorisation but does not attribute such power to the symbols he identifies, which he calls 'terms' (Price, 1998, 113). These signify both words or statements used to express political concepts or ideas,

---

41 Both Saussure and Barthes revised their 'levels' of signification; Barthes came to believe that denotation was the true location of 'ideology', while Saussure decided that the 'arbitrary' nature of the sign could be split into 'relative' and 'absolute' conditions (Price, 1996, 458).

42 This book argues that sender-receiver models provide, at the very least, a useful initial focus for enquiry.

43 It may be reasonable to argue that the practices and language of McCarthyism form the background to the experience of this generation of American writers; Edelman mentions, and briefly analyses this phenomenon in his text.

and a 'set of conditions for public conduct and debate' (*ibid.*); this model suggests in essence a symbolic version of agenda-setting.

A more extended conception is presented by Connolly, who proposes by 'terms' first 'the vocabulary commonly employed in political thought and action', second the way in which the meanings attaching to such concepts set the conditions (the 'frame') for political enquiry, and last the effect – the judgments or commitments sanctioned when the required criteria are met (Connolly, 1993, 2).

Edelman, concerned more with dramatic effects than the functions of discourse, attempts also to establish the idea that 'ritualistic' use of language (such as 'chronic repetition of cliches') prevents critical thinking, supporting Orwell's remarks about politicians who recite material almost unconsciously. Such a 'reduced state of consciousness' is in Orwell's words 'favourable to political conformity' (in Edelman, *ibid.*, 125). The conviction that the strategic use of terms can elicit a behavioural response, seen in many of this chapter's examples, has a long history, attested by Thomson who cites the content of the Crusader recruitment text of 1216, 'Ordinato de predicatione Sancti Crucis in Anglia', filled with 'simple metaphors' and the repetition of the exhortation 'Arise, therefore, take up my cross and follow me' (Thomson, 1999, 136).

Linguistic cues, therefore, are imagined as powerful triggers, but despite the undoubted insight of writers like Orwell and Edelman, their observations remain at the level of assertion, positing once more a docile or easily influenced populace, but offering little insight into the process in political or, especially, social-psychological terms. Even work dedicated to the study of persuasion and propaganda imagines the creation of 'naive supporters of an invisible institution' (Jowett and O'Donnell, 1986, 217). At this point, it is interesting to note that audience compliance may not actually indicate 'persuadability' *per se*, or any necessary belief in the positions it is asked to condone.

Compliance with address

As an example of the above, Ng and Bradac, attending more closely to the psychology of persuasion, argue that there are certain kinds of messages which produce significant outcomes, messages which manage to 'deflect attention and scrutiny while at the same time achieving their desired effect' (Ng and Bradac, 1993, 133). In other words, there is a class of address which attains an end without being subjected to detailed processing.

The reference here is not, at least initially, to political communication, but to ordinary life, a useful insight if the basis of rhetoric is believed to emerge from the strategies deployed during everyday exchange. These authors describe the existence of messages 'that convey to hearers specific injunctions or beliefs but remain unexamined and thus beyond criticism'; they refer to ordinary messages, the effect of which 'is probably typically innocuous' (*ibid.*) but nonetheless marked.

The next stage is to ask what conditions or contextual structures ensure compliance with such linguistic directives. Ng and Bradac give the example of a queue for tickets, in which someone in line steps in front of an acquaintance, offering the inadequate reason that he must do this because he requires *two* tickets. This explanation is manifestly weak and even nonsensical, considering that all those in the line are waiting to purchase the same commodity. The recipient of this message, however, cedes her place in the queue, but the reason for such a response can be found in 'the kind of compliance itself' (*ibid.*) and, crucially for the work of the present study, *not entirely in the message itself.* Ng and Bradac believe it to be a 'routine, overlearned reaction' (*ibid.*) to a familiar episode, similar to uncontroversial acts of compliance made in response to everyday commands such as 'close the door' (*ibid.*, 132).

These authors claim that little close attention is paid to the *semantic details* of such utterances; citing the work of Langer, Blank, and Chanowitz (1978), Ng and Bradac note that many messages are processed 'relatively mindlessly', and that in certain situations refusal is just as likely to be the outcome. Whichever reaction is elicited (compliance or rejection), the focus of the enquiry remains the concept of a relatively automatic and uncritical *processing* of a message.

The factors which determine this type of response, highlighted by Ng and Bradac (and based on Petty and Cacioppo's model, 1986), are as follows: low personal involvement in the issue; lack of forewarning of message content; and a low cognitive need. The exposure of individuals to what Cialdini (1984, in Ng and Bradac, 1993), calls 'an information laden environment', also helps to divert message processing 'away from the particular argument of a message to the message form' (Ng and Bradac, 1993).

When the message *form* suggests that the act of communication offers an explanation or apology, then this may provide reason enough to elicit either acceptance or refusal in a relatively automatic fashion, thus avoiding the use of critical thought. This notion of dominant form is echoed within pragmatics and conversation analysis, where interaction is often described as a series of 'moves' (Nofsinger, 1991), which in some cases act to establish general conditions over and above the apparent purpose or integrity of content.

Edelman, on the other hand, offers only the notion of reduced consciousness through linguistic manipulation, as an explanation for audience compliance, while Thomson speaks of the 'amazing credulity' displayed by individuals and groups in supporting outrageously pernicious social systems (Thomson, 1999, Preface). Thomson cites as evidence only vague notions of 'mass attitude change' before offering finally the 'content of propaganda material' (*ibid.*, 6) as an indicator of its power. The survival of historical propaganda in the form of text, however, proves little about its effectiveness within its original context. The problem with Edelman's observation, in contrast, is that it is not developed into a general theory of address or ideology; in other words, there is no consideration of the way in which individual statements within a single address either emerge from, or implicitly compose, a coherent position or point of view.[44] There is, however, some description of 'the prevailing political sign structure' which is defended by an elite which gains 'both the material and symbolic rewards of politics' (Edelman, 127). The basic mode of analysis suggested by this model remains very much in force within contemporary social theory. A prime example is Herman and Chomsky's 'Manufacturing Consent' (1988).

They propose the idea that 'the mass media serve as a system for communicating messages and symbols to the general populace' (in Tumber, 1999). This model envisages a media which works to socialise individuals, and to promote values which will 'integrate' people into the institutional structures of society (*ibid.*, 166). Such positions assume the existence of a dominant force which exercises power through forms of symbolic intervention. The Althusserian model of interpellation also constitutes a model of directive address, yet is one in which the state uses individual subjectivity to maintain social cohesion. Althusser's hostility to humanism sought, in the words of Howarth, 'to "de-centre" the subject by drawing attention to its production in and through ideology', yet assumed through interpellation 'an already constituted subject which subsequently 'recognises/misrecognises' itself' (in Scarbrough and Tanenbaum, 1998).

Disengagement from the political realm

Running alongside views of visual media as an affective or integrative 'spectacle', and the existence of linguistic 'cues', a counter-narrative seems to emerge, one which however leaves intact the notion of a powerful elite and an impressionable populace. This centres on the apparent limitations of certain types of expository form, especially party or election broadcasts, in securing the kind of measurable impact imagined by theories of stimulus and response, or alternatively promoted by notions of 'psychic' effect. It is again partly a question of generic form; television is thought to lack the aura attributed to Cinema, and is located within a consumer culture that is both domestic and public (Morley, 1992, 201).

This, and the uses of television content as 'popular festival and ritual' (Brunsdon *et al.*, 1997, 11) may reduce its usefulness as an instrument for persuasive outcomes. Another token of that position which argues the ineffectiveness of party/election broadcasts, may be found in the absence of any opposition to such material *per se* as a serious threat to the democratic process,[45] while film as a genre has been accused

---

44 See van Dijk, 1998, who formulates the relationship between discrete statements and discourse; a series of statements can suggest an underlying discourse, just as a discourse/ position in turn can generate statements.

45 It is the conduct of electioneering in general which has been subject to criticism; individual broadcasts have been discussed within this context (see for example Ansolabeher and Iyenrar, 'Going Negative', 1995).

of carrying hidden ideological intentions (see Cooke in 'An Introduction to Film Studies' 1996).[46]

The ineffectiveness of political messages was also suggested by T.C. Worsley, a television critic for the *Daily Telegraph* who, writing in the late nineteen-sixties, identified 'the superfluity of Party Political Broadcasts' which 'created more boredom than enlightenment' (Worsley, 1970, 176). Worsley exemplifies a certain attitude to the genre, but part of the problem lay perhaps in the transference of expectation from the experience of wartime broadcasting.

During the Second War, radio broadcasts were made from an authority to a public which trusted the source (Price, 1996, 345; Rosenbaum, 1997, 43), a source which was seen as a reliable 'information provider' (Lenart, 1994, 7) yet was more than a conduit for knowledge about events; it engendered a sense of solidarity and cultural association. It was inevitable then that 1945 became 'a radio election' (Rosenbaum, 1997, 43) and that the form itself remained the primary mode of electoral address for the next ten years.[47] Once election broadcasts on television became the predominant means of communication, the decision to put them out at the same time in the evening across all channels, reflects the assumption that dedicated attention might be devoted to an event of national significance. Worsley's response was that 'the sound of the switching off of sets at 9.30 of an evening could be heard all over the land' (Worsley, 1970, 176).

Yet this was at a time when, according to Rosenbaum, television broadcasts were making a significant impact, at least in the sense that they became more notable than radio messages; British political parties, impressed with the potential of television, allowed radio broadcasts to be reduced in length (Rosenbaum, 1997, 45).

Research undertaken by Blumer, Gurevitch and Ives into the 1974 British general election also addressed, among other issues, the problem of disengagement (Blumer, *et al.*, 1978). Blumer noted that 'over four successive General Elections between 1959 and 1970, there was a distinct downward trend in popular appreciation of party broadcasts' (*ibid.*, 46). This was also explained as follows; 'the prevalent disrespect for political talk itself' (*ibid.*). 'Many people', they observed, 'seem to be in a frame of mind where political discourse is almost automatically expected to be off-putting' (*ibid.*, 47). Here then is an indication that content, where it assumes a 'political' form, reduces public interest. The earlier view of political messages (including that taken by Blumer himself), as mechanisms for the production of powerful psychological effects or attachments, stands in contrast to this depiction of an electorate distinctly unimpressed by the mundane realities of public address. It also shows a marked difference to the study carried out by Trenaman and McQuail on the 1959 General

---

46 Television series, however, have been attacked for the inappropriate creation of propaganda within forms, like drama, which are supposed to prioritise entertainment. Offence is caused by the use of certain genres or formats in ways which offend against their paradigmatic borders (see the discussion in Price, 1998).

47 The broadcasts themselves assumed the form of public 'talks' of sometimes 30 minutes length for the major parties (Rosenbaum, 1997, 44).

Election campaign, in which they reported fairly significant interest in such material (Trenaman and McQuail, 1961, 86).

One party publicist interviewed by Blumer and his co-authors, declared that 'voters formulate their impressions in rather vague terms ... the ordinary person comes home tired from work, and all he wants to do is put his feet up and watch the telly' (Blumer, *et al.*, 1978, 10).[48] Lack of commitment is noted throughout such studies, apart from the earlier enquiry of 1959 mentioned above. The departure from set patterns of political loyalty is advanced as one major reason for disengagement (this problem, defined as 'apathy', became a major theme within the 2001 British General Election). While Lazarsfeld, Berelson and Gaudet in the landmark 'The People's Choice', argued that political campaigns '*activate* latent predispositions' (Lazarsfeld, Berelson and Gaudet, 1948, 74), Blumer and his fellow writers acknowledge that, while it was assumed in the earlier post-war period that 'most voters could be counted on to tune in to political affairs through some underlying party allegiance' (Blumer, *et al.*. 1978, 45), the discovery of 'late deciders' and the disillusioned, pointed to an era in which parties had to contend more stridently for votes.

Within the British context, concern with issues of triviality and cultural decline also appear as significant factors, evidenced by commentators like Groombridge, whose 'Television and the People' appeared in 1972. This author makes a distinction between serious and inconsequential uses of television as a medium, using the notion of spectacle to produce the following paradox; that television works by 'distracting people from what matters with shows' (light entertainment) and by 'distorting what matters into a show' (1972, 58). Some American commentators take this concern further, identifying negative campaigning (within televised political advertisements) as the source of voter disillusionment (Ansolabehere and Iyengar, 1995). This raises again the question of the relationship between media forms and the world of events they mediate.

Boorstin (1963) held the opinion that contemporary culture was infested with 'pseudo-events', manufactured occurrences such as news conferences and 'photo-opportunities', connecting the rise of what he called 'image-thinking' with technologies of mass communication (in Leiss, *et al.*, 1990, 27). Boorstin's vision suggests a dysfunctional or highly restricted democratic culture, though 'reality' can at least be distinguished here from the mediated falsification of events. What does seem reasonable, however, is the view that the media 'play a constitutive role in British political life' (Garton *et al.* in Scannell, *op. cit.*, 100), rather than merely reflecting an entirely separate process.

In plain terms, the debate about where exactly campaigns occur, whether in an autonomous reality of space and time (meeting halls, streets, public rallies), or within the forms and discourses of the electronic media (studio interviews and talk shows), is further complicated when political parties orchestrate 'live' events in anticipation

---

48 These researchers received the full co-operation of over one hundred and fifty politicians, academics, broadcasters and party apparatchiks, but ultimately produce a rather limited and restrained overview.

of their public scrutiny through television, radio and the press. Worsley takes a purist stance, stating that 'the medium should be judged solely by its success in involving us in the struggle going on outside'; he praises its success in extending the public's field of 'vision and awareness' (Worsley, 1970, 176).

Again, defending a straightforward concept of unimpeded access, Brian Cox,[49] argued that 'the role of television, once an election got under way, was primarily to enable the contestants to use this new medium to put their policies and their arguments before the public' (Cox, 1995, 178). Worsley agrees; 'television has been put in its place ... that place is to act simply as an explainer and a disseminator' (1970, 176). It should not, therefore, in any way create the events it is supposed to be monitoring. Cox also argues that the General Election of 1964 marks the point at which the medium dominated the message; it was 'the first truly television election' (Cox, 1995, 171).[50] Some commentators, by comparison, appear to maintain a belief in (the admittedly limited) power of those who compose the message itself. Scannell notes, perhaps a little impetuously, that broadcasters, while they control the discourse, 'do not control the communicative context' (Scannell, 1991, 3). This does not take into account the interdependence between the two, or indeed the difficulty in establishing a consistent discourse. Blumer takes up the theme of a mediated 'location' for public events in a remark which seems to prepare the ground upon which many postmodern accounts of the social are constructed, asserting that 'it seems more misleading to assume that there is an election campaign taking place "out there", which television is merely reflecting and reporting, than to assume that modern election contests have to a very considerable extent become fully and truly television campaigns' (Blumer *et al.*, 1978, 43).

This provides some continuity with the view that news and other material is formulated in anticipation of a new mode of political production and 'consumption'. As early as 1942, for example, Schumpeter had argued that 'the ways in which issues and the popular will on any issue are being manufactured is exactly analogous to the ways of commercial advertising' (1962, 263), a position later held by Boorstin (*op. cit*). Within the tradition of critical theory established by the Frankfurt School, particularly the line of reasoning followed by Marcuse as a 'second-generation' theorist, it is the fusing of culture and political economy which allows the manipulation of individuals by 'affirmative forces' (Agger, 1992, 132).

The 'superstructural' sphere (which includes art, politics and everyday experience), becomes therefore increasingly 'economised' in line with the requirements of social control and the profit motive (*ibid.*). The corollary to overwhelming influence – disenchantment and withdrawal – may be attributed within this perspective, to the appearance of political messages within the broader process of commodification, in line with the familiar dictum that 'politics is sold like washing powder'. In other words, this position may attribute the supposed revulsion from politics, to a single

---

49 Editor of ITN news from 1956 to 1968.

50 Assertions to the effect that specific elections are the most 'mediated' occur with regularity; see for example Cole, cited in Garton *et al*, in Scannell, 1991, 100.

cause; its inappropriate occurrence within a mode of discourse previously reserved for commercial address.

Marketing, publicity and ideology

Maarek, writing from an American perspective, describes the advent of 'political marketing', a hybrid form of public and commercial address (Maarek, 1995, 28) There appears therefore a general convergence between various forms of 'publicity', described in Outhwaite's words (following the work of Habermas) as the 'colonization of the lifeworld by the market economy and legal-bureaucratic regulation' (Outhwaite, 1994, 9). In tandem with this development is the growth of private concerns with a 'quasi-political character'[51] (Habermas, in Outhwaite, *ibid.*, 8).

The increasing strength of these private organisations encourages the development of what Fairclough calls 'an international neo-liberal discourse' (Fairclough, 2000, 76) within British political debate. This form of discourse plays down the role of a reforming, redistributive state in favour of a more positive assessment of a 'globalised' economy, appearing to threaten what Garton *et al.* perceive as Britain's retention of 'an element of old-fashioned verbal debate and commentary' (in Scannell, 1991, 100).

Commodification itself may, indeed, be represented as a form of social discipline, paralleled by the rise of a linguistic formation suited to presenting its exigencies in the best light. Such a development would lend credence to Baudrillard's conception of a mediated sphere which comes to inhabit or even replace a once autonomous reality; he writes of the way that consumption 'exalts signs on a basis of denial of things and the real' (though leading ultimately to a 'pathetic redundancy of signs' themselves (Baudrillard, 1998, 99)).

Applied to the order of political discourse, this view would either suggest the emptying of meaning, or instead an attempt at linguistic discipline intended to serve the needs of capital; in either case, the wider context is a condition in which 'promotion' in general becomes 'a rhetorical form diffused throughout our culture' (Wernick, 1991, vii). The proliferation of symbolic forms within a 'global' economy provides, within this perspective, evidence for a universal system of references which individual locales or communities are powerless to affect, thus ensuring the transition to what Baudrillard calls 'the political economy of the sign' (1981). The once-vaunted stability of capitalist society and its linguistic formations, and the established security of 'the political order' (Mueller, 1973, 7) may be seen in the context of powerful, directive Western states served by social-democratic parties. The consequent retreat from the post-war commitment to redistributive politics allowed the growth of a 'new' capitalism, one which was increasingly able to 'evade political control' (Bennett, 2001, 142).

Following the logic of this rather pessimistic analysis, the supposed strength of the 'commodified' message (always perceived within consumer society in general)

---

51 See for example Chapter 4 on Corporate address.

lies in its much deeper penetration into each individual psyche; this, in Marcuse's terms, is more difficult to contest than the operation of ideological address in the earlier industrial period.

The 'new reality of domination' is found, in Agger's opinion, within the 'instinctual structure of individuals' (Agger, 1992, 131). In this scenario, alienation becomes an inextricable part of the human personality. Such a thesis would provide an explanation both for models of domination and for an increasing disenchantment with forms of political publicity. What it does not explain or accommodate is evidence of rebellion or resistance; it remains therefore within the broad category of a dominant ideology thesis, with the individual imagined as the local executor of his/ her own oppression. Such an idea is reminiscent of Weber's depiction of the triumph of another instrumental force, rationalisation or bureaucratisation, producing a 'polar night of icy darkness and hardship' (in Bennett, 2001, 5).

Chapter 6

Politics and Electoral Address

A model of ideology

Departures from theories of dominant ideology appear in a number of sources, most notably in Abercrombie *et al.*, whose challenge[1] was to the common belief that the dominant economic class 'set the dominant values of society ... to win the consent of subordinates' (Abercrombie, *et al.*, 1980, xv). Since this intervention, a less inflected model of ideology has gradually appeared. The proponents of this position nevertheless acknowledge that, in abandoning theories of dominance, they may be accused of reducing the critical purpose of the entire notion (Price, 1997; van Dijk, 1998). This development is particularly relevant to studies of political discourse, if political messages are understood to represent manifestations of 'belief'.

A simpler idea is advanced within this book; that political discourse *is a pragmatic condition* in which 'propositions' are advanced concerning the status of various phenomena, thus severing the connection between expression and the necessary existence of particular beliefs. The purpose of political address seems to be to achieve outcomes, rather than to build core beliefs in audiences.[2]

Conversely, this does not mean to say that propositions cannot be founded on 'ideological' positions. van Dijk, in defending the 'neutral' definition of ideology, however, appears to weaken the term further by insisting that ideological critique may continue under certain conditions – namely, through the use of supplementary references, rather as the study of power does not preclude 'a critical analysis of power *abuse*' (van Dijk, 1998, 11). In effect, this proposes the use of an extra qualifying term and does not solve the issue of definition itself. As Connolly argues, by retaining certain terms but 'drastically redefining the *concept* for technical purposes' (his example is in fact also 'power'), political scientists risk equivocation (Connolly, 1993, 129).

Price attempts to retain a sense of the negative valence that persists in everyday use of ideology, by characterising all ideologies as 'incomplete' and therefore inadequate rather than necessarily pernicious (Price, 1997, 111). Another strategy which posits opposition to the notion of dominance, is to argue that *systems of belief* can also be promoted by the subordinate, thus removing ideology from its association with 'ruling ideas'. van Dijk offers just such an explanation, arguing that 'there are

---

1   See Abercrombie *et al.* 'The Dominant Ideology Thesis', 1980.
2   This idea appears to be strengthened by the perception of political parties that definite positions on specific issues will become hostages to fortune (see below).

good theoretical and empirical reasons to assume that there are also ideologies of opposition or resistance', going on to propose other variants, such as competitive and 'internally cohesive' models (van Dijk, 1998, 11).

This riposte to the established wisdoms does not, however, deal with the central problem of ideology (its conceptual status as either 'neutral' or 'negative'); it merely extends the notion of systematic world-views to other social actors. The deciding factor in judging ideology therefore becomes the point at which it is used 'unjustly [in] legitimating power abuse or domination' (*ibid.*, 11), returning in effect to a negative conception through a sub-division of the 'ideological'. van Dijk proceeds to the next point, the argument that legitimation as such is not necessarily negative, because most forms of ethics would recognise a difference between 'the legitimation of resistance against domination' (*ibid.*).

This completes the move in which the evaluation of a term is made according to a set of external criteria, leaving the internal integrity of the concept under-theorised. In addition, it also seems a dubious tactic to argue that, just because legitimation is employed by a subordinate group, it becomes less problematic than when it is used by more powerful social forces, such as political parties. Legitimation is of itself, a flawed attempt at promoting social cohesion (evidenced by the 'myths' created by liberation movements to reinforce shared attitudes and goals). van Dijk offers fewer hostages to fortune when he argues that the main function of ideologies is the 'co-ordination of the social priorities of group members' (in Bell). Zizek pursues this course, in that he dispenses with ideas about the truth or falsehood of an expressed position while supporting the strong thesis of ideology, arguing that 'an ideology is ... not necessarily 'false' ... it can be 'true', quite accurate, since what really matters is not the asserted content as such but *the way this content is related to the subjective position implied by its own process of enunciation*' (Zizek, 1994, 8).

In other words, the important duty of analysis is to contrast 'asserted content' with the assumed position of the enunciator. I take *assumed* here as 'simulated' (or 'taken on') as it applies to the speaker, and *assumed* in the sense of 'taken to be the case' with regard to the listener. The mode of enquiry suggested in this case, however, would only make sense if there is a point from which to judge the relative value of what is 'asserted' against what is *subjectively implied* during the process of expression; this suggests ultimately a return to an opposition between truth and falsehood.

The present work is therefore more concerned to establish a model of ideology which, while it is prepared to accept van Dijk's dictum that it constitutes the basis of the 'social representations shared by members of a group' (van Dijk, 1998, 8), argues that it is always founded on an incomplete and thus potentially harmful world-view. This means that to be 'ideological' is exactly to ensure that one's utterances will assume a partial form; put another way, that they will be characterised by 'partiality' in the sense of both *bias* and *lack of completion*.

The other conviction here is that the concrete *expression* of ideology is always problematic: first, because the directive aspect of ideological explanation (its 'interventionist' character, its orientation to achieving political or commercial goals), leads to the rhetorical inflection of particular ideas at the expense of others; second because discourse, as a means of 'delivery' (propositions must be created from 'available discourses'), can only function with reference to other relevant 'points of view'. Opposing points of view, for example, must be constructed or 'referenced' within the course of an argument. This indicates an uncertain process and an 'impure' end result. Equally, the concept of a separate realm of beliefs, distinct in nature from the symbolic forms in which they are clothed, should be treated with caution. Beliefs certainly create and re-compose linguistic and other forms, but are themselves partly created through currently available means of expression, and are hence to some degree already constituted in pre-existing discourses. However, this does not mean that general ideas or attitudes cannot be motivated (brought to mind) by either novel or quite arcane references.

Enoch Powell's racist speech attacking the Conservative government's immigration policy, for example,[3] contained a reference to classical antiquity: 'like the Roman, I seem to see "the River Tiber foaming with much blood"', which although in itself obscure to many, succeeded within the larger context of the speech. It linked a sufficiently violent image to the general issue of 'race', and although ostensibly intended to warn against negative consequences, derived increased effectiveness from the fact that it could also be interpreted as a threat; in effect, the speaker composes a sort of instrumental ambiguity. Powell's diatribe demonstrated the recognition of an opposing point of view, and was explicitly constructed as an answer to its precepts.[4]

Rhetorical argument and simulated speech

The way in which argument in general achieves coherence can be attributed to its rhetorical nature (Billig, 1991). Standing against the psychological tradition, in which attitudes[5] are regarded as simple and unvaried 'stances', Billig proposes that they be understood as 'a complex mixture of positions' (Billig, 1991, 171). The reason for this is found, according to Billig, in the various discourses used by individuals (*ibid.*), which are composed from a variety of sources. Proponents of attitude theory, originating with Allport's assertion of 1935 that the concept was 'the most distinctive and indispensable' in social psychology (in Jowett and O'Donnell, 1986, 101), argue that the possession of strong views will act to exclude alternative points of view. In contrast to this position, the rhetorical approach to social psychology

---

3   Delivered on April 22nd 1968 at the annual meeting of the West Midlands Conservative Political Centre, and written in a style designed to provide easy transference to the public prints (Jones).

4   Referring to the words of one of his constituents, Powell wrote: 'I can already hear the chorus of execration. How dare I say such a horrible thing? How dare I stir up trouble and inflame feelings by repeating such a conversation?'

5   An attitude is 'a person's general evaluation of an object ... person ... an event, an incident, a commodity, an institution' (Price, 1998, 78).

insists that the expression of deeply-held beliefs, within interactive situations, will display considerable complexity (Billig, *ibid.*, 179). Speakers therefore construct their views 'rhetorically from matters of agreement' (*ibid.*).

Such insights apply also to the production of speeches and other more unidirectional discourses, in the sense that a hearer or audience is assumed not only to exist, but to have opinions of which some account must be taken. So, for instance, utterances which are shaped for public consumption must adapt to circumstance. A useful example is the speech made by the U.S. President Bush to Congress on 20 September 2001, following the attack on the World Trade Center, from which the following short excerpt is taken:

> Tonight, we are a country awakened to danger and called to defend freedom ... whether we bring our enemies to justice or bring justice to our enemies, justice will be done.

The opposition between bringing enemies to justice or 'justice to enemies' is rhetorically legitimate but semantically redundant, in the sense that the original phrase does not really describe spatial movement; yet the key term 'justice' made an important impact on Western policy-makers and politicians. As Andrew Grice in *The Independent* of 22nd September argued:

> Blair aides were particularly pleased that the President closed by summing up his strategy as pursuing 'patient justice'. In the immediate aftermath of the atrocities, Mr. Blair was keener than Mr. Bush on the word 'justice' but it now features regularly in Washington.[6]

The point here is that 'justice' was considered part of a larger discourse of rights and fairness, more suited to gaining support from the international community than talk of taking terrorist leaders 'dead or alive'. Grice cites the words of one of Blair's advisers; 'It's a question of using the language most likely to help you achieve your objectives and get as many other countries on board as possible'.[7]

Overall, the existence of an intersubjective realm is found in both conversational argument and directive/persuasive speech, suggesting in turn the close relationship between 'internal' (message-construction) and 'external' (expressive) aspects of discourse. As I have argued, the use of 'everyday' propositions lies at the heart of political intervention, and continuing adherence to a 'conversational' mode of presentation is evident in party election material. Once again, the Conservative Party has employed this technique within political broadcasts. In the following extract, it is evident that propositions about the failures of the Labour opposition are couched in 'ordinary' language and try to reproduce concerns that individual citizens will recognise:

> *Young white woman 2*: It was a difficult decision because I voted Tory before I thought they really had learned their lesson the Labour party ... erm ... the Tories had that slogan ...

---

6   Grice, *The Independent*, 22 September, 2001.
7   Grice, *The Independent*, 22 September, 2001.

erm ... Britain's booming don't let Labour mess it up and I thought you know they won't do that, Blair won't do that ... erm ... but they have.

Young black man: Things were nice and calm, I mean how much damage can you do eh? Interest rates have gone up, unemployment is rising, I'm having to pay an extra thirty or forty pounds a week because of them.

Young white man: Yeah, well, they had their chance and they made a complete mess of it. Me mortgage has gone through the roof, and they put tax up almost straight after they got in, when they promised they wouldn't. You know. Don't worry, they said, we're different now. I suppose it was our fault for trusting them in the first place. Basically we're back in recession, ain't we?

Middle-aged Asian woman: My son is looking for a job for all the year, now he can't get one because of minimum wage. Nobody can afford to take him on. I don't know how long he'll have to wait.

Middle-aged white man: Well democracy you know – the Tories had had their day, we thought maybe somebody else. See what they've done, I mean it's just been a total downhill, total downhill, for three years. But what gets to me you see is I went for it, we all went for it, we thought you know a change equals something better. Of course it wasn't [*inaudible*] something heck of a lot worse'.[8]

There are certain tensions here between the ordinariness of speech (which is in reality scripted) and the appearance of unlikely utterances, the occurrence of which can be attributed directly to the quirkiness of political dogma. In this case, the Conservative Party's opposition to a minimum wage appears as a more obviously ideological reference, inserted into a more colloquial context; 'my son is looking for a job for all the year, now he can't get one because of minimum wage. Nobody can afford to take him on'. It sticks out exactly because it concurs with any proposition's character as an 'abstract' manifestation of semantic force (see Chapter 1), which can be re-modelled in a different order or structure without departing from its essential meaning. The problem in this case is that the change of form from policy to conversational speech cannot disguise the ideological inflection which still prevails in terms of content.

There are also important lessons to be learned from such exercises in the presentation of meaning, concerning the character of discourse. As Harre and Gillett argue, discourse may be public or private; 'as public, it is behaviour; as private, it is thought' (1994, 27). Behaviour here would include performative speech, while thought may assume a linguistic mode. In other words, a difference need not necessarily be constructed in the nature of speech and mental activity when considering language-based activities (as does Pinker, in his 'mentalese' thesis, 1994).

If there has been (within political debate) the growth of a more controlled form of discourse-production, in which special bodies are set up to create and monitor

---

8   Conservative Party Broadcast of 9 April 1997; transcribed by Michael Pearce. Synopsis by Pearce: The broadcast consists of 10 'talking heads' filmed in generally gloomy settings, such as an underground car-park and a desolate housing estate. The talking heads are linked by captions on a blank screen. The opening caption reads, 'Imagine if the polls were right. Imagine if Labour won the election'.

linguistic output, then it may be reasonable to expect a very close relation or even convergence in theme and expression within political speeches. While this does not provide evidence to support the 'end of ideology' thesis (Bell, 1965), it does suggest that there has been a move away from radical positions of left and right, in order to embrace a more managerial or bureaucratic attitude, reflecting in particular the consolidation of a pro-business consensus amongst politicians.[9]

Subjectivity and authority

The theme of this chapter turns on the question of dominance and subordination within social theory, but more particularly on the nature of directive communication and the ways in which its impact is calculated. This implies the need to characterise both expression and reception. Goran Therborn, within an interesting account of post-war social formations, posits a more dialectical model, founded on an equation between *qualification* and *subordination* (Therborn, 1980). Although his theory of the social is not primarily concerned with linguistic structures, he explores complementary meanings within the term 'subject' as a means of indicating the existence of a more complex relationship between authority and the individual.

His position turns on the difference between an active, self-defining subject (the 'subject of history') and a more circumscribed manifestation, a social being constructed as the 'subject' of royal power.

Therborn offers here an insight into both the operation of purposive discourse and the reproduction of a class system within post-industrial modernity. He notes that a social system acts to reproduce itself, but that a contradiction arises between its need to order the existence of its citizens (by instituting forms of social control), and the requirement to fulfil its own overall development by training individuals capable of autonomous action. The first condition appears as *subjection*, the second as *qualification*. An increase in qualification (amongst certain groups) may in some respects decrease subjection, but a subsequent turn towards repressive social measures could produce imbalances. In Therborn's words, 'the effects of a contradiction between subjection and qualification are opposition and revolt or underperformance and withdrawal' (1980, 17).

This conception, though its intended reference is to wider societal conflicts, nonetheless offers a useful if rather simplified model of interaction within the political sphere. It stands as an alternative to those perspectives which, for example, characterise lack of voter engagement as 'apathy'. It might, however, require re-adjustment as managerialism places linguistic and thus behavioural conformity at the centre of organisational and political strategy (Cameron, 2000). Existing control-oriented disciplines, such as neuro-linguistic programming, together with corporate training courses in customer relations (emphasising as they do the use of standard responses designed to maintain forms of instrumental politeness), mean that older

---

9   See for example the remarks made by Johnson and Steinburg, cited in Chapter 4.

modes of authoritarian or hierarchical control are supplemented by attempts to get employees to internalise or at least *functionalise* certain values. In politics, this process may be called the 'functional' motivation of attitude, i.e. where the point of address is to enable representations of policies to be 'sanctioned' by an electorate, rather than to *broaden attitudes* as part of a general commitment to 'educating' voters.

Returning to the commercial example, the graded steps to greater qualification are in effect, also stages in more intensive subjection to the official mantra of service, quality, or whatever notion is deemed most serviceable to control symbolic output. Thus, if the actual condition achieved by the insistence on propagandistic address or disciplinary speech, is one of psychological withdrawal, even while an apparent linguistic or behavioural conformity is maintained, then theories of subjectivity and the persistent issue of effects should be examined.

The backlash against direct effects

The idea of direct effects exercised on a *mass* scale has prompted, in Britain at least, an academic backlash (couched in polemical terms) against the concept of effects in general (Gauntlett, 1995; Barker and Petley, 1997).[10] There are problems, however, in discounting the notion of 'effects' altogether, as Gauntlett does in 'Moving Experiences' (1995, 1). The debate itself acts as a conduit for other important discussions, including ideas about the relationship between the public and authority. The controversy may even express, in Buckingham's words, concerns about 'the shortcomings of capitalism' (in Barker and Petley, 1997, 45).

There is also the sense, analysed by Price (1998), that the issue has always proceeded as a form of shadow-boxing, in which British media researchers found the 'unsophisticated' reasoning of moral campaigners a useful justification for their own agenda. Jensen, surveying the field in 1993, had already decided that the classic approach to effects had been 'reformulated to state broader issues concerning the role of mass media in the production and circulation of meaning in society and, significantly, the role of audiences in that process' (Jensen, 1993, 3). Yet, many years before this statement, it is possible to find Halloran expressing the simple conviction that mass communication 'does not serve as a necessary and sufficient cause of audience effects' but works instead 'through a nexus of mediating factors and influences' (Halloran, 1964, 30).

The excerpt from Jensen's work, however, reveals a parallel development to the effects debate; this is the 'turn to audience'. The contention behind the work of many who adhere to, or at least still discuss theories of dominance, is that a preference for investigating subjective aspects of communication (in particular, reception analysis), has taken place within a broader political context. This is assumed to be a general retreat from an 'emancipatory' project within the social and political sciences, and

---

10 Barker and Petley announce that their book 'is not a standard academic book. It is a polemic drawing on a body of academic research' (1997, 10).

to mark a departure from the interrogation of institutional power, replacing such discussion with speculation about audience gratification and sub-cultural choice (Fiske, 1987, 1989b).

This tendency was noted with distaste by Barker and Beezer (1992). These authors argued that established paradigms of political and textual enquiry had been replaced by a new interest in 'active' audiences and strategies of interpretation. They were supported by Robins and Webster, who perceived a shift 'away from the idea of powerful media towards an acknowledgement of the active receiver' entailing the abandonment of the 'hypodermic' model[11] with the unfortunate consequence that 'any concern with propaganda evaporated' (1999, 133). Kitzinger also argued that 'interrogations of media power' have been superseded by 'faith in textual polysemy and semiotic democracy' (in Philo, 1999, 3). Lack of engagement with issues of effect becomes therefore, for some writers at least (Price, 1998; Philo, 1999), evidence of a refusal to examine power relations or questions about the morality of public discourse.[12]

The change in focus from institutional power to audience behaviour may demonstrate an attempt to achieve some balance between the construction and interpretation of meaning, but in both projects the central conception of a 'dominant' address is left intact. Audience resistance in this model is posited exactly because theorists still adhere to the concept of a dominant ideology which is met with a kind of 'graded' response, ranging from dominant readings (those which agree with the message of the text), through negotiated positions, to outright opposition (Hall *et al.*, 1980).

As Hodge and Tripp recognised in 1986 (see 'Children and Television', 132), the effects issue remains at least a useful starting point for the development of a more sophisticated consideration of ethics within mediated discourse. In sum, the concept of 'direct effects' represents, however crudely, a paradigmatic example of what McQuail calls 'source-receiver' relationships (1987, 262). It recognises, in other words, the existence of differential power relations between sender and recipient. The nature of this relationship, and especially the way it is characterised, is illustrated by party political messages and a by-election campaign held in 2004.

Media and the creation of meaning

Mulgan describes the media as 'the paramount place where elections are conducted and fictions disseminated' (in Wheeler, 1997, 1).[13] This statement bears comparison with Blumer's description (above), which envisages the media as *the* location or space

---

11 An alternative term for 'direct effects'.

12 Barker and Philo agree about the inadequacies of contemporary audience studies, but differ on the issue of effects; Philo's work for Barker's 'Ill Effects' (1997) failed to appear in the volume, leading to the production of his own 'Message Received' in 1999.

13 The idea of 'fictional' presentations (ideas and perspectives which mis-describe existing conditions, or which invent new ones) receives critical assessment below.

where elections take place ('modern election contests have to a very considerable extent become fully and truly television campaigns', 1978, 43). Such perspectives appear at one level to do no more than describe an increasingly salient development; the growing importance of media as the essential ground for the administration and/ or symbolisation of *a process of electoral choice* (set apart from but conceptually linked to the act/practice of voting itself).[14]

Yet these remarks seem also to reproduce ideas about the *assumption by media* of functions previously conducted and 'publicised' in other ways. If they reproduce observations familiar from theorists like McLuhan (1967) on the modification of culture by technology (and in particular the cultural impact of television), they also appear to prefigure postmodern narratives (witness Mulgan's 'fictions' above) concerning the role of electronic mediation in forming spectacular realities.[15] So, according to this conception, media forms are no longer a mere resource available to issue proponents for the transmission of ideas (the source for which is an entirely independent sphere), but the true location of events themselves.

The concern of this book, in line with its adherence to discursive realism, is certainly the 'reality' or otherwise of campaigns (their verifiable existence both within and beyond mediation[16]), but also the way in which their structure anticipates their own *exemplification* for an imagined public. That implies more careful consideration of the relationship between 'event' and 'location'. All mediated events occur in real spaces; that is to say, they may present a front of various sorts, composed perhaps of scenery and certainly of discourses, but are nonetheless firmly bound within a material, situational context. In television debates or reports, for example, what the camera 'sees', and by extension what the viewer perceives, unless computer-generated, is actually there, in the sense that there is an original presentation in three dimensions.

Its artificiality owes more to its reduction in dimension, the imposition of a frame, and the enhancement of sound, familiar from visual/auditory media, than any production of a *consistent* 'hyper-reality'. Advocates may turn an appropriate 'face' to the viewer, but this choice is based on their ability to make representational and discursive choices from a range of materials that all participants recognise as meaningful. This is not intended to reinforce the observation that there is a *political consensus* between 'rulers' and 'subjects' (Mueller, 1973, 4) rather that there is a common understanding of the boundaries which exist between a limited public participation in political affairs, and the exigencies of the political system itself.

---

14 This may further be theorised by arguing that the individual is first 'placed' in the role of subject (a physical point of reception and within the space of the social system), addressed in the light of a general model of subjectivity, then motivated in some way (for example, through processes of identification), before being allowed to carry out certain sanctioned activities (voting).

15 Bringing to mind, once again, Blumer's view that it is 'misleading to assume that there is an election campaign taking place "out there"' (1978, 43).

16 Where mediation itself is understood as an aspect of social reality.

If these factors are considered in tandem with the conduct of professional politicians, it may become clear that any agreement is over differentiated roles and interests, rather than the existence of a shared conviction over ideological demands or the general direction of society. A simple form of analysis which might illustrate this point, may be a study of the roles taken by political advocates and by media in 'creating' the spectacle identified earlier in this chapter; it seems apparent, however, that the resulting amalgam of references provides an electorate with a complex conception of the overall 'event'.

While Corner, for example, notes that a central question is the way in which the media have both 'transformed the character of political activity and in the process changed the nature of political institutions' (Corner, 1995, 33), it is possible to argue that parties and interest groups' fore-knowledge of representational forms and institutional constraints, together with the jaundiced view expressed by many journalists (Price, 1998), produces in effect a critical metadiscourse about the political process itself.

Post-structuralism and address

The notion that the media are the primary operatives in the political world is taken further in post-structuralist theory. This challenge to the perceived separation and independence of media, public, state, capital and the lifeworld, removes the requirement of a normative consensus about public conduct and political decency, advocated by social scientists like Blumer and theorists such as Jurgen Habermas. Although Spivak in particular chafes against this tradition of normative theory, rightly arguing that Habermas treats rhetoric unimaginatively, she also insists that the practice of deconstruction (as a variant of post-structural analysis) is a 'political safeguard' against the construction of narratives through 'masterwords' (in McQuillan, 2000, 398).

Interestingly, examples of these masterwords suggest leftist and (possibly) feminist paradigms of reference, such as 'the worker' and 'the woman' (Spivak, *ibid.*). Spivak distrusts 'fundamentalisms and totalitarianisms ... however seemingly benevolent' (*ibid.*), a statement which reveals a critical dissatisfaction with the Enlightenment tradition rather than hostility towards the expressive output of the accomplished political rhetorician. Deconstruction moreover, argues that there is no referent 'exterior to effects of textuality', and that politics itself is always textual because 'the literal political referent is to be found only within the text' (Readings, in McQuillan, 2000, 392). This may be regarded as reasonable, if all experience becomes textual at a certain point. The tendency here, however, in positing all symbolic expression as a form of 'achieved' textuality rather than attending to its moment of production, is to collapse the temporal/spatial conditions in which meaning is produced (the specificity of context and discourse), and to deny the validity of the *pre-textual* materialisation of events (speech, material symbolisation, acts such as voting, etc.). The limits of deconstruction as a practice, which it not only recognises but advocates in its own defence, lies in the scope of its aims. While it seems reasonable to declare that 'deconstruction cannot found a political program of any kind' (Spivak, in McQuillan, *ibid.*, 397), the circumscribed nature of its ambitions is more fully explicated in Derrida's reference to its the fact that it is 'strategically useful at a given moment' (in Readings, McQuillan, 392). The next remark is particularly revealing; 'I believe that it has in fact been useful' (*ibid.*). This comment reveals the operative capabilities of the deconstructive position; it is 'useful' in revealing the textual character of phenomena, of reminding the onlooker of the constructedness of events, but attains little else beyond this modest achievement.

It has also certain negative effects: in particular, Derrida's list of various texts levels out the range of possible characteristics within each example; the body, the table, Wall Street, and nuclear arms are all texts, according to this position (*ibid.*). The sense of their quite different textual power, as well as their extra-textual character, is not discussed. As Katz argues, postmodernism in general treats what he calls the politics of culture as 'a site of indeterminacy' in the belief that 'the most radical act is resistance to closure' (Katz, 2000, 1).

The conviction expressed in this book, that the exposition of theory is by its very nature 'universalistic' in character (i.e. that the point of theory is not to be particular or ephemeral, but inclusive in range), suggests that deconstruction should be rejected as a mode of analysis. In more extreme examples of poststructuralist theory, the barriers between message and individual psyche seem to have broken down entirely; Baudrillard, for example, perceives exposure to 'the instantaneous retransmission of all our facts and gestures on a channel' (Baudrillard, in Thomas, 2000, 198). Despite this re-conceptualisation of the relationship between spectator and display, the fact that Baudrillard has to over-state his case ('instantaneous retransmission'), means he is engaged more in assertion than description. Without due consideration of temporal, narrative and discursive constraints which mark the production of those signs he believes to be immediate, Baudrillard demonstrates a wilful avoidance of the mundane; everyday exchange, bottom-line economics, deadlines, institutional determinants, party manifestos, all disappear in the seamless specularity of contemporary existence. Surveillance, or its simulation (Bogard), replaces the political narrative of progress.

In contrast to this position, I would adhere to the belief that such postmodern scenarios are insecurely founded projections or extrapolations of present conditions; awareness of the camera as an instrument of social and political control (in Baudrillard's terms, no longer a police action but instead more like 'an advertising promotion', *op. cit.*) does not motivate every act, precisely because human beings are not at present subject to universal surveillance in the Orwellian sense.[17] In sum, the argument of this book is that institutions like the media are not all-pervasive, and

---

17 The dramatisation of close observation through the production of programmes like 'Big Brother', simulate (in a heavily narrative form) how such a process might appear to an onlooker. However, this text is also marked as a 'professional' treatment of a controlled event, edited and re-presented for the purposes of entertainment. It may invoke a past narrative

are still 'named' and recognised as distinct and *circumscribed* forces, indicating an acceptance of a continued institutional separation from the events they represent. The character of contemporary media forms may in fact be judged through their ability to promote Boorstin's 'pseudo-events', in the sense that this function depends on maintaining stable relationships with other centres of power and influence, other 'players' or 'issue proponents' (Dearing and Rogers, *op. cit.*). The political system in which the media operate is above all 'energy-efficient'. That is to say, all the major centres of political dissemination (parties, policy institutes, analytical programmes) are geared to intervention when required,[18] and apply pressure at spatial and temporal points regarded as most productive. Rather than accept the idea that the media have 'infected' reality, in Baudrillard's terms, 'from the inside' (see above), this posits a configuration of events and representations, put into action to meet specific purposes.

Emergent meanings and a 'framework of expectations'

The alternative is to treat talk of standards in public debate (formal disapproval of sensationalism, hostility to 'spin', etc.), as irrelevant, either because the age of total assimilation is at hand, or because 'aporia' produces 'an irresoluble hesitation between competing meanings', where aporia is a kind of indeterminacy or the impossibility of establishing 'ultimate meaning' (Nash, 2001, 8). A contrasting position, espoused in the present work, is that meaning is an *emergent* quality of symbolic forms, revealed as such phenomena are employed within each particular context of use. The objection to this position is revealed in arguments to the effect that the meaning of political (or any other) messages cannot be reliably established because context itself is 'boundless' (Culler, 1985, 123). However, if context is composed of a series of identifiable elements[19] which provide structure for events and which can in turn be used as a mode of analysis, then a fairly reliable description of events may be made.

This does not mean that context is always proscriptive or somehow able mechanically to produce entirely predictable outcomes (as may be suggested by 'strong' social semiotic positions; Egging and Martin, in van Dijk, 1997, 231). It does, however, suggest that Culler is mistaken in arguing that context is boundless merely because it is 'open to further description' (Culler, 1985, *ibid.*). The difference between the two positions is that the realist would regard further description as a

---

of 'total control' (Orwell's '1984') but also projects a possible future in which the political significance of surveillance is diminished.

    18 A parallel example is the appearance of police in sufficient strength to meet a threat whose public characteristics have been drawn in advance by various issue proponents, including protesters, police, politicians, and the media. A demonstration is made to all observers that, should similar 'offences' be committed, the same deployment of strength could be made.

    19 Hymes' system is used here as it appears in Coulthard, 1985, Price, 1993/8, and Georgakopoulou and Goutsos, 1997.

move towards greater verifiability, whereas the deconstructionist would believe it proved the indeterminacy of meaning. The point of the realist argument is to make a case for the continued existence of distinct spheres of action within social reality, despite the predominance (at certain times and places) of *forms of mediation which partially bring events into being.*

An example of the latter, which also illustrates my belief in the continued separation of institutions and their respective spheres of action, is cited in Corner (1995). This is the 'MacArthur' study made by Lang and Lang (1953). The recall by President Truman of United States General Douglas MacArthur from the Far East, resulted in the expression of strong popular feeling, in support of the General and his strident 'anti-communist' stance. Lang and Lang discovered that the media anticipated MacArthur's arrival in Chicago by creating a 'framework of expectations' about what was to occur (Corner, 1995, 35).

This framework was then used to construct the dynamics of the event itself; this observation reinforces the view advanced by Connolly, in his discussion of conceptual 'frames', generated from the meanings of specific terms (1992, *op. cit.*). One interesting example of such construction is found in the way that MacArthur was shown on television surrounded by cheering crowds, as though they were in constant attendance. However, television cameras recorded only that portion of the assembly which MacArthur passed at the time, failing to show those individuals who waited quietly for his appearance, or groups which began to disperse once he had passed.

The process of political communication should not, therefore, be seen as a simple problem of transmission; other factors must be taken into account. These elements are revealing, in that they demonstrate the ways in which social actors are obliged to make adjustments to their behaviour to meet contingencies and to conform to structures within which they seek advancement, an insight which may be applied in particular to personal conduct during elections. In addition, and most crucially for present purposes, they demonstrate the various constraints upon communication, and the existence of *modes of exchange* which do not appear within the generally rather abstract overviews of 'messages' and 'receivers'.

In essence, accounts of media influence offer typifications of actors and events, such as 'direct' effect or even influence based on 'two-step flow' (Lazarsfeld, *et al.*, 1940), which may neglect the operation of more pragmatic processes. To a great degree therefore, mediated elections have become self-referential, and the mechanics of the campaign, while not replacing the 'issues', are foregrounded to a significant extent. Such processes are, from time to time, revealed in the political analysis written by journalists; one useful instance appears in Jones' 'Sultans of Spin' (1999), in which he describes the behaviour of the New Labour victors of 1997.

The accusation that its policies were 'more spin that substance' may be useful as shorthand, but it is the actual pattern of media use which requires analysis. Jones speaks of Labour's predilection for perpetuating 'a kind of feeding frenzy', in which the media were sought out and presented with stories as though an election were still in progress (Jones, 1999, 18). Interpreting this observation from an academic perspective, the party here pre-empts the role of the enquiring journalist, making instead a presentation from which salient points are meant to be passed on to the public. There are other observations, however, about the processes at work.

Crucially, the use of media may not simply be to contact or influence the public; this may in fact be a secondary aim to establishing a high profile within influential circles. In this case, media forms are employed to gain the attention of other professional advocates within a 'community of practice' (Scollon, 1998). In other words, politicians act for a primary audience of their peers (including pollsters, journalists and other commentators) with the larger purpose of advancing their own interests. This line can certainly be over-played (see the argument in Chapter 1), yet there is some element of truth with regard to the career trajectory of journalists and politicians. An example appears in Jones, where a high media profile and success in shadow cabinet or NEC elections are said to be linked (Jones, 1999, 19). One effect of individual politicians exerting such energy on their own behalf, is that other colleagues are actually seen as competitors.

Public address and rhetorical technique

In the case of election campaigns themselves, the ideal situation for the delivery of direct address, certainly from an advocate's point of view, is one in which a high degree of control is exercised by the speaker; the concept of 'allocution', taken from antiquity, provides the paradigmatic instance of this particular condition. In such a situation, a person in recognised authority speaks to his or her followers, urging the assembled audience to do, say, feel, or think something (Price, 1997).

The more common or general term for the actual practice of persuasive communication, often used in a pejorative sense, is rhetoric; this derives from the Greek word rhetor, which means 'speaker' or orator. Rhetoric may thus appear simply as the art of persuasive speech or writing.[20] Burton, of Brigham Young University, notes that the Ancient Greeks spoke in terms of *kairos*, a term that means something like 'generative timeliness', or 'occasion', (Burton, 1999).[21] Burton goes on to argue that a given *kairos* calls forth certain kinds of appropriate utterance. The Romans spoke of 'decorum', a significant, overarching principle of rhetoric, meaning appropriateness of discourse; the point was to fit words not only to the subject matter, but to the audience in a given place and at a given time. In effect, this reveals an understanding of context.[22]

However, there are some differences in the value and moral worth accorded to the term 'rhetoric', originating both in variations in definition, and in the actual practice

---

20 Price, after Atkinson (1984) lists the following techniques used in rhetorical address: the rule of three or the three-part list; the use of contrast or juxtaposition; the biased presentation of a rival's position; rhetorical questions; repetition; negative identification (Price, 1997).

21 In 'Silvae Rhetoricae', internet site.

22 Sensibility to the kairos enabled a speaker to exercise decorum in choosing to say the right thing to an audience in the most appropriate way.

of the skill itself. Aristotle, for example, describes rhetoric as an *ability* to perceive, in any given case 'the available means of persuasion' (Gill and Whedbee, in van Dijk, 1997, 157). Campbell believes it to be an art or talent 'by which discourse is adapted to its end' (*ibid.*). The tension, then, is between conceptions of rhetoric as argumentation and as an eloquent (and morally doubtful) form of language (Gill and Whedbee, 1997). The tendency to identify rhetoric only with highly inflected, and thus suspect speech events (the privileging of form over truthfulness) may often be justified, but has created an automatic association between rhetoric and equivocal communication.[23]

Distrust of the rhetorical tradition is also motivated by its increasing employment within academic writing, a form of enquiry which was supposedly driven purely by rationality and a search for truth, and which assumed an appropriate logical form. Mason addresses this issue when he notes that 'philosophical speech and writing imply the existence of truths which transcend the beliefs and opinions of individual writers and readers, speakers and hearers' (Mason, 1989, 65). This conviction, reminiscent of Habermas' position, leads to a highly critical view of rhetoric, particularly at the point at which it is seen to assume the function of philosophical enquiry *per se*; the consequent fear is that philosophy will 'collapse into rhetoric' (Mason, *ibid.*). However, as indicated above, more positive or sympathetic accounts of rhetoric do appear, in for example the work of writers like Thomas Farrell, who argues that rhetoric is 'the *collaborative art* of addressing and guiding decision and judgement' (Farrell, 2).

Farrell maintains that the best instances of rhetorical practice are found in antiquity and the early Christian period, providing a 'public language' for successful cultures (*ibid.*, 8). In advancing the goal of public rationality, Farrell's aim is to suggest compatibility rather than opposition between Aristotelian rhetoric and 'emancipatory reason' (*ibid.*, 12). Before the issue of rhetoric's place in public culture is addressed in more detail, another significant point should be discussed; although conceived as a specialised form of language-use, rhetoric may be an 'exalted' version of everyday exchange.

As Nofsinger explains, all social actors 'have goals, make moves, take turns, employ tactics and work out strategies' (Nofsinger, 1991). His rationale for speech analysis is therefore to focus 'on what people *do* in conversation (their 'moves') rather than merely on what they *say*' (Nofsinger, 1991, 13). Thus, the art of effective or persuasive speech or writing, is not confined to the realm of politics, and certain rhetorical techniques may be found in 'ordinary' interaction. Again, as Nofsinger argues, conversation is 'a rational activity having a strategic dimension' (Nofsinger); strategy implies the existence of linguistic techniques designed to persuade.

This is not to negate entirely Gill and Whedbee's judgement that the essential activities of rhetoric are located on a political stage (in van Dijk, 1997, 157), but to

---

23 Equivocal communication can be described as a form of 'strategic ambiguity', in which a speaker is evasive or obscure in order to disguise the true state of his/her feelings of opinions (Bavelas *et al*, 1990, 28).

argue that this sphere of action is a product of the ways in which people compose positions in defence of interests. It is also an arena which provides one important setting for what Moravcsik calls projective uses of thought (and by extension language). These, in contrast to the use of descriptive or representational codes, belong to the realm of imaginative statements which attempt to describe new possibilities in the arrangement of social life (Moravcsik, 1992, 266). Another tendency within political exposition may be found in what Jameson (in an interpretation of Frye) calls the production of *mythic patterns* in modern texts intended to reinforce a sense of 'the affinity between the cultural present of capitalism and the distant mythical past' (Jameson, 1981, 130).

Although this insight refers to the literary text (and more especially the romance) it may be applied to other forms of textual expression such as the 'social narratives' (Price, 1996) created by public speakers in order to effect particular aims. Habermas, in a critique of Piaget, produces a theory of mythic communication in which the lifeworld of distinct social groups is reinterpreted through a 'mythical worldview', one which in this case has certain negative effects, including the removal of the 'burden of interpretation' from individuals and, as a consequence, the reduction of a society's ability to reach the critical zone in which verifiable validity claims can be made (Habermas, 1984, 71).

Publicity, and by implication rhetorical forms of communication, are here diametrically opposed to Habermas' conception of communicative action, which demonstrates 'an orientation to reaching understanding' (Habermas, 1984, 98). Language is therefore presented ultimately as a medium for establishing forms of shared knowledge, a mode of expression in which participants 'reciprocally raise validity claims that can be accepted or contested' (Habermas, 1984, 99). These claims include the truth of the statement, the degree of its conformity to the existing normative context, and the sincerity of the speaker (the idea that expression is in accordance with intention; Habermas, *ibid.*).

Within rhetorical public speech, these validity claims are known and understood, but their existence is treated not as a coda to be obeyed, but as elements which must be taken into account in the production of messages; in other words, they must appear as references, key terms designed to elicit the favourable assessment of an audience, rather than as normative goals. The tension between Habermas' larger concepts, those of strategic and communicative action, can be brought, if not to resolution, then at least into a more productive focus by examining Habermas' interesting reference to the 'reciprocal' nature of exchange.

If this is taken for the moment, not as an 'ideal' state to be attained, nor as a normative principle in the manner of Grice's conversational maxims (1989, 26-27) – precisely because these approaches are composed as a standard against which the quality of a communication event may be judged – then a less 'judgmental' conception may emerge. This turns upon the idea that those who contribute to an event (as speakers, hearers, witnesses, etc.) will understand at the very least the constraints under which the event is produced, including as Grice recognised, the possible appearance of violations of and offences against interactive norms (Grice,

1975). In the case of political speeches, where actual exchange is not possible, it is nevertheless evident that speakers will provide references to the presence of hearers/ audiences, through the use of inclusive reference (terms such as 'we' which carry a larger ideological implication), and rhetorical questions (Price, 1996, 253).

In addition, established *social norms* are used as moral touchstones in order to establish a discursive framework for the delivery of particular utterances. On the one hand, these criteria are used by rhetoricians to signal their awareness of and presumed agreement with public values; on the other, the very perception that they must be used in order to provide normative references, helps to re-circulate specific values and to re-establish the general domain of moral conduct. In other words, while it is possible to alter the significance of terms, references, and propositions, they continue to reproduce some part of their original social force.[24]

Reference, identity and address

Close analysis of the ways in which political parties alter the range of their references and *symbolic identities* is one method of plotting the development of currents of discourse. Janda and his co-authors provide an overview of such a process, offering the initial observation that the identity of a political party is 'the image that citizens have in mind when they think about that party' (Janda, *et al.*, 1995, 171), and going on to mention some detail of research findings. Although not an attempt to engage with qualitative forms of textual analysis (specifically, critical discourse analysis), they cite changes in linguistic references; the German Social Democratic Party, for instance, signalled its intention to advance 'technology and infrastructure' fairly consistently, presenting this concept between ten and eleven per cent of all statements made (extrapolated from overall references made within their 1983 and 1987 election manifestos), and reducing an already low incidence of appeals in 1983 to 'national effort and social harmony' to a complete absence of such ideas in 1987 (*ibid.*, 179). In all such cases, political aims must appear within a referential system equivalent to Jackendoff's third level of linguistic structure, the conceptual[25] (in Cruse, 2000, 129). Jackendoff argues that there is an 'expressive constraint' on meaning, in that it is limited by the available means of discourse.

Representational strategy: content and thematic analysis

This section examines the discursive strategies employed by politicians in the contest to capture the Parliamentary seat of Leicester South, in a by-election contest of 2004.

---

24 For a critique of the associated notion that 'resistive discourses' can be entirely emptied of their radical significance, see Price, 1998, 184-6.

25 The three levels are the phonological, syntactic, and conceptual.

The material used in this study consists of election leaflets[26] which, as a distinctive part of a wider publicity campaign, represent a record of the strategic priorities of each political group.[27] All political interventions are treated here as problematic, not on the basis of any lack of purpose or clarity. Leaflets are 'appeals' which, within the constraints of electoral politics, are at least logical in their basic intentions. It is the selection of *persuasive devices* (instruments for purposes, see above) which is fraught with difficulty.

The point here is not that reception and interpretation are uncertain processes, but that the *choice of ground* itself will entail the production of controversies which may undermine an intended aim. As a result, electoral appeals represent a calculated risk. There is, for each party, a 'hierarchy' of preferred topics (Alasuutari, 1992), in which the relative salience of themes (Kavanagh, 1995, 70/71) is the product of a trade-off between the perceived benefits and perils of bringing an issue to public attention.

It is not, therefore, simply a matter of recording the incidence of aggregated subject-matter, but also of calculating whether it is addressed defensively or employed aggressively; to paraphrase Alasuutari, how an issue is either exhibited or excused. This may account for the perennial appearance of another notion; the distinction made between positive and negative campaigning. The choice of stance also reveals, in the case of serious contenders at least, consciousness of an established record against which an appeal can be measured. Parties with less political credibility in this particular contest and thus with little perceived chance of gaining election (Conservative) seemed to produce more inconsequential appeals than those with little hope of success but less political history (Respect).

Content analysis, used to make 'valid inferences from text' (Weber, 1998, 23), begins with the identification of individual units of meaning. It then distinguishes amounts or degrees of substance; in other words, constituent parts, once recognized, can be quantified. There are two problems, however; one is knowing the significance of what has been categorized (multiple appearances of one concept may carry less power than a single strategically-placed appeal), while the other is the character of symbolic content. This can include terms, catch-phrases, logos, photographic images, charts, drawings and abstract designs, which taken together produce themes.

Themes are not just topics, but as Barker writes 'meanings with social purposes attached to them' (Barker, 1989, 267). It is the identification and evaluation of themes which may provide a more *concrete* alternative to the more general references usually found to 'discourses'. The search here is for 'discourse coherence', the

---

26 The initial sample was composed of: 9 Conservative, 10 Labour, 19 Liberal Democrat, 3 Respect and 1 Save Our Schools communiqués, collected or received during the campaign. However, since the material must be seen to represent the general distribution of leaflets in a typical ward, items which appeared in the local newspaper or which were distributed in the street, were excluded from the sample, and only those received within one ward were retained. This brought the sample down from 42 items to 36.

27 No assumption is made about successful transmission, a notion which authors like McQuail treat with caution because they suggest 'an underlying rationality and purposefulness about communication' (McQuail, 1975, 14).

sense of a unifying subject or narrative proposition within and between individual representations. The leaflets demonstrate the point made above; that an address must appeal to more than the positions it intends to represent. Political parties must demonstrate, in this case based on notions of local issues, that they understand common knowledge and perception.[28] Discursive *practice*, therefore, is always 'reproductive and transformative', because the particular configuration of discourses produces a 'new, changed, transformed arrangement' (Kress and van Leeuwen, 2001, 32).

The *themes* which were deployed in the by-election represent well-known and substantial aggregations of subject-matter, used in an attempt to reinforce a core message while weakening the appearance of its rivals as *credible* or *reliable* alternatives. Such themes may be, as indicated above, inflected in a particular way (defensively or aggressively), and will reveal much about a party's perception of its own strengths and weaknesses. In sum, a theme is bigger than a simple reference and a single 'subject'. In each case, the propositional content (the essential meaning which can assume different forms), is a function of the basic demand to make an impact on an audience within a known discursive context. So, for example, a piece which describes how the Tory candidate was in the process of applying for a three-story extension to his house in Lincoln, was not primarily about house-extension, but about the *negative* value 'non-local', combined with an *undeveloped theme* of class prosperity (a perception *attributed to* constituents).

Categories for analysis

In the case of the Liberal Democrats and Labour, the relative salience of distinct themes was assessed for each face or side of fifteen Liberal Democrat and seven Labour communiqués. Categories for analysis included *content* (items, situations, individuals and events, all appearing as *representations*), *form* or the generic arrangement of content,[29] *rhetorical devices*, *context* including the broader discursive context), *discourse* (statements which generate point of views or points of view which generate statements), and *reception* at least in terms of the *imagined subjectivity* suggested in the text.

The references and themes which follow have been placed in an approximate order of importance, judged on the amount of space devoted to distinct issues appearing across all publications from each individual party.

---

28 Hence, perhaps, the use of the Conservative slogan 'Chris 4 leicester', appealing to those who recognize a reference to text-messaging.

29 Forms in this study included leaflets, 'letters' presented as personal missives, and 'newspapers' or news-sheets (*Leicester South Rose, South Leicester News, Leicester Mirror* and the *Leicester Fox*).

Liberal Democrat

'Straight Choice': a pragmatic appeal to see the election as a contest between Liberal and Labour, with other parties discounted (nearly four times as much space was allocated to this as was devoted to the second most important heading).

'Allegiance': a contrast between the positive/moral allegiance of the Liberal Democrat candidate Parmjit Gill to his leader Charles Kennedy, and of the negative/immoral allegiance of Blair to Bush; this represents a transfer from the local to the national. The Iraq war is presented as something Labour improperly initiated, with a call to vote 'lib dem as the only effective way to show opposition to the war'.

'Unfair Tax': a reference to the Council tax, usually illustrated with pictures of pensioners.

'Unfair Fees': a comment which refers to fees for university students, introduced by Labour, supported by a 'questionnaire' which might be regarded as somewhat loaded;

'Top Up Fees
Do you support Labour's plan to force thousands of students into massive debt?
Yes – I support top-up fees
No – I think the highest earners should pay a bit more instead'.

'Closures/Cuts': more usually a reference to the proposed closure of Post Offices and the Labour candidate's past involvement, as Council leader, in the closure of schools, than to budget cuts (a sensitive case which could be attributed to the deficiencies of local Liberal Democrat councillors). The 'questionnaire' again presented biased choices to the electorate;
'Do you support Labour's policy of closing 3,000 more Post Offices including a further 18 here?
Yes – close 3,000 Post Offices
No – keep them open'.

'Local Credentials': the validity pf the candidate's local status is contrasted with the negative value accorded to the Conservative's origin. Parmjit Gill is described as:
'The local choice who will fight for us'.
'Parmjit Gill was born and brought up here. He went to school here. His family lives here … the Tory from Lincoln can't win here'.

'Fighting Crime': a very small proportion of the material, but cast in terms used by both Labour and Conservative'.

Labour

'Local Political Credentials': a contrast between the Labour candidate, Sir Peter Soulsby, and his rivals, emphasizing his record and making a set of promises based on national policy. The position is more political than the Liberal Democrat strategy, yet presents national policies as always beneficial for the local area. Soulsby refers to his '37 years living and working in this constituency', promising 'real influence for Leicester South people' and emphasizing his desire to make 'a difference where it matters for local people'.

'Straight Choice': a pragmatic appeal to see the election as a contest between Labour and Liberal, with other parties discounted.

'Cuts': is a reference to cuts in local services. The term 'closures', linked with the Post Office controversy, is avoided.

'Hypocrisy': the supposedly two-faced character of Liberal Democrat promises.

'Liberal Democrats Soft on Crime': an attack on the opposition of Liberal Democrats nationally to ID cards and other initiatives.

'Anti-war': a very limited proportion of the material, presented defensively.

Certain issues of public concern, such as the financial interests and career-paths of MP's, appear in leaflets as references to opponents only. There is only one instance in all the material of the proposition that politicians may not 'know best', and this thee remained undeveloped. All candidates campaigned against reductions in services, but used different terms to describe their aims. In Labour's case, this was combined with attempts to deflect criticism of its record. So, for example, the Labour candidate used his position on the Iraq war defensively, and never used the issue as an aggressive gambit against another party.

On the whole, the Liberal Democrat strategy mobilized its chosen themes in order to attack the Labour party for being destructive and treacherous, withdrawing community services and invading Iraq; in so doing, it made particular use of Soulsby's local record. Soulsby, dubbed 'Mr Leicester' in his own literature, became 'tony Blair's man' in that of the Liberal Democrats. In a number of cases, the Liberal Democrat was described by Labour as 'Parmjit Singh Gill', in response to what it described as his tactic of playing on his ethnic background when addressing Asian voters. The faint spectre of racial categorization featured as an implicature within the campaign.

The commonplace and 'common sense'

All forms of political address are composed within a general discursive context, a constantly evolving range of ideas and opinions which constitute the resource for the production of coherent messages. Drawing on established themes, such communiqués attempt to reflect the subjectivity of their audiences within the structure of each address. The values to which politicians allude appear in forms designed to represent a *common-sense* understanding of life, in the belief that such an approach will accord with the attitude of the electorate. Yet the actual expression of well-known points of view (on crime, locality, war, etc.) depends in the first instance on two fairly immutable factors: linguistic rules which ensure *coherence* and the *generic qualities* of the selected form, which generate 'typical' appearances (headlines, appeals, 'personal' requests, and so on).

In other words, the first step in trying to achieve an effect is to make recognizable, *coherent references* within an *established format*. So, in linguistic terms, the assertion produced by one candidate that 'taxes keep going up, yet the quality of local services keeps going down', relies in the first instance on the negative resonance of the term 'tax', immediately reinforced by an untested yet semantically valid contrast or juxtaposition, in which an endophoric or internal link (made through 'yet') is established between rising taxes and declining services. The implicature (financial exploitation of ordinary people through the tax system) is produced through an ironic contrast which is given force by its apparent status as a commonplace.

Activity and passivity

The purpose of all discursive interventions is to establish understanding and subsequently an agreement which lasts long enough to secure votes. The role of the electorate is otherwise largely passive, with the exception of minor actions (signing petitions, answering surveys, putting up posters) designed to reinforce this desired end. Candidates, on the other hand, are presented as dynamic; their actions past and present are designed to foreshadow a future in which they will work tirelessly to serve their constituents. Their passage to Westminster is represented exclusively in these terms, with no acknowledgement of personal ambition, private consultancies, or other selfish motives.

There are as a result seemingly endless photographs of these characters *in situ*, shown in various local contexts. In the June issue of Leicester South Rose, Soulsby was shown clearing rubbish from Queen's Park Way, supported by a nameless resident who was reported as saying 'I like a politician who's prepared to get his hands dirty to make a difference'. Other material showed Soulsby in front of Saffron Resource Centre and in a local shop. The Conservative candidate appeared outside a post office, crouching over a dangerous hole in Aylestone, gesturing towards burnt-out car and leaning on a graffiti-daubed wall. The Liberal democrat was placed in many similar situations, but appeared unable to bend at the waist.

The fundamental issue is that if a party is going to employ representational forms, in which accepted features of the social world are reproduced in a directive manner, then they must accord with the public's sense of moral and symbolic values. Yet the challengers, the Liberal democrats, based the bulk of their argument on the simple observation that they were best placed *in terms of existing support* to win the seat; happily for the party, this was in fact the outcome, although Gill lot the seat to Soulsby in the General Election of 2005. All this must be seen in a broader social and political context, in which the political 'mean' or centre lies to the right, in the sense that traditional rightist issues on crime are used alongside more social democratic appeals for the maintenance of good public services.

As indicated above, certain issues are completely absent; neo-liberal economic policies which all but one of the parties appears to support, are never set out as a *programme of action*. The most 'left' of the parties, Respect, produced material which seemed like a mild version of Labour's election propaganda in 1983 and 1987; it too reproduced the strategy of 'localism', in which the candidate Yvonne Ridley revealed that she 'started my working life as a fifteen-year-old 'tea girl' in a local works canteen' and would consider it 'the greatest honour of my life to go from Leicester tea girl to Leicester South MP'.

Historical speech and reference: US Presidents

It is also possible to illustrate the salience and value of rhetorical interventions through reference to historical speeches, especially as differences to contemporary social attitudes are likely to be more obviously apparent. For example, the inaugural speech of George Washington (made President of the United States on 30 April, 1789), uses the productive tension between private retirement and public duty, referring to God as a presiding and actively beneficent deity whose particular care is extended to the new nation. Twentieth-century political discourse contains far fewer purposive references to a supreme being; to take a brief example, no remarks about God appear in the Conservative Party's 1955 election manifesto, while the only reference to religion reinforces an anodyne definition of the cultural diversity of the Commonwealth.[30] Washington begins by making a reference which actually remains a commonplace within contemporary political discourse; an appeal to a shared sense of correct or appropriate behaviour. He begins therefore with an introduction based on the *propriety* of what is to follow, arguing that:

> ... it would be peculiarly improper to omit in this first official act my fervent supplications to that Almighty Being who rules over the universe.[31]

The evocation of God is not a mere figure of speech, but an essential touchstone for the moral legitimation of the nation as a whole, standing it must be noted in stark contrast to the attitude of the French revolutionaries of 1789:[32]

> ... that Almighty Being ... whose providential aids can supply every human defect, that His benediction may consecrate to the liberties and happiness of the people of the United States a Government instituted by themselves for these essential purposes (*ibid.*).

---

30 'The British Commonwealth and Empire is the greatest force for peace and progress in the world today. It comprises a quarter of the world's population. It contains peoples of every race, of every religion, of every colour, and at every stage of political and economic advance': Conservative manifesto, 1955; website.

31 Washington, 1789; Bartleby.com website.

32 See Hunt, 1996, for descriptions of the 'de-Christianisation movement'.

As the speech proceeds, the interests of speaker and audience are identified, a common rhetorical technique set out below:

> in tendering this homage to the Great Author of every public and private good, I assure myself that it expresses your sentiments not less than my own (*ibid.*).

The particular virtue of the American democracy is expressed through the assertion that 'no people can be bound to acknowledge and adore the Invisible Hand which conducts the affairs of men more than those of the United States', as every step of its progress in achieving the character of an independent nation 'seems to have been distinguished by some token of providential agency' (*ibid.*).

Direct address appears in the invocation to 'join with me' in considering the form and proceedings of 'a new and free government' (*ibid.*). An important point here is the material circumstance in which the speech is delivered; this is a leader who addresses a nation which has cast aside a colonial status in favour of economic and political independence. Thus the sense of good fortune and divine guidance is not a formality, but a reference to recent and verifiable experience. In analysing this kind of text, a multitude of approaches may be employed (see below). In the first place, however, there are certain clear differences between a text of this nature and the exercise of rhetoric during and in the run up to modern election campaigns.

Using examples of Hymes' system of contextual categories to illustrate the composition of any speech event (Coulthard, 1985; Price, 1996; Price, 1998), an initial assessment can be made. In terms of *structure* (the form of the event) for instance, the Washington passage evokes a singularly important moment; the first inaugural address made by an American President. Its historic status was, one could argue, known to contemporary participants and onlookers. Thus its overall *purpose* (that which brings the participants together) may be conceived as a potent mixture of national verification, a celebration of survival, and a personal testament made by Washington himself. The *key* is formal and exhortative, while also attempting to produce a sense of national destiny. The analysis of this particular example uses therefore a *combined* contextual and linguistic model of interpretation.

Approaches to the political text

Based upon the survey of theories of effect given above, a summary of possible approaches to the political text may now be set out. Metaphors concerning the visual appearance of politics as 'spectacle' seem to pertain to an era which imagined the Cinema as a dominant and psychologically effective social force; running parallel to this was a conception of dramatic effects, associated with the use of strident political propaganda within a turbulent international context. With the onset of televised political address, however, this model was tempered by the domestic character of the new medium, and by the sometimes mundane and mis-directed content of election broadcasts themselves.

Thus, a counter-discourse seemed to emerge, in which the realities of campaigning and the actual consumption of politics, suggested a disengagement with the entire process. Yet the notion of direct effects continued to achieve some prominence, through those theories which advanced the idea of linguistic 'triggers', key terms capable of drawing forth strong public responses. This did not however produce linguistic or discourse theory as such, relying instead very often on a simple opposition between rationality and emotion. The transference of linguistic models from pragmatics, did however demonstrate some advance, so that the moves of everyday conversation could be applied to the structures of political speech. At the same time, the development of linguistic analysis of events in general, provided a model for enquiry based on a linguistic-contextual theory of the generation of meaning. In addition, the construction of political address in rhetorical form, suggested that the precepts of rhetoric could themselves be re-applied as a mode of critical analysis.

The approach which follows combines therefore certain aspects of the 'turn to language' (most vitally, the use of critical discourse analysis) with a theory of address and 'imagined subjectivity', but does so within the wider tradition of realist hermeneutics and a more 'neutral' view of ideology. Thus, ideology does not, as it appears in Zizek's work, assume an all-pervasive power at the point at which it also seems to 'disappear' as a subject of public interest. He notes that, just at the moment when the expansion of the new mass media 'enables ideology effectively to penetrate every pore of the social body', individuals do not act 'primarily on account of their beliefs or ideological convictions' (Zizek, 1994, 14).

Here, the system is thought here to 'bypass' ideology, relying instead upon the use of economic coercion, and legal and state regulations (*ibid.*). Zizek recognises, however, that the supposedly 'extra-ideological mechanisms' that regulate social reproduction seem to become sources of ideology (*ibid.*). This is partly solved by re-appraising the argument made earlier, that discourses are not necessarily based upon language, but may recirculate in other practical-symbolic forms.

Election broadcasts, utopias and public discourse

Following Abercrombie's remarks about the nature of 'dominant ideology' (1980) as actually a force which helps to maintain the cohesion of the 'ruling' groups, we may understand, for example, the New Labour project as representing a double-pronged intervention; while not 'ideological' in the traditional sense, and rather more of a pragmatic adjustment to circumstance, this very pragmatism has to be 'sold' to those who wish to cohere around it, and to those who have at certain points to sanction the presentation itself (during an election). Thus, following Zizek's explanation, it becomes a form of ideological project whose core intention is to 'represent' only what 'works for Britain', without examining the complexity of the social structure itself.

Within contemporary political discourse in general, references are often made to the concept of national improvement; this may be read as one element which draws upon a larger structure or theme. This is the idea of *futurity*, a concept which appears as a staple of political rhetoric, partly owing to the fact that politics itself is an institutionalised expression of the everyday comparison made between the present and the possibilities of future development.[33] Yet the recurrence of this theme may also be traced to the persistence of Utopian ideals within national communities. Since at least the appearance of More's 'Utopia' in 1516 (quite apart from the older tradition represented by Plato's 'Republic'), political rhetoric has depended upon the positive representation of existing individuals and institutions, while still relying upon the notion of an ideal social order which might be attained.

Levitas argues that early utopias are 'not located in the future, but in a spatial rather than a temporal elsewhere' (Levitas, in Mackay and O'Sullivan, 1999, 259). The point is however that the 'location' of such ideal places is the space of the imagination. Yet even within works supposed to represent pragmatic materialism, the processes of idealisation provide a necessary resource for the construction of persuasive discourses. Mill,[34] for example, bemoaning the misuse of the term 'utilitarianism', defends the philosophy as one devoted to 'the happiness ... of all concerned' in which 'as the means of making the nearest approach to this ideal, utility would enjoin ... that laws and social arrangements should place the happiness, or ... the interest, of every individual ... in harmony with the interest of the whole' (Mill, 1863/1910, 16).[35] Levitas offers a definition of Utopia based on the principle of improvement, describing it as 'the desire for a better way of living expressed in the description of a different kind of society that makes possible that alternative way of life' (Levitas, in Mackay and O'Sullivan 1999, 257). She argues that the 'political importance of utopia' rests on the argument that 'a vision of a good society located in the future may act as an agent of change' (*ibid.*). In demonstrating the continued referential strength of this paradigm, it is possible to begin with following statement, taken from Blair's speech to the Labour party conference of 2000:

All we need is the confidence to make the right choice for the future.

One concept runs throughout this address, generating its forward momentum; that is the notion of a 'destination' or journey's end ('our journey's end – that strong, fair and prosperous Britain for all') and the obstacles which must be overcome in order to reach it. Within this form or genre audiences *expect* certain propositions to be advanced. In this speech, Blair goes on to mention the achievements of the government and attacks the retrogressive policies of the Conservative party. He

---

33 Price, 'Text and Context' lecture course, 2001.

34 J.S. Mill constructed a less rigid account of Utilitarian philosophy than that offered by either his father James, or his other political mentor, Jeremy Bentham.

35 In 1872, Butler published the satirical work called Erehwon (the word 'Nowhere' written backwards) while from 1885-90 the socialist thinker William Morris produced, in serialised form, a work called 'News from Nowhere' concerning a perfect socialistic society.

repeats the overall goal again later in the speech, this time in an echo of previous instances of public rhetoric:

> Our journey's end: a Britain where any child born in this Millennium, whatever their background, race or creed, wherever they live, whoever their parents, is able to make the most of the God-given ability they bring into this world.

These references are not merely to current perceptions of childhood and ideas about equality, but depend for their resonance upon the most prominent example of such discourse, Martin Luther King's speech, 'I have a dream'.[36] In this address, King refers to his own children and his hope that one day they will be judged by the content of their character, not by the colour of their skin, cherishing the hope that little children in the state of Alabama, both black and white, will one day be able to 'hold hands as sisters and brothers' (see Gill and Whedbee, in van Dijk, 1997, 180).

Yet Blair's speech, though an apparent plea for equality, reveals limitations which critical discourse analysis is able to discern. Certain phrases may appear to qualify or in effect *operationalise* other material. In this case, the essential qualifying agent is the reference to *ability*; children are born with individual degrees of capacity or talent, in this case provided by God. The role of the social order with regard to this situation, is to provide appropriate conditions for each child to make the best of his or her own merits. It is, in other words, the provision of 'a level playing field'; it is up to the individual, not the state, to ensure the full attainment of capacity.

It is worth noting that, because of the tight adherence to themes expressed in and operationalised through certain terms, it is possible for the politician to repeat phrases in a manner which acts to reinforce his/her convictions (expressed as propositions) in line with theories of rhetorical psychology; according to this approach, public discourses shape belief rather than inner states (Billig, 1991). In this case, Blair repeated similar injunctions in another context. In a speech made a year later, during the General Election Campaign of 2001, he attacked Conservative Party values by characterising their outlook as 'narrow, selfish, individualist' whereas his own party had 'cast aside' this view in favour of a perspective which knew 'a person's place' to be 'wherever his or her talents take them' (Klein, Guardian, 7.6.01). The repetition of basic themes may be seen both as attempts at reinforcement, but may also demonstrate as West argues 'how important it is for leaders to conserve their political capital and focus their attention on a limited number of issues' (West, 1993, 102).

Pursuing once again the use of children as symbols of hope and future development, the United States Green Party broadcast an advertisement during the Presidential election of 2000[37] which featured a group of children who explained that they wanted a future in which everything remained the same, from pollution in the environment and corruption in politics, to the familiar appearance of empty promises:

---

36 Delivered on 28 August 1963, in Washington D.C.
37 The Green Party candidate was Ralph Nader.

When I grow up, I want the government to have the same problems it has today ... when I grow up, I want politicians to ignore me[38]

The broadcast works as an ironical message in which children have absorbed and reproduce the dominant yet unspoken values of the political establishment, thus making the point that it is the Green Party which offers real change and hope for the future. Within the introduction to the 'Believing in Britain' manifesto, which appeared in 2000, the Conservative leader William Hague[39] made a number of references which bear a strong similarity to the agenda suggested by New Labour; once again, references to the future provide the frame for the generation of meaning. Hague asserts that:

> We could have prosperity on a scale unknown to any previous generation, with more people than ever before sharing in its benefits and opportunities ... we could have a healthier, better educated population than ever before in our history ... we could have greater stability and stronger communities than for many years past. We could be a leading nation in a more peaceful, freer and more democratic world than it has ever been possible to achieve.[40]

This represents an attempt not just to gain votes, but to re-interpret experience in a particular light; the technique here is to describe a goal which may be reached but to provide no firm point or verifiable data against which success or failure can be measured. This kind of appeal to a poorly-defined progress can be used in reverse, retaining the same kind of propositional content; that is to say, a state of decline and despair can be attributed to a previous administration, while the current government is represented as the saviour of the national economy and the harbinger of a new spirit. This is very much the case in the following excerpt, produced by the Conservative Party as a Party Election Broadcast in 1992:[41]

> '[A sunset with the Last Post playing]
> Did the sun set on Britain? The country which once had an empire that covered one third of the planet.
> [Black and white photographic images of strikers, rubbish and other scenes from the 1979 'winter of discontent']
> A country wrecked by internal strife, too busy disputing to collect its refuse, to care for its sick, or to bury its dead
> A people that seemed too tired to work hard, too keen to take handouts, too happy to slip into the dreams of power and greatness. Did the sun set on Britain?
> [Footage of beautiful countryside, fishing boats, the sun rising over London, milk being delivered, bread being baked]

---

38 U.S. Green Party website, 2000.

39 Replaced on 14 September 2001 by Iain Duncan-Smith. Subsequent leaders were Michael Howard and David Cameron.

40 Conservative Party Election Manifesto: Believing in Britain, 2000.

41 Transcript made by the author.

Today sees the sun rise on a different Britain. It hasn't always been an easy task. Yet today, despite a worldwide recession, over 1 million more British people go to work than in 1979. It hasn't been easy.

Yet today, Britain has gone from the highest level of strikes in 50 years, to the lowest. Confrontation has been replaced by co-operation. It hasn't been painless, and for some it's still tough.

Yet Britain today is conquering the inflation that causes unemployment. Today the British are no longer punished for working hard, by high taxation ...

Because Britain works harder, we have more money to spend on our families. In fact, since 1979 our living standards have overtaken those of Italy, Sweden, Australia, Belgium, Holland – and because Britain earns more, we're spending more on our social services ... to put it another way, one day in every two weeks, you're working for the NHS'.

The 'before' and 'after' comparison which sustains the initial premise of this broadcast, following the rhetorical question about the nation, is familiar from the practices of advertising. The type of image chosen and the presentation of a comfortable, semi-rural, and united Britain working to the same end despite differences in class and occupation, may be almost unrecognisable to its city-dwellers, but works as an overall proposition in that it provides visual 'evidence' of the points being made. Its internal consistency, however, makes reference to external knowledge essential, and it is here, in the 'exophoric' nature of comparison, that some contradictions may emerge. However, there are statements within this material which are open to question even within the frame of the broadcast itself, especially where the provision of visual reference is more difficult. A particularly noticeable instance is the claim that 'over 1 million more British people go to work than in 1979'. This could be accounted for by the increase in the available workforce within the population overall, rather than an indication of greater employment *per se*.

The existence of some form of 'convergence' in political messages, as mainstream parties fight for the 'centre ground', is a common theme in recent works of political analysis (Jones, 1999). An example occurs in the piece cited above; it seems remarkable that, more than the mere sharing of a key term such as for example 'family' (used by both New Labour and the Conservative Party as an ideological touchstone[42]), larger and more self-contained units of discourse can be employed. The Tory party broadcast which uses the reference 'it hasn't been painless, and for some it's still hard', is echoed by Blair's declaration in a speech at the Labour Party conference, Brighton 2000, which in describing the economic circumstances faced by his government, uses an almost identical reference:

---

42 An institution which seems considered to be part of a shared public ethos, and which supposedly animates a range of values. Whenever a reference to the concrete economic or social category related to this concept is required, then the wide divergence in living arrangements is subsumed within the term 'families'. The degree to which it refers to a traditional understanding of 'nuclear' families is less important than the assumption that it is thought to motivate a positive response.

For many families life's still a struggle. It's tough, balancing work and family. Jobs can be insecure. There's the mortgage to pay; the holiday to save for. Inflation may be lower but the kid's trainers don't get any cheaper.

In both cases, the recognition accorded to those who have not shared in economic prosperity, appears to be a carefully controlled reference which must not be allowed to expand too far, with the result that it might constitute an agenda on its own terms. These references are made in order to anticipate and defuse criticism; they are both answered within the texts themselves. In the Conservative's case, the broadcast moves on to assert that 'Britain today is conquering the inflation that causes unemployment', as though inflation is the only or at least the chief cause of unemployment, while Blair goes on to envisage the other problematic issues his government will consider. One way of addressing the supposed convergence between political parties is to depict both sides as though they are indistinguishable.

This tactic was employed by the SDP and Liberal Democrat Alliance in a broadcast of 1987, in which John Cleese presents the supposedly lamentable situation of 'see-saw' politics, the notion that the Labour and Conservative parties merely undo each other's policies when each succeeds the other, and that there is no balance in Parliament, only extremes. The problem is one of unintended effects, which appear because those involved in the creation of messages concentrate to closely on their own mode of interpretation; a prime example of such 'aberrant decoding' (Eco, 1960) appears in this instance.

Two puppets in little suits sit astride either end of a wooden see-saw, one wearing a red rosette, the other a blue one. The puppets are identical white males, apart from this symbol. They look like anodyne and rather sinister twins, political clones. Cleese demonstrates the repetitive motion as each gains a brief ascendancy when the see-saw moves their way. To show how a more sensible system might be put in place, Cleese introduces a third puppet, wearing a yellow rosette. It is identical to the others. It stands at the fulcrum of the see-saw and the whole structure remains inert. The three puppets may thus appear to the viewer as representative of a political class, all involved in the same pointless and exclusive exercise.

The success of propositions within political presentations of this kind depends on security of reference (the sense of an accurate match between the symbols and their referents) and the credibility of proposition. Propositions do not necessarily have to be, as Fairclough believes, 'ideologies' which 'generally figure as implicit assumptions in texts', and which 'contribute to producing or reproducing unequal relations of power, relations of domination' (Fairclough, 1995, 32). They may be explicit in their attempt to produce positions on public issues.

Based on the study of political address, the process of transmission would appear to obey the following pattern. First, an instrumental purpose is produced as a consequence of established structures and practices, but is in formal terms at least, held in advance of the expressive event. Second, the construction or adaptation of an appropriate setting is created (partly composed through discourse but also constructed as *physical theatres for address*). Third, the composition of an address is made, which attempts to reconcile the imagined subjectivity of the listener with both purpose and the purported (formal) system of belief favoured by the party concerned; this, sometimes called ideology, represents conscious acknowledgement of one's own and opposing positions (an opinion pre-supposes that there are alternative opinions). Fourth, explicit *characterisation of the qualities of opposing beliefs* is made, rather than mere reference to them (whether they are effective, moral, rational, etc.). Fifth, an individual articulation (based on an 'idiolect', a personal form of utterance) is reproduced from a general ideological resource.

Conclusion

Overview

The general purpose of the enquiry conducted within the course of this book, was to investigate the character of public communication,[1] together with various academic perspectives on its role in the production of meaning. A more particular aim was the analysis of directive[2] or 'strategic' modes of address within the broader context of public interaction. The texts which constitute this category (a class partially composed, inevitably, by the act of selection itself) were taken from both commercial and political sources, in the conviction that they demonstrate enough shared resemblances to represent a 'promotional' genre (Wernick, 1991).

The existence of a cross-generic promotional discourse appears to provide a resource for the conduct of what may at first sight appear to be quite distinct practices; yet certain commercial, 'corporate' and political projects share important characteristics and draw upon similar rhetorical techniques. Directive forms of address, therefore, are regarded here as a typical practice within a social order which, while hierarchical in structure, must employ discursive techniques which reflect public adherence to informal, democratic and 'conversationalised' types of interaction.

The present work regards the appearance of strategic communication as evidence of a desire to intervene in public life to secure goals which are not primarily of benefit to the community as a whole, but which nonetheless, in a formal democracy, are subject to assessment and evaluation. Therefore, powerful groups or 'issue proponents' (Dearing and Rogers, 1996), must 'give an account' of their purposes, even if these descriptions are incomplete or partial.[3] 'Public relations' may then, in essence, be regarded as the strategic anticipation of critical enquiry, as well as a distortion of the more exalted normative standards envisioned by theorists like Habermas (1989) Grice (1989). Individual utterances made by corporate bodies may therefore be seen as attempts to create favourable symbolic conditions for the attainment of quite elitist social, cultural and political ends. Such interventions, despite their 'multi-modal' appearances, are broadly discursive in nature, if discourse

---

1   Recognition of the continued relevance of 'public' as a description of significant, society-wide message-production, appears in Corner, 1995, 11.

2   A resolution to move an audience to think or act in a certain way. In linguistics, the 'directive' function is based upon the grammatical mood known as the imperative (Coulthard, 1985, 26).

3   The position taken here is that all 'social narratives' or interventions are bound to be incomplete, and that this is related to the condition of ideological address; see Chapter 1 for a fuller discussion.

is understood as a general symbolic resource for the production of meaning. I have argued, therefore, that the 'end product' of any discursive strategy, whatever symbolic elements are employed, is a 'social narrative' (Price, 1996), an attempt to present a coherent account of various phenomena in such a way as to convince an audience of its relevance and validity.

Academic theories which offer accounts of linguistic and symbolic influence were thus particularly relevant to the development of the debates covered in the six chapters of this book. Perspectives on the nature of discourse, ideology and address, were evaluated with regard to their worth as explanations for the power of mediated communication. Four broad currents of thought, in particular, were assessed in the course of the overall exposition; these were theories of ideological dominance (sometimes associated with traditional Marxist outlooks), constructionist or relativist views on language and society, post-structuralist beliefs regarding the breakdown in referential stability, and tendencies which support a realist account of reference and meaning. It is this last position, manifesting itself variously as discursive, critical or ontological realism, which has provided the matrix both for the development of theory and for a closely related analytical description.

In addition, those linguistic traditions which provide close descriptions of grammatical and semantic processes, have provided an important link between the structure of messages, the strategies which authors may adopt, and the 'ideological' positions which utterances may represent. The notion of 'exophoric' reference for example, while perhaps suggesting a rather artificial distinction between internal and external elements of meaning-production, at least provides support for the idea that texts must 'point away' from themselves in order to establish validity and, more especially, resonance in argument. If this insight is combined with a realist account of referentiality, what is 'indicated' by terms or concepts (in general terms, by units of meaning above the level of the sentence) is thus a whole range of material-symbolic 'events' in the social and natural world.

As a further consequence of this relationship between the symbolic and the 'real', this book also advocates a distinction between the discursive and the extra-discursive. This was not to suggest a mechanical transfer of meaning between two separate realms of experience, but to demonstrate the productive/material character of reference as a social action, rather than those alternatives which suggest an enclosed system of semiosis. Positing a relationship *between* discourse and the 'material world' proposed by Pujol, *et al*, it is perhaps a necessary first step in establishing a position which is better expressed by these authors as a 'discourse/material assemblage', a concept much closer to the lived experience of human subjects (Pujol *et al*, in Burr in Parker, 1998, 20).

Modernity and discourse

The social, cultural and political context in which meaningful address takes place, was characterised by a term used by a number of commentators, that of 'late modernity' (Jameson, 1981; Giddens, 1991; Fornas, 1995; Hughes, 1998; Chouliaraki and Fairclough, 1999; Young, 1999). Preference for this term as a label for the contemporary social formation, as opposed to 'modernity' pure and simple, or 'postmodernity' as an alternative, may be explained as a way of recognising epochal developments, without conceding that an entirely new state of affairs has ensued. In other words, the pressure of change within 'modernity' itself calls for some acknowledgement of further altered circumstances, without necessarily requiring a radical departure from procedural continuity.[4] In all such discussions, the uses and dangers of regarding periodicity as a structuring agent should be acknowledged.

While recognising, in turn, the challenges which accompany attempts to identify textual phenomena as representative examples of historical periods or ideological conjunctures, the particular focus of the present work (textual manifestations of 'directive' address (see above)), must be located within a broader field of communicative practices and events. Yet at the same time, while it is important to emphasise that this type of address is the product, like other mediated forms, of industrial production and hierarchical modes of organisation, the present work contends that they are also marked by a number of distinctive features.

If care is not taken to discriminate between types of communication, then it may seem as though the directive form has become entirely dominant. This difficulty is found in Fairclough, who writes of 'the colonization of discourse by promotion', and who argues that 'we are ... all constantly subjected to promotional discourse', to the degree to which it becomes difficult to judge the sincerity of an utterance (Fairclough, 1995a, 139). In reply to Fairclough's question, 'how can we be sure what's authentic?' (ibid), I would suggest that individuals are always aware when institutionalised discourses are in operation, despite or perhaps because of their appearance as 'quasi-mediated interaction' (Thompson, 1995). Furthermore, human subjects are able to gauge the quality of a communicative act from the circumstance in which it is delivered, and are used to experiencing dramatic exhortation on a range of issues which nonetheless do not require any particular active commitment or action on their part.[5]

In cataloguing, therefore, the distinctive features of directive address, it is possible to include certain formal qualities (both structural and semantic), the use of rhetorical technique as a means of persuasion, the deployment of 'multi-modal'

---

4   The presence of different, yet co-existing tendencies, suggests that it is not yet clear what kind of social order may become predominant; 'late modernity' allows therefore some flexibility in this respect, despite its difficult suggestion of a periodicity the 'lateness' of which can only be demonstrated by reference to what has gone before.

5   Many questions posed at a national level are far enough removed from everyday responsibility to allow responses which entail little personal consequence: for example, the question posed by the BBC web-site at the end of September 2001; 'are we right to be cautious' (with regard to the use of force in Afghanistan) can be answered easily by most citizens either way in the knowledge that a professional army will assume the role designated by the term 'we', when and if any action is taken.

discourses,[6] and a carefully articulated relationship between reference (what the text 'points' to within and beyond itself), proposition (what it says is the case about any issue), and implicature (what associations the text may animate through the supposed relationship between reference and proposition).[7] It may be worth asking why propositions, as explicit forms of evaluation of objects, events, persons, etc., are thought to motivate individuals. Therborn is useful in this respect, arguing that the social order functions through a kind of operative address, which proposes the recognition of three simple qualities; what exists, what is good, and what is possible (Therborn, 1980, 18). All these elements, however, are given semiotic life within a general context. This context is made up of the generic form to which the particular text belongs, combined with the social conjuncture in which the text appears. The 'ideological' thrust of such material is shaped, therefore, by more than a simple intention held in advance of utterance or textual expression.

Yet while it is entirely reasonable to argue that the process of analysis must therefore consider the 'institutional and discoursal practices within which texts are embedded' (Fairclough, 1995a, 9), it is exactly such practices which are difficult for outsiders to examine and verify. This may explain, for example, the tendency of academics to attribute certain institutional practices to media workers.[8] It also means that 'intention' is usually described through the process of textual interpretation; Fairclough admits, for instance, that 'analysis of practices of production and consumption' were not adequately covered in his landmark account of critical discourse analysis (ibid). The work of this book, however, has not been concerned to investigate the entire cycle of 'mediation', but has searched for an explanation for the production of textual meaning as it appears both in academic discourses and within texts themselves.

Norms of address

If strategic intention is understood within the context of a generic, 'promotional' form, which itself appears within the social conjuncture of late modernity, then it is possible to argue that its didactic or interventionist character may be softened by the 'conversational' norms which seem to be a feature of contemporary society (Grice, 1989; Fairclough, 1989, 1995a). Yet the present work has argued that it may still be characterised by a more clearly 'inflected' voice than everyday exchange. Barker calls this quality an 'evaluative accent' (Barker, 1989, 269), and relates it to the

---

6   'Multi-modal' in the sense of drawing upon a range of representational techniques or symbolic resources (Kress and van Leeuwen, 2001).

7   Directive address produces a large number of propositions, while also using techniques intended to increase the incidence of identification between audience and message content. Implicature is sometimes used when it is thought wise to avoid making an unambiguous statement.

8   The paradigmatic case is probably the academic description of journalistic 'news values' made by Galtung and Ruge in 1973 (see Price, 1998, 218).

ideological work of the text. It carries, in other words, a particular emphasis, using some aspects of contemporary discourse, while neglecting or suppressing others. In Clegg's words, following insights generated by Laclau and Mouffe, ideology appears as a 'set of practices', primarily of 'a discursive provenance', which attempt to foreclose the possibilities of signifying elements 'in determinate ways' (Clegg, in Mumby, 1993, 26). This book has argued that such attempts to determine meaning has a notable consequence; that the finished product can never produce a message free from contradiction.[9]

Any individual mode of communication can only appeal to its audiences through reference to pre-existing discourses, which must be represented with enough accuracy to provide a series of implicit or explicit contrasts with the overall 'direction' of the address itself.[10] Although 'exophoric' references sometimes appear to form a consistent theme, and can even suggest 'alternative' readings which may be brought to bear on the message itself, their actual purpose is to enable the production of a coherent textual position by providing a contrasting set of themes or values against which the dominant perspective can be measured.

This book has proposed, therefore, the existence of *directive intention* as an essential motive force for the production of the material described above, doing so in the belief that it represents a more important factor for the production of address in this instance than would be the case, for example, in texts which are presented as 'entertainment' *per se* (whatever didactic purposes might be discovered within the course of the latter's exposition). Having made this point, it is nonetheless important to recognise the quality which exists within all social utterances, a feature which helps to solve the problem of where to draw boundaries between the textual and those acts and events which are either random or which stand outside formal symbolic systems; this is the character of texts as *purposes* rather than merely their existence as 'bodies' of work. In sum, all texts have purposes, even where that is merely to draw attention to 'brute' facts which would otherwise be discovered in a more dangerous or traumatic fashion; the warning on a fuse box, for example, to the effect that the electricity supply must be disconnected before the cover is removed, is clearly 'directive' yet would not usually be regarded as 'ideological'.

The present work adheres, therefore, to the perspective offered in the Introduction, in which intention or purpose is imagined as a universal quality of all texts; yet it also notes the existence of a form of address constituted by an essential imbalance of power between the message source or author, and its recipients, and the consequent use of a more 'inflected' accent in its delivery.

---

9 I would contend that a text will not advance a 'dominant' conception of social relations merely as a consequence of its place within a dominant mode of production.

10 By 'direction' I mean the purpose of the communicative act, as that is gradually made concrete during the course of the address itself.

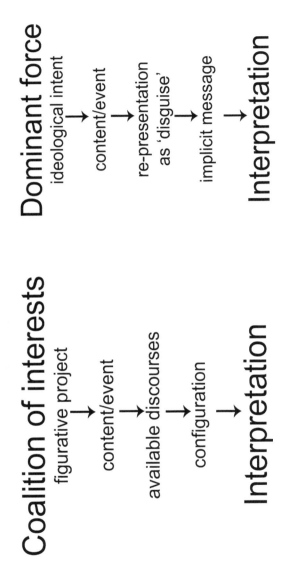

Illustration 7: Two Models of Ideology and Address

Text, form and ideology

Rather than conduct a search for hidden belief-systems behind examples of address, I have assumed that reference to beliefs and principles is partly pragmatic, or designed to achieve a goal (election, sales, an improved image) which could be achieved in other circumstances by a different set of references. In one sense, this may beg the question, in that pragmatic conduct may serve ideological ends, ends which may themselves be represented as the inevitable products of *a realm of necessity* in which there is a struggle over the allocation of resources. The appearance of pragmatic strategies in authors is often matched by pragmatic responses in audiences. Resistance to forms of address which attempt to make subjects alter their conduct or belief in some way, may indicate an attempt to protect the 'lifeworld' from the sphere of the political. This debate was notable, indeed, during the rise of a particularly virulent form of partisan discourse; one which emerged from the authoritarian practices of 'Thatcherism'. Golding, for example, explained that this system of belief was not necessarily taken up wholeheartedly as a creed by the British people, precisely because they still adhered to an 'opportunistic and pragmatic' outlook (Golding, 1992[11]).

Such an approach, essentially concerned with the ideological conditions of reception, runs parallel with another important insight into the constraints at work in the construction of meaning; that textual coherence is only achieved by producing a sufficient range of meaningful references, and that this principle may act to undermine or qualify the strategic goal of the individual message itself. The present work, therefore, is not overly concerned at the difficulty of reconciling the work of textual analysis with evidence of audience response. Its theoretical framework supports the proposition that models of audience subjectivity are necessary to the composition of any message, and therefore provides a model for analysis which not only takes the reciprocal movement of ideas between source and recipient into account, but moves this back to the point of textual origin.

Another closely related issue is thus the notion of the 'text' itself and, in tandem with this concept, the idea of the various 'forms' in which it is generally thought to appear. Part of the reason for the present work's emphasis on identifying a directive tendency within a promotional genre, is its interest in drawing attention to more general features of the communication process, and in particular what I have called the social effects of 'the circulation of broad genres of text' (see Chapter 1). In plotting the development of text from a single utterance or inscription of meaning, to a purpose embodied in a form (see above), it may also be possible to imagine a movement from individual to more general social meanings. In other words, ideological intent may not appear in discrete messages, but in *the habitual or regulated production of forms of address*.

---

11 Golding, P., 'Communicating capitalism', in *Media, Culture and Society*, vol. 14., no. 4., October, 1992.

This is not identical to the argument which posits the production of entertainment as a suppressive or compensatory act; rather, it is to acknowledge the value of broad genres of communication to the maintenance of the social system itself. So, for example, the reason for the similarities which exist between various types of content in advertising, politics, and corporate announcements, lies less in their use of 'propagandistic' declarations (they often clearly obey more 'dialogic' principles), than in their appearance as formal contributions to the mediation of public values.

It is in this sense, therefore, that they reproduce the conditions under which 'concensual' social control may be effected. Jameson argues that this process carries a radical implication; 'at this level', he argues, '"form" is apprehended as content' (Jameson, 1981, 99). Using this insight, it is possible to return, again, to the question of ideology and the notion of the 'pragmatic' composition and reception of public communication. If, as argued above, the important question in the maintenance of any symbolic order, is the 'formal' appearance of communication genres, and if ideology can exist not only as specific content but as the regular (and regulated) appearance of form, then the question of 'dominance' versus 'resistance' (outlined in van Dijk, 1998), becomes less important than the following observation; that consensus is as much a *recognition* of structural inequalities as conflict.

This book has therefore attempted to refute the conception of ideology as the propagation of false belief, while retaining the notion that it is partial or incomplete. This makes it possible to question the power of those 'inherited interpretive traditions' which Jameson believes produce limited readings of public texts (Jameson, 1981, 9). Language use and the various constraints upon its employment, whether contextual or more broadly political, forms a recurrent theme within both academic and journalistic studies, which suggests reappraisal of the questions asked in the Introduction; to what extent does the act of address make social relations 'concrete', and to what degree are texts mechanisms of social cohesion?

Texts are clearly manifestations of a range of social practices, of politics, of commerce, and of human relationships in general. While it may not be possible to recover the original 'specialised institutional practice' (Bernstein in Chouliaraki and Fairclough, 1999, 118), through textual analysis alone (a more extreme goal than the one proposed within the present work), it is still possible to argue that 'social control' in any society is actually effected by the simple existence of communication and interaction. In other words, all societies must function in terms of reciprocal exchange including, to take two examples of central relevance to this book, the exchange of goods and symbols.

Kurke, for example, explains how 'in the embedded economy of Ancient Greece, exchange went far beyond concrete economics', encompassing even a 'traffic' in ritualised forms of praise (Kurke, 1991, 8). Following Bourdieu, it is possible to discover the enduring power of ritual forms of language use which are *'formally* impeccable but semantically empty'(Bourdieu, 1991, 41). Such observations suggest, as outlined above, a direct relationship between the existence of a 'concensual' realm and the notion of a pragmatic, everyday acceptance of existing power relations, in which more coercive or directive forms of address are possible because the 'public' and the 'private' each retain at least a formal division in their respective sphere of operations. The problem remains, however, that promotional genres and directive address do not appear to restrict themselves to one theatre of operation alone; as Fairclough notes (above), they seem to infect every aspect of exchange.[12]

Ideology and discourse: future directions

The present work also recognised that, within contemporary social formations, the commodification of human relationships has formed a consistent theme;[13] alongside Marx's 'immense collection of commodities' (in Mosco, 1996, 140), there appears to exist a vast range of texts or forms of address. In many cases, it is possible to argue that the point of such phenomena is to 'sell' goods. I would suggest, however, another purpose; the production and maintenance of a culture within which transnational capital and its political allies are able to promote a favourable interpretation of events and trends, the 'resistive' tendencies of which appear already sewn into the fabric of address. In the course of this process, however, the conditions under which all such advocates must operate, should be recognised. The uncertain nature of any attempt to persuade is at the centre of this issue.

In addition, the opportunity for uninterrupted, uni-directional address is limited, and the attitude of audiences or referent groups has been described as cynical or sceptical (despite or because of what Beck calls the loss of 'class consciousness'; Beck, 1999, 98). Yet there is nonetheless a perception that late modernity represents a 'traumatic' field of social action, one in which directive address may achieve some success because the identities it both composes and speaks to are themselves insecure. That is to say, modernity is based on flux and change (a state of affairs Giddens calls 'post-traditional', 1991), in which transactions between individuals and groups have become impersonal, to such a degree that, in Bauman's words, 'the need of personal relationships becomes ... poignant and acute' (Bauman, 1990, 96). This may account in turn for the proliferation of what Fairclough calls 'the "conversationalisation" of public discourse' (Fairclough, 1995a, 138) in which individuals are presented, perhaps as a compensatory measure, with highly 'interactive' and informal modes of address.

This is to some degree confirmed by the quality of political speech and rhetoric set out in Chapter 4, and by the method of dramatisation (the use of actors who express 'everyday' beliefs in colloquial terms) found in some of the examples. What Fairclough calls 'the modelling of public discourse upon the discursive practices of everyday life' (Fairclough, ibid), therefore, suggests that the production of 'quasi-interactive' modes is actually a means of regaining attention lost by more traditional genres.

---

12 Chouliaraki and Fairclough, in an appraisal of Habermas, speak of 'the colonisation of lifeworlds by systems, the defensive and offensive reaction of social movements to this colonisation' (Chouliaraki and Fairclough, 1999, 88).

13 See in particular the discussion in Chapter 2.

This has also become part of the strategic practices of corporations which follow '"routinised" customer service interactions' (Leidner, 1993, in Cameron, 2000, 54). These represent symptoms of continued authoritarian intervention in the construction of contemporary subjectivity, in which the existence of 'domination and subjection' is maintained in particular by 'the symbolic order of texts' (Fornas, 1995, 225). The ability of 'issue proponents' (Dearing and Rogers, 19),[14] to change their mode of address yet to retain the same *propositional* content may serve as a reminder both of the abstract nature of any proposition and the character of discourse as a *resource*, the full extent of which is never fully revealed within any individual utterance or expressive intervention.

The ultimate issue here, is the degree to which texts represent identities which are composed from more than one source, through interaction between commodified culture and the lifeworld. There is indeed an essential similarity to be found amongst the texts and genres which have appeared within the present work, over and above their shared status as persuasive interventions within the everyday 'flow' of commodified communication. This is their political character. 'Political' here does not necessarily refer to formal adherence to established groups or parties, but rather to a general principle that unites a variety of textual practices. This principle is superficially marked as a form of common sense which dramatises its own attempts to come to terms with certain 'realities' of life within late modernity.

As common sense, these texts do imitate some of the everyday understandings (homilies, moral narratives, apocryphal tales, re-worked stories from media sources), which occur within 'ordinary' diatribes, and are not automatically to be characterised as acts whose true (malevolent) character is disguised. Such discourses, however, are political insofar as they are directed towards a specific goal which marks them out from those activities which emanate from the lifeworld itself; their ultimate purpose is to re-orientate public sensibility towards a dynamic of far-reaching social 'change'.[15] This is not to argue that there are no new 'realities' in for example, social and economic life, or that all that is being offered is a series of discourses which are ultimately equivalent to the seamless production of entertainment. Such a position would only serve to beg the question; to what do such discourses refer, or why are such 'distractions' produced? Zizek identifies the tendency referred to here, when he argues that 'the ruling ideology endeavours to sell us the insecurity' caused by the dismantling of the welfare state, in the guise of an 'opportunity for new freedoms' (Zizek, 2001, 116).

---

14 The authors of many of the texts studied within the main body of this work are not always presented in such neutral terms; they are shown in a less than favourable light by Hobsbawm, for example, who describes them as 'a special-interest group of professional politicians, journalists, lobbyists and others whose occupation ranked at the bottom of the scale of trustworthiness in sociological inquiries' (in Dahlgren, 1995, 1).

15 Such change includes, for example, major alterations in security of employment; see for example Brindle's discussion of the dramatic decline in the numbers of older workers in Britain since 1979 (Brindle, *Guardian*, Society section, 26 September 2001).

Yet when such impulses assume a concrete, textual form, they have their positive uses, in so far as they alert individuals to the existence of change; nonetheless, the accuracy of their *reference* ('there are major social changes in progress'), must be set against the less than altruistic nature of their *propositions* ('we can all thrive in this new environment, provided we buy or believe X or Y'). Refusing on the one hand to treat all public communication as a form of ideological subterfuge (which causes theorists like Dyer to search for meaning 'beneath the surface gloss' of advertisements; Dyer, 1982, 21), and refusing on the other to give credence to the notion of a 'total system' in which the penetration of capital has evacuated all forms of contestation or even meaning from the realm of the symbolic (as Foster characterises Baudrillard's late theory in Quinn, 1999, 68), *Discourse Power Address* recognises a different process at work, and new possibilities for the development of theory and research.

The perspective upon which this is based may be described as follows: that directive address in the present context of semiotic 'de-regulation' owes its existence to changed material conditions; or, more accurately, that discursive strategies within the current period form an integral part of material existence, acting both to reflect changes in the nature of social organisation and, through texts' creative or transformative capacity, to prefigure new developments in social relationships.

In attempting to make the nature of social change more palatable (in Zizek's view, it is ultimately presented as a chance to remould individual personality; 2001, 119), directive forms of address will accentuate opportunity. Two simple and brief examples may be found within a statement of Conservative policies introduced by William Hague in 2000, under the rubric 'Believing In Britain'. First, this document notes that 'as the world becomes more competitive, countries will be forced to find new strategies to ensure strong, stable societies as well as prosperous economies'. In a faint echo of the mantras emerging from self-help manuals (ultimately traceable to what Lau calls 'new age capitalism'; Lau, 2000), the passage goes on to argue that 'we are well placed to succeed, if we believe in ourselves'. Second, in signalling their wholesale retreat from centralised funding for British universities, the Conservative party declares a *positive* attachment to freedom as a principle, citing this as the reason for a policy of one-off endowments; 'we want to set the universities free to grow and to recover their global pre-eminence'.

Text, structure and resistance

Recalling the notion that all 'issue proponents' must work with discourses which they inherit and then reconfigure, it is nonetheless possible to repeat the observation that the references they carry will inevitably contain not only opportunities for 'polysemic' readings, but some of the enduring qualities of the social relationships they once described. In other words, just because corporate organisations and political parties use 'radical' references, or seem attracted to notions of freedom and equality, does not mean that such terms no longer animate critical, resistive or progressive associations.

Indeed, some companies have attempted to associate themselves with positive forms of *identification*, taking 'one world' discourses of love and unity and making them an associative sign of the commercial enterprise itself, so that, in turn, the *raison d'etre* of one form of capitalism appears to be the growth of mutual understanding and respect, exchanged through the product which is presented as a moral signifier.[16]

From what has been established above, 'modernisation' as a process, discussed in Chapter 3, remains particularly dependent upon its ability to address and reconstitute contemporary subjectivity, which is in Fornas' opinion, as much the product of historical developments as are 'social spheres and symbolic modes' (Fornas, 1995, 224). The role of academic enquiry must therefore be to show an acute awareness of what Fowles among others calls 'the project of the self' (Fowles, 1996), and its place within a broader social goal designed (from above) to engineer forms of public awareness which are intended to create support or at least acquiescence in response to authority's pursuit of symbolic regeneration.

From this observation, further research may be conducted into the growth of socially constitutive discourses, such as the 'corporate citizenship' outlined in Chapter 4; the purpose would be to establish a contextual study of both discourse and extra-discursive events, a method already pre-figured in the comparative analysis used within the work on advertising and corporate promotion.

With regard to the use of textual analysis in general, a more refined system, combining the strengths of critical discourse analysis, with the realist philosophies of language outlined in the course of the present work, could also yield new insights into text as a site of dramatised conflicts and partial resolutions. From what has been said above, it remains the case that certain 'adventurous' forms, such as advertising, retain a transformative capacity, producing new themes from 'sedimented' meanings. The present enquiry would not attribute this to a 'postmodern' turn within commercial representation, but would locate this within a longer established tendency of the 'avant-garde' to re-configure public meanings.

Another aspect of such a project might encompass closer enquiry into the authorship of texts, pursuing more closely the issue of who speaks on behalf of whom, and in what range of guises such forms of address are made (Grice, 1989). The tensions which exist within the process of production and the 'temporary' solution represented by the appearance of the advertisement within its 'frame' (see Fowles, 1996), could lead to a closer inspection of production itself. Another approach worth pursuing, would be ethnographic studies of audience reception.

It is the nature of ideology and its relationship to discourse, however, which might provide an opportunity to develop the primary concerns of this book. In particular, the character of form and its regulated appearance as 'content' within the realm of commodity production, may offer new directions in the study of genre, meaning and public expectation. The present work would contend that too much

---

16 Benetton is probably the prime example of this tendency, producing a multiplicity of symbolism through a concept which is also a principle and a 'campaign' in all its senses – 'united colors'.

emphasis has been placed upon the notion of an ideological address which attempts to establish particular meanings, positions which are then supposed to constitute enduring markers in future hegemonic struggles, or which are imagined as ensuring the 'complete' dominance of subaltern groups.

I would advocate the principle that realist perspectives on the character of symbolic intervention should in future consider texts as *configurations of meaning* (Buxton, 1990), designed as attempts to establish favourable grounds for the success of specific and often temporary ideological alliances, and thus producing a variety of meanings within particular moments of contested action. A sense of the provisional and contingent, in which intended outcomes are uncertain and in which events may change so radically as to throw established generic production into crisis (observed whenever 'breaking news' gives advocates little time to prepare a 'script'), must nonetheless be seen in the larger context of meaning and action. Symbolic resources are mobilised for a purpose; to achieve particular ends within finite periods of time. Thus the uncertain power of directive address is not an indication of the 'over-organised' character of the powerful (Fiske, 1989), or of a crisis in meaning, or of the wily resistance shown by the subaltern. It is instead characteristic of messages created for present use; in a social system marked by the exclusion of the majority from 'mediated' authorship, a highly inflected mode of address will remain a useful strategic weapon.

Cultural enquiry should therefore attempt to delineate the relationship between those unequal forces which interact to produce textual configurations, understanding their contradictions not as play or confusion, but as the result of conflicts which are only ever partially resolved. As Buxton argues in a critique of structuralism, 'the text must be related to something other than its own structure: in other words, we must explain how it comes to be structured' (Buxton, 1990, 13). From this observation I would end with Lukes' blunt judgement on the conduct of research and the creation of abstract models, whatever theoretical perspective they embrace; 'no social theory merits serious attention that fails to retain an ever present sense of the dialectics of power and structure' (Lukes, 1977, 29).

Bibliography

Abercrombie, N., Hill, S., and Turner B.S. (eds) (1980) *The Dominant Ideology Thesis* London: Unwin Hyman

Abercrombie, N., Hill, S., and Turner B.S. (eds) (1990) *Dominant Ideologies* London: Unwin Hyman

Adam, B. (1990) *Time and Social Theory* Cambridge: Polity Press

Adam, B. (1998) *Timescapes of Modernity:the environment and invisible hazards* London and New York: Routledge

Adbusters www.adbusters.com

Adorno, T.W. (1991) *The Culture Industry: selected essays on mass culture* London: Routledge

Agger, B. (1992) *The Discourse of Domination* Evanston: Northwestern University Press

Alasuutari, P. (1992) 'The Moral Hierarchy of Television Programmes', in *Media, Culture and Society* vol 14 no. 4, October 1992

Alasuutari, P. (1995) *Researching Culture* Thousand Oaks, London, Delhi: SAGE

Alasuutari, P. (ed) (1999) *Rethinking the media audience: the new agenda* Thousand Oaks, London, Delhi: SAGE

Aldridge, A. (2005) *The Market* Cambridge: Polity Press

Allen, G. (2000) *Intertextuality* London and New York: Routledge

Althusser, L. (1984) *Essays on Ideology* London: Verso/NLB

Andersen, R. and Strate, L. (2000) *Critical Studies in Media Commercialism* Oxford and New York: Oxford University Press

Andriof, J. (1998) 'Managing Uncertainty through Stakeholder Partnerships Building' in *Warwick Business School Research Briefing* www.warwick.ac.uk

Andriof, J. and McIntosh, M. (eds) (2001) *Perspectives on Corporate Citizenship* Sheffield: Greenleaf

Ang, I. (1985) *Watching Dallas: soap opera and the melodramatic imagination* London: Methuen

Ang, I. (1991) *Desperately Seeking the Audience* London and New York: Routledge

Ang, I. (1996) *Living room wars: rethinking media audiences for a postmodern world* London and New York: Routledge

Ansolabehere, S. (1995) *Going Negative* London and New York: Free Press

Ashcroft, B. (2001) *Post-Colonial Transformation* London, New York: Routledge

Atkinson, M. (1984) *Our Masters' Voices* London: Methuen

Austin, J.L. (1962) *Sense and Sensibilia: reconstructed from the manuscript notes by G.J. Warno* London and Oxford: Oxford University Press

Austin, J.L. (1971) *How to do things with words* Oxford: Oxford University Press

Ayer, A.J. (1936) 'The Principle of Verification', in Nye, A. (ed) (1998) *Philosophy of Language: the Big Questions* Oxford UK. and Cambridge, Mass: Blackwell

Axford, B. and Huggins, R. (2001) *New Media and Politics* Thousand Oaks, London, Delhi: SAGE

Backstrand, K. (2001) *What Can Nature Withstand?* Lund: Lund University

Barker, M. (1989) *Comics* Manchester: Manchester University Press

Barker, M. and Beezer, A. (eds) (1992) *Reading into Cultural Studies* London and New York: Routledge

Barker, M. and Petley, J. (eds) (1997) *Ill Effects* London and New York: Routledge

Barnet, B. (2000) 'Hypertext and Association' in *Convergence* Autumn 2000, vol. 6, no. 3 Luton: University of Luton Press

Barrett, C. (1998) 'BP: On the side of Human Rights' in *Shield* BP Amoco Group, December 1998

Barrett, M. (1991) *The Politics of Truth: from Marx to Foucault* Cambridge: Polity Press

Barthes, R. (1977) *Image, Music, Text* London: Fontana

Barwise, P. and Ehrenburg, A. (1988) *Television and its Audience* Thousand Oaks, London, Delhi: SAGE

Baudrillard, J. (1981) *For a critique of the political economy of the sign* New York: Telos Press

Baudrillard, J. (1990) *Fatal Strategies* New York and London: Semiotxt(e)/Pluto

Baudrillard, J. (1993) *Symbolic Exchange and Death* Thousand Oaks, London, Delhi: SAGE

Baudrillard, J. (1998) *The Consumer Society* Thousand Oaks, London, Delhi: SAGE

Bauman, Z. (1990) *Thinking Sociologically* Oxford UK and Cambridge Mass: Blackwell

Bavelas J.B., Black A., Chouil, N., Mullet, J. (1990) *Equivocal Communication* Thousand Oaks, London, Delhi: SAGE

Beck, U. (1997) *The Reinvention of Politics* Cambridge: Polity

Bell, B. and Garrett, P. (1998) *Approaches to Media Discourse* Oxford UK and Cambridge Mass: Blackwell

Bell, D. (1965) *The End of Ideology: on the exhaustion of political ideas in the fifties* New York: Free Press/London: Collier-Macmillan

Bennett, A., Mercer, P. and Woollactt, J. (1986) *Popular Culture and Social Relations* Milton Keynes: Open University Press

Bennett, O. (2001) *Cultural Pessimism* Edinburgh: Edinburgh University Press

Bensel, R. (1990) *Yankee Leviathan* Cambridge: Cambridge University Press

Benson, C. (2001) *The Cultural Psychology of Self* London and New York: Routledge

Bergalli, R. and Sumner, C. (1997) *Social Control and Political Order* Thousand Oaks, London, Delhi: SAGE

Berlin, I., Fields, B.J., Miller, S.F., Reilly, J.P., and Rowland, L.S. (1997) *Free at Last* Edison, New Jersey: Blue and Grey Press

Berman, M. (1983) *All that is solid melts into air* London: Verso

Bernstein, R.J. (1985) *Habermas and Modernity* Cambridge: Polity Press

Bernstein, R.J. (1991) *The new constellation: the ethical-political horizons of modernity/postmodernity* Cambridge: Polity Press

Bhaskar, R. (1978) *A Realist Theory of Science* Hassocks, Sussex: Harvester Press

Bianchini, F. (1992) 'Cultural Policy and the Development of Citizenship' in *Leisure and New Citizenship* Congreso E.L.R.A.

Bignell, J. (1997) *Media Semiotics: An Introduction* Manchester: Manchester University Press

Billig, M. (1991) *Ideology and Opinions* Thousand Oaks, London, Delhi: SAGE

Blair, A. (2000) Speech to Labour Party Conference, Brighton

Bloch, M. (1965) *Feudal Society* London: Routledge

Blunden, E. (1982) *Undertones of War* London: Penguin Books

Blumenberg, H. (1983) *The Legitimacy of the Modern Age* Cambridge: MIT Press

Blumer, J.G., Gurevitch, M., and Ives, J. (1978) *The Challenge of Election Broadcasting* Leeds: University of Leeds

Blumer, J.G., and McQuail, D. (1968) *Television in Politics: its Uses and Influence* London: Faber and Faber

Bobbio, N. (2001) *Old Age and other essays* Cambridge: Polity Press

Bogard, W. (1996) *The Simulation of Surveillance* Cambridge: Cambridge University Press

Boorstin, D.J. (1963) *The Image or, What happened to the American Dream* Harmondsworth: Penguin

Boothroyd, J. (2000) 'The Battle of Wellfleet' in *Adbusters* Winter 2000

Bottomore, T.B. and Rubel, M. eds. (1963) *Karl Marx: Selected Writings in Sociology and Social Philosophy* London: Penguin

Bourdieu, P. (1991) *Language and Symbolic Power* Cambridge: Polity Press

BP www.bpamoco.com

Brandist, C., Shepherd, D and Tihanov, G. (2004) *The Bakhtin Circle* Manchester: Manchester University Press

Branigan, E. (1992) *Narrative Comprehension and Film* London and New York: Routledge

Branston, G. and Stafford, R. (1999) *The Media Student's Book* Arnold

Brierley, S. (1995) *The Advertising Handbook* London and New York: Routledge

Brindle, *Guardian*, Society section, 26 September 2001

Brooker, P. (1992) *Modernism/Postmodernism* London and New York: Longman

Brooker, P. (1999) *A Concise Glossary of Cultural Theory* London and New York: Arnold

Brown, G. and Yule, G. (1983) *Discourse Analysis* Cambridge: Cambridge University Press

Bruck, P.A. (1992) 'Discursive Movements and Social Movements' in Wasko, J. and Mosco, V. *Democratic Communications in the Information Age* New Jersey: Garamond/Ablex Publishing Co

Brunsdon, C., D'Acci, J., and Spigel, L. (1997) *Feminist Television Criticism: a Reader* Oxford: Oxford University Press

Buckingham, D. (1993) *Children Talking Television* London: Falmer Press

Burton, G.O. (1999) *Silva Rhetoricae* http://humanities.byu.edu/rhetoric/silva.htm

Business for Social Responsibility (2000) *Introduction to Corporate Social Responsibility* www.bsr.org/resourcecenter/topic

Butler, R. (1999) *Jean Baudrillard: The Defence of the Real* Thousand Oaks, London, New Delhi: SAGE

Buxton, D. (1990) *From the Avengers to Miami Vice: form and ideology in television series* Manchester: Manchester University Press

Calabrese, A. and Sparks, C. (2004) *Toward a Political Economy of Communication* Lanham, Oxford: Rowan and Littlefield

Calinescu, M. (1987) *Five Faces of Modernity* Durham: Duke University Press

Cameron, D. (2000) *Good to Talk?* Thousand Oaks, London, New Delhi: SAGE

Catephores, G. (1989) *An Introduction to Marxist Economics* London: Macmillan

Chouliakari, L. (2002) 'The Contingency of Universality', *Social Semiotics*, 12:1, 2002

Chouliaraki, L. and Fairclough, N. (1999) *Discourse in Late Modernity* Edinburgh: Edinburgh University Press

Clarke, J. and Newman, J. (2004) 'Governing in the Modern World?' in Steinburg, DL and Johnson, J (eds) *Blairism and the war of persuasion* London: Lawrence and Wishart

Clegg, S.R. (1993) 'Narrative, Power and Social Theory', in Mumby, D.K. *Narrative and Social Control* Thousand Oaks, London, New Delhi: SAGE

Clifford, M. (2001) *Political Genealogy after Foucault* London: Routledge

Coates, J. (1993) *Women, Men and Language* London and New York: Longman

Cobley, P. (1996) *The Communication Theory Reader* London and New York: Routledge

Cohen N. in *Observer*, 28th November 1999

Coles, R. (2005) 'The wild patience of radical democracy' in Tonder, L. and Thomassen, L. (eds) *Radical Democracy* Manchester: Manchester University Press

Collier, A. (1998) 'Language, Practice and Realism', in Parker, I (1998) *Social Constructionism, Discourse and Realism* Thousand Oaks, London, Delhi: SAGE

Collin, F. (1997) *Social Reality* London and New York: Routledge

Collins Dictionary (1987)

Connolly, W.E. (1993) *The Terms of Political Discourse* Oxford UK and Cambridge Mass: Blackwell

Corporate Citizenship Company www.bitc.org.uk

Cooke, L. in Nelmes, J. (1996) *An Introduction to Film Studies* London and New York: Routledge

Corner, J. (1995) *Television Form and Public Address* London and New York: Arnold

Couldry, N. (2000) *The Place of Media Power* London and New York: Routledge

Coulthard, M. (1985) *An Introduction to Discourse Analysis* London: Longman

Cox, G. (1995) *Pioneering Television News* London: John Libbey

Crewe, I. and Gosschalk, B. (1995) *Political Communication: Election 1992* Cambridge: Cambridge University Press

Crewe, I. and Harrop, M. (1989) *Political Communication: Election 1987* Cambridge: Cambridge University Press

Crowley, D. and Heyer, P. (1995) *Communication in history: technology, culture, society* London and New York: Longman

Crowther, P. (2003) *Philosophy after Postmodernism* London, New York: Roultedge

Cruse, A. (2000) *Meaning in Language* Oxford: Oxford University Press

Culler, J. (1985) *On Deconstruction* London and New York: Routledge

Curran, J. and Seaton, J. (1997) *Power without Responsibility* London and New York: Routledge

Czerniawska, F. (1998) *Corporate Speak: the Use of Language in Business* London: Macmillan

Dahlberg, L. (2001) 'Extending the Public Sphere through Cyberspace: the case of Minnesota e-Democracy' in *First Monday*, vol 6 no. 3

Dahlgren, P. (1995) *Television and the Public Sphere* Thousand Oaks, London, New Delhi: SAGE

Dant, T. (1999) *Material Culture in the Social World* Buckingham, Philadelphia: Open University Press

Davidson, M. (1992) *The Consumerist Manifesto* London and New York: Routledge

Davis, R.H.C. (1970) *A History of Medieval Europe*, London: Longman

Deacon, D., Pickering, M., Golding, P., Murdock, G. (1999) *Researching Communications* London, Sydney, Auckland: Arnold

Dear, P. (2001) *Revolutionising the Sciences* Houndmills: Palgrave

Dearing, J.W. and Rogers, E.M. (1996) *Agenda-Setting* Thousand Oaks, London, New Delhi: SAGE

Debord, G. (1997) *Comments on the Society of the Spectacle* London: Verso

de Mooij, M. (1998) *Global Marketing and Advertising* Thousand Oaks, London, New Delhi: SAGE

Derrida, J. (1981a) *Dissemination* London: Athlone Press

Devitt, M. and Sterelny, K. (1987) *Language and Reality* Oxford UK and Cambridge Mass: Blackwell

Dillon, M.C. (1995) *Semiological Reductionism* New York: State University of New York Press

Dodd, N. (1999) *Social Theory and Modernity* Cambridge: Polity Press

Dowis, R. (2000) *The Lost Art of the Great Speech* New York: Amacom

Drummond, P. (ed) (1993) *National identity and Europe: the television revolution* London: British Film Institute

Durham, M.G. and Kellner, D.M. (2001) *Media and Cultral Studies: Keyworks* Oxford UK and Cambridge Mass: Blackwell

Dyer, G. (1982) *Advertising as Communication* London and New York: Routledge

Edelman, M. (1964) *The Symbolic Uses of Politics* London, Chicago: University of Illinois Press

Edmonds, C. (1929) *A Subaltern's War* London: Peter Davies

Edwards, D. and Potter, J. (1992) *Discursive Psychology* Thousand Oaks, London, New Delhi: SAGE

Eggins, S. and Martin J.R. (1997) 'Genres and Registers of Discourse', in Eldridge, J., Kitzinger, J. and Williams, K. (1997) *The Mass Media and Power in Modern Britain* Oxford: Oxford University Press

Eldridge, J.E.T., Kitzinger, J. and Williams, K. *The Mass Media and Power in Modern Britain* Oxford: Oxford University Press

Elsaesser, T. (1990) *Early Cinema* London: BFI

Evelyn-White, H.G. (1914) Hesiod*, the Homeric Hymns and Homerica* Harvard University Press

Fairclough, N. (1989) *Language and Power* London and New York: Longman

Fairclough, N. (1995a) *Critical Discourse Analaysis* London and New York: Longman

Fairclough, N. (1995b) *Media Discourse* London and New York: Arnold

Fairclough, N. (2000) *New Labour, New Language?* London: Routledge

Farrell, T. (1993) *Norms of Rhetorical Culture* New Haven: Yale University Press

Featherstone, M. and Lash, S. *Spaces of culture: city, nation, world* Thousand Oaks, London, Delhi: SAGE

Fiske, J. (1982) *An Introduction to Communication Studies* London: Methuen

Fiske, J. (1987) *Television Culture* London and New York: Routledge

Fiske, J. (1989) *Understanding Popular Culture* Boston, London: Unwin Hyman

Fiumara, G.C. (1992) *The Symbolic Function* Oxford UK and Cambridge Mass: Blackwell

Fornas, J. (1995) *Cultural Theory and Late Modernity* Thousand Oaks, London, Delhi: SAGE

Fowler, R. (1991) *Language in the News* London and New York: Routledge

Fowles, J. (1996) *Advertising and Popular Culture* Thousand Oaks, London, Delhi: SAGE

Frank, T. 'The Conquest of Cool', in *Red Pepper*, September 2001, 24-25

Freedman, R. (1961) *Marx on Economics* London: Penguin

Friedman, J. (1994) *Cultural Identity and Global Process* Thousand Oaks, London, Delhi: SAGE

Fuery, P. (2000) *New Developments in Film Theory* Houndmills: Macmillan Press

Galbraith, J.K. (1958) *The Affluent Society* Boston: Houghton Mifflin

Garnham, N. (2000) *Emancipation, the Media, and Modernity* Oxford: Oxford University Press

Gauntlett, D. (1995) *Moving Experiences* London: John Libbey.

Georgakopoulou, A. and Goutsos, D. (1997) *Discourse Analysis: An Introduction* Edinburgh: Edinburgh University Press

Gerbner, G. (1977) *Mass media policies in changing cultures* Wiley: New York and London

Gerbner, G. and Gross, L. (1976a) 'Living with television: the violence profile' in *Journal of Communication* 26, 2: 173-199

Giddens, A. (1990) *The Consequences of Modernity* Cambridge: Polity Press

Giddens, A. (1991) *Modernity and Self-Identity* Cambridge: Polity

Giddens, A. (1993) *Sociology* Cambridge: Polity Press

Giddens, A. (1998) *The Third Way* Cambridge: Polity Press

Gill A.M. and Whedbee, K. (1997) 'Rhetoric', in van Dijk, T.A. (ed) (1997) *Discourse as Structure and Process* Thousand Oaks, London, Delhi: SAGE

Gill, D. and Adams, B. (1992) *ABC of Communication*

Gill, G. (2003) *The Nature and Development of the Modern State* Basingstoke: Palgrave Macmillan

Gillespie, M. (1995) *Television, Ethnicity and Cultural Change* London and New York: Routledge

Goldhaber, M.H. (1997) 'The attention economy and the net', in http://www.first-monday Issue 2

Golding, P. (1992) 'Communicating Capitalism', in *Media, Culture and Society* vol. 14 no. 4 October 1992

Goldman, R. (1992) *Reading Ads Socially* London and New York: Routledge

Graham, P., Keenan, T. and Dowd., A-M 2004 'A call to arms at the end of history: discourse-historical analysis of George W. Bush's declaration of war on terror', in *Discourse and Society* 15 (2-3) 199-221 Thousand Oaks, London, New Delhi: SAGE

Gramsci, A. (1971) *Selections from Prison Notebooks* London: Lawrence and Wishart

Graves, R. (1960) *Goodbye to All That* London: Penguin

Graves, R.P. (1990) *The Years with Laura Riding* London: Weidenfeld and Nicolson

Grayson, D. (1999) Speech to Leadership Conference on Global Corporate Citizenship, 23.2.99 www.bitc.org.uk

Green, K. & LeBihan, J. (1996) *Critical Theory and Practice* London and New York: Routledge

Greenwood, J.D. (1994) *Realism, Identity and Emotion* Thousand Oaks, London, New Delhi: SAGE

Grene, D. and Lattimore, R. (1959) *The complete Greek tragedies* Chicago, London: University of Chicago Press

Grice, P. (1989) *Studies in the Ways of Words* Cambridge, Mass., London: Harvard University Press

Gripsrud, J. (1999) *Television and Common Knowledge* London and New York: Routledge

Groombridge, B. (1972) *Television and the People: a programme for democratic participation* Harmondsworth: Penguin

Gumperz, J.J. (1982) *Discourse Strategies* Cambridge: Cambridge University Press

Gunnarsson, B-L., Linell, P. and Nordberg, B. (eds) (1997) *The Construction of Professional Discourse* London: Longman

Habermas, J. (1984) *The Theory of Communicative Action: Vol 1* Boston: Beacon Press

Habermas, J. (1989) *The Structural Transformation of the Public Sphere* Cambridge: Polity Press

Hall, S. (ed) (1980) *Culture, media, language: working papers in cultural studies, 1972-79* London: Hutchinson/Centre for Contemporary Cultural Studies

Hall, S., Held, D., and McGrew, T. (eds) (1992) *Modernity and its Futures* OUP and Polity Press

Halloran, J.D. (1964) *The Effects of Mass Communication* Leicester: Leicester University Press

Hansen, H.K. and Salskov-Iversen, D. (2002) 'Managerialised patterns of political authority' in MacCabe, C. (ed) *The rise and rise of Management Discourse* Critical Quarterly, 44, 3 Autumn 2002

Harootunian, H. (2000) *History's Disquiet* New York: Columbia University Press

Harre, R. and Gillett, G. (1994) *The Discursive Mind* Thousand Oaks, London, New Delhi: SAGE

Harris, D. (1992) *From Class Struggle to the Politics of Pleasure* London and New York: Routledge

Harris, D. (1996) *A Society of Signs?* London and New York: Routledge

Hart, S. and Murphy, J. (1998) *Brands: the New Wealth Creators* Basingstoke: Macmillan

Hartley, J. (1982) *Understanding News* London and New York: Routledge

Hartmann, G.W. (1936) 'A Field Experiment on the Comparative Effectiveness of 'Emotional' and 'Rational' Political Leaflets', in Rosnow, R.L. and Robinson, E.J. (1967) *Social Psychology* New York and London: Academic Press

Harvey, D. (1990) *The Condition of Postmodernity* Oxford, UK and Cambridge, Mass: Blackwell

Harwell, R.B. (1958) *The Confederate Reader* U.S.A.: Konecky and Konecky

Hawkes, D. (2001) *Idols of the Marketplace* Basingstoke, New York: Palgrave Macmillan

Hayward, S. (1996) *Key Concepts in Cinema Studies* London and New York: Routledge

Hearfield, C. (2004) *Adorno and the Modern Ethos of Freedom* Aldershot, Burlington: Ashgate

Heater, D. (1993) *What is Citizenship?* Cambridge: Polity Press

Heertz, N. (2001) *The Silent Takeover: The Rise of Corporate Power and the Death of Democracy* New York: Random House

Heritage, J. (1984a) *Garfinkel and Ethnomethodolgy* Oxford: Basil Blackwell

Herman, E.S. and Chomsky, N. (1988) *Manufacturing Consent: the political economy of the mass media* New York: Pantheon Books

Hill, C. (1975) *The World Turned Upside Down* Harmondsworth: Penguin

Hindess, B. (1996) *Discourses of Power* Oxford, UK and Cambridge, Mass: Blackwell

Hirsch, F. (1977) *Social Limits to Growth* London: Routledge and Kegan Paul

Hirschkop, K. (1999) *Mikhail Bakhtin: an aesthetic for democracy* Oxford: Oxford University Press

Hirschkop, K. and Shepherd D. (1989) *Bakhtin and Cultural Theory* Manchester: Manchester University Press

Hodge, R. and Kress, G. (1988) *Social Semiotics* Cambridge: Polity Press

Hodge, B. and Tripp, D. (1986) *Children and Television* Cambridge: Polity Press

Holquist, M. (2002) *Dialogism* London, New York: Routledge

Horrocks, C. and Jevtic, Z. (1996) *Baudrillard for Beginners* Cambridge: Icon

Hovland, C.I., Lumsdaine, A.A., and Sheffield, F.E. *Experiments in Mass Communication* Princeton: Princeton University Press

Howarth, D. (2000) *Discourse* Buckingham, Philadephia: OUP

Hughes, G. (1998) *Understanding Crime Prevention: social control, risk and late modernity* Buckingham: Open University Press

Hufton, O. 'In Search of Counter-Revolutionary Women' in Kates, G. (1998) *The French Revolution* London and New York: Routledge

Hunt, H. (1996) *The French Revolution and Human Rights* New York: Bedford Books

Huizinga, J. (1955) *The Waning of the Middle Ages* Harmondsworth: Penguin Books

Inaugural Addresses of the Presidents of the United States (2001) Bartleby.com

Isin, E.F. (2000) *Democracy, Citizenship and the Global City* London, New York: Routledge

Jameson, F. (1981) *The Political Unconscious* London: Methuen

Janda, K., Berry, J.M., Goldman, J. and Hula, K.W. (1995) *The Challenge of Democracy* Boston: Houghton Mifflin

Jaworski, A. and Coupland, N. (1999) *The Discourse Reader* London and New York: Routledge

Jensen, K.B. (1995) *The Social Semiotics of Mass Communication* Thousand Oaks, London, New Delhi: SAGE

Jones, N. (1997) *Campaign 1997* London: Indigo

Jones, N. (1999) *Sultans of Spin* London: Victor Gollancz

Jones, N. (2002) *The Control Freaks* London: Politico's

Jowett, G. and O'Donnell, V. (1987) *Propaganda and Persuasion* Thousand Oaks, London, New Delhi: SAGE

Kaid, L.L. and Holtz-Bacha, C. (1995) *Political advertising in western democracies* Thousand Oaks, London: SAGE

Kates, G. (1998) *The French Revolution* London and New York: Routledge

Katz, A. (2000) *Postmodernism and the Politics of Culture* Boulder: Westview Press

Kavanagh, D. (1995) *Election Campaigning* Oxford UK and Cambridge Mass: Blackwell

Klapper, J.T. (1955) in Schramm, (ed) *The Process and Effects of Mass Communication* Urbana: Illinois

Klein, N. (2000) *No Logo* London: Flamingo

Klein, N. (2001) in *Guardian* 7.6.01

Kress, G. and Hodge, R. (1979) *Language as Ideology* London and New York: Routledge and Kegan Paul

Kress, G. and van Leeuwen, T. (2001) *Multimodal Discourse* London and New York: Arnold

Kuper, A. and Kuper, J. (eds) (1985) *The Social Science Encyclopedia* London: Routledge and Kegan Paul

Kurke, L. (1991) *The Traffic in Praise* New York: Cornell University Press

Labov, W. (1972a) 'Rules for ritual insults' in Sudnow, D. (ed) *Studies in Social Interaction* Mouton: The Hague

Laclau, E. (1977) *Politics and Ideology in Marxist Theory* London: Verso

Laclau, E. and Mouffe, C. (1985) *Hegemony and Socialist Strategy* London: Verso

Landlow, G.P. (1992) *Hypertext: The Convergence of Contemporary Critical Theory and Technology* Baltimore: John Hopkins University Press

Lash, S. (1999) *Another Modernity, A Different Rationality* Oxford: Blackwell

Lau, K.J. (2000) *New Age Capitalism* Philadelphia: University of Pennsylvania Press

Lazarsfeld, P.F., Berelson, B. and Gaudet, H. (1948) *The People's Choice* New York: Colorado University Press

Lefebvre, H. (1995) *Introduction to Modernity* London: Verso

Leiss, W. Kline, S. and Jhally, S. (1990) *Social Communication in Advertising* London and New York: Routledge

Lenart, S. (1994) *Shaping Political Attitudes* Thousand Oaks, London, New Delhi: SAGE

Levin, C. (1996) *Jean Baudrillard: a study in cultural metaphysics* London: Prentice Hall

Lichtenberg, J. in Weiss, T.G. (1993) *Collective Security in a Changing World* Boulder, London: Lynne Rienner

Livingstone, S. 'Mediated Knowledge', in Gripsrud, J. *Television and Common Knowledge* (1999) London and New York: Routledge

Lopez, J. and Potter, G. (2001) *After Postmodernism* London and New York: Athlone

Lovell, T. (1983) *Pictures of Reality* London: BFI

Lukes, S. (1986) (ed.) *Power* New York: New York University Press

Lunt, P.K. and Livingstone, S.M. (1992) *Mass Consumption and Personal Identity*

Lury, K. (2001) *British Youth Television* Oxford: Oxford University Press

Luthar, B. (1993) 'Identity Management and Popular Representational Forms' in Drummond, P. (ed) (1993) *National identity and Europe: the television revolution* London: British Film Institute

Matelart, A. (1996) *The Invention of Communication* Minneapolis: University of Minnesota Press

McArthur, T. (1996) *The Oxford Companion to the English Language* Oxford: Oxford University Press

McChesney, R. 'The Global Media Giants', in Andersen, R. and Strate, L. *Critical Studies in Media Commercialism* Oxford: Oxford University Press

McCombs, M. (2004) *Setting the Agenda* Cambridge, Malden: Polity

McGuigan, J. (1996) *Culture and the Public Sphere* London and New York: Routledge

McLellan, D. (1995) *Ideology* Buckingham: Open University Press

McLuhan, M. (1967) *The Medium is the Message* London: Penguin

McPherson, J.M. (1988) *Battle Cry of Freedom* Oxford and New York: Oxford University Press

McPherson, J.M. (1997) *For Cause and Comrades* Oxford and New York: Oxford University Press

McPherson, J.M. (1996) *Drawn with the Sword* Oxford and New York: Oxford University Press

McQuire, S. (1998) *Visions of Modernity* Thousand Oaks, London, Delhi: SAGE

McQuail, D. (1987) *Mass Communication Theory* Thousand Oaks, London, Delhi: SAGE

McQuail, D. (1993) *Communication models: for the study of mass communications* London: Longman

McQuillan, M. (2000) *Deconstruction: a Reader* Edinburgh: Edinburgh University Press

McSpotlight (1998) 'Trial News 1' in www.mcspotlight.org/media

Maarek, P.J. (1995) *Political Marketing and Communication* London: John Libbey

MacDonnell, D. (1986) *Theories of Discourse* Oxford: Basil Blackwell

Macherey, P. (1978) *A Theory of Literary Production* London, Boston and Henley

Mackay, H. and O'Sullivan, T. (1999) *The Media Reader: Continuity and Transformation* Thousand Oaks, London, New Delhi: SAGE

Mandelson, Peter (2004) *Opening Speech: Progressive Governance Conference* Policy Network

Manning, P. (2001) *News and News Stories: A Critical Introduction* Thousand Oaks, London, New Delhi: SAGE

Manville, B. (1990) *The Origins of Citizenship in Ancient Athens* New Jersey: Princeton University Press

Marchand, R. (1986) *Advertising the American Dream* California: University of California Press

Marcuse H. (1964) *One dimensional man: studies in the ideology of advanced industrial society* London: Routledge and Kegan Paul

Martin, H-P., and Schumann (1997) *The Global Trap: globalization and the assault on prosperity and democracy* London: Zed Books

Marx, K. (1954) *Capital* London: Lawrence and Wishart

Marx, K. and Engels, F. (1967) *The Communist Manifesto* Harmondsworth: Penguin Books

Marx, K. and Engels, F. (1974) *The German Ideology* Lawrence and Wishart: London

Mason, J. (1989) *Philosophical Rhetoric* London and New York: Routledge

Mattelart, A. (1991) *Advertising International* London and New York: Routledge

Mattelart, A. (1996) *The Invention of Communication* Minneapolis, London: University of Minnesota Press

Mattelart, A. and Mattelart, M. (1998) *Theories of Communication* Thousand Oaks, London, New Delhi: SAGE

Mattelart, A. and Mattelart, M. (1992) *Rethinking Media Theory* Minneapolis, London: University of Minnesota Press

Mazzoleni, in Kaid, L.L. and Holtz-Bacha, C. (1995) *Political Advertising in Western Democracies* Thousand Oaks, London: SAGE

May, J. and Thrift, N. (2001) *Timespace: Geographies of Temporality* London and New York: Routledge

Meijer, I.C. (1998) 'Advertising Citizenship: An Essay on the Performative Power of Consumer Culture' in *Media, Culture and Society*, vol. 20 (2) 235-249 SAGE

Metz, C. (1982) *Psychoanalysis and Cinema: the Imaginary Signifier* London: Macmillan

Mill, J.S. (1910) *Utilitarianism* London and New York: Everyman

Miller, D. (1987) *Material Culture and Mass Consumption* Oxford, UK and Cambridge, Mass: Blackwell

Mills, C.W. (1956) *The Power Elite* Oxford: Oxford University Press

Mills, S. (1997) *Discourse* London and New York: Routledge

Milward, A.S. (1992) *The European rescue of the nation-state* London: Routledge

Montag, W. (2003) *Louis Althusser* Basingstoke, New York: Palgrave Macmillan

Moravcsik, J.M. (1992) *Thought and Language* London and New York: Routledge

Moores, S. (1993) *Interpreting Audiences* Thousand Oaks, London, Delhi: SAGE

Morley, D. (1992) *Television, Audiences and Cultural Studies* London and New York: Routledge

Morley, D. and Robins, K. (1995) *Spaces of Identity* London and New York: Routledge

Morton, A.L. (1975) *Freedom in Arms* London: Lawrence and Wishart

Mosco, V. (1996) *The Political Economy of Communication* Thousand Oaks, London, Delhi: SAGE

Mueller, C. (1973) *The Politics of Communication* New York: Oxford University Press

Muller-Doohm, S. (2005) *Adorno: a biography* Cambridge, Malden: Polity

Murdock, G. (1993) 'Communicating Modernity', in *Media, Culture and Society* October 1993, 523

Murphy, C. 'Is BP Beyond Petroleum? Hardly' in *Fortune*, September 30th, 2002

Murphy, J. (1998) 'What is Branding?' in *Brands: the new wealth creators* Basingstoke: Macmillan Business/Interbrand

Musson, G. and Cohen, L. (2000) 'Entrepreneurial Identities: Reflections from Two Case Studies' in *Organisation* vol 7 (1) 31-48 London, Thousand Oaks, New Delhi: SAGE

Myers, G. (1999) *Ad worlds: brands, media, audiences* London: Arnold

Myerson, G. (1994) *Rhetoric, Reason and Society* Thousand Oaks, London, Delhi: SAGE

Nash, C. (2001) *The Unravelling of the Postmodern Mind* Edinburgh: Edinburgh University Press

Neale, S. (1980) *Genre* London: BFI

Negrine, R. (1998) *Television and the Press since 1945* Manchester: Manchester University Press

Negroponte, N. (1995) *Being Digital* London: Hodder and Stoughton

Nelmes, J. (1996) *An Introduction to Film Studies* London and New York: Routledge

Ng, S.H. and Bradac, J.J. (1993) *Power in Language* Thousand Oaks, London, Delhi: SAGE

Nike (2000) 'Nike responds to 'horror' concerns' *Nike Press Releases* October 2000 nikebiz.com/media/news

Nofsinger, R.E. (1991) *Everyday Conversation* Thousand Oaks, London, Delhi: SAGE

Norris, C. (2000) *Deconstruction and the Unfinished Project of Modernity* London: Athlone Press

Norris, P., Curtice, J., Sanders, D., Scammell, M., and Semetko, H.A. (1999) *On Message* Thousand Oaks, London, Delhi: SAGE

Nye, A. (ed) (1998) *Philosophy of Language: the Big Questions* Oxford UK. and Cambridge, Mass: Blackwell

Ober and Strauss (1990) 'Drama, Political Rhetoric and the Discourse of Athenian Democracy' in Winkler, J. and Zeitlin, F. (ed) *Nothing to do with Dionysus?* New Jersey: Princeton University Press

O'Brien, M. 'Theorising Modernity' in O'Brien, M., Penna, S., and Hay, C. (1999) *Theorising Modernity* London and New York: Longman

O Siochru, S. and Girard, B. (2002) *Global Media Governance* Lanham, Oxford: Rowan and Littlefield

O'Sullivan, T., Hartley, J., Montgomery, M. and Saunders, D. (1998a) *Key Concepts in Communication and Cultural Studies* London and New York: Routledge

O'Sullivan, T., Dutton, B. and Rayner, P. (1998b) *Studying the Media* London and New York: Arnold

Osborne, T. (1995) *Aspects of Enlightenment* London: UCL Press/Taylor and Francis

Outhwaite, W. (1994) *Habermas: a Critical Introduction* Cambridge: Polity Press

Outram, D. (1995) *The Enlightenment* Cambridge: Cambridge University Press

Packard, V. (1957) *The Hidden Persuaders* London: Longman's Green

Packard, V. (1962) *The Hidden Persuaders* London: Penguin

Parker, I. (1992) *Discourse Dynamics* London and New York: Routledge

Parker, I. (1998) *Social Constructionism, Discourse and Realism* Thousand Oaks, London, Delhi: SAGE

Parker, I. (1999) *Critical Textwork* Open University Press: Buckingham and Philadelphia

Perkins, A.B. (2000) 'A time for cautious optimism in the global village' in *Red Herring* No. 86 4.12.2000

Philo, G. (ed) (1999) *Message Received* Harlow: Longman

Pinker, S. (1994) *The Language Instinct*

Pointon, M. (1999) 'Materializing Mourning: Hair, Jewellery and the Body', in Kwint, M., Breward, C., and Aynsley, J. *Material Memories* (1999) Oxford, New York: Berg

Postan, M.M. (1975) *The medieval economy and society: an economic history of Britain in the Middle Ages* Harmondsworth: Penguin

Potter, J. and Wetherell, M. (1987) *Discourse and Social Psychology* London, Thousand Oaks, New Delhi: SAGE

Poulantzas, N. (1974) *Classes in Contemporary Capitalism* London: Verso

Preston, P. (1995) *Franco* London: Fontana Press

Price, S. (1996) *Communication Studies* London: Longman

Price, S. (1997) *The A-Z Media and Communication Handbook* London: Hodder & Stoughton

Price, S. (1998) (2nd. ed) *Media Studies* London: Longman

Price, S. (2001) 'Involvement of the Citizen in Local Life?' in *As Grand Questoes da Comunicacao Municipal Para o sec XXI* Lisbon: Forum de Municipios Europe

Price, S. (2003) 'Competing Discourses on the Web? Diversity, Anarchy and Corporate Address' in Ralph, Manchester and Lees *Diversity or Anarchy?* Luton: University of Luton Press

Price, S. (2006a) 'Brute Reality' in Barker, A. (ed) *Television, Aesthetics and Reality* Cambridge: Cambridge Scholars

Reicher, S. (2000) 'Mass Psychology and the (Re) Analysis of the Self', in Wheeler, W., *The Political Subject*, London: Lawrence and Wishart

Renckstorf, K., McQuail, D. and Jankowski, N. (1996) *Media Use as Social Action* London: John Libbey

Rengger, N.J. (1995) *Political Theory, Modernity and Postmodernity* Oxford, UK and Cambridge, Mass: Blackwell

Rheingold, H. (1994) *The Virtual Community* London: Secker and Warburgh

Rivett, M. (2000) 'Approaches to Analysing the Web Text' in *Convergence*, vol 6, no. 3, Luton: University of Luton Press

Robins, K. and Webster, F. (1999) *Times of the Technoculture* London and New York: Routledge

Rosenbaum, M. (1997) *From Soapbox to Soundbite* London: Macmillan

Rosenthal, R. and Rosnow, R.L. (eds) (1969) *Artifact in Behavioral Research* New York, London: Academic Press

Sacks, H., Schegloff, E.A. and Jefferson, G. (1974) 'A simplest systematics for the organisation of turn-taking for conversation', in *Language*, 50 (4)

Sarup, M. (1993) *An Introductory Guide to Poststructuralism and Postmodernism* New York, London, Toronto, Sydney, Tokyo, Signapore: Harvester Wheatsheaf

Sassoon, S. (1965) *Memoirs of an Infantry Officer* London: Faber

Saunders, P. and Harris, C. (1994) *Privatization and Popular Capitalism* Open University Press: Buckingham and Bristol

Saussure, F de. (1960) *Course in general linguistics* London: Owen

Scannell, P. (1991) *Broadcast Talk* Thousand Oaks, London, Delhi: SAGE

Scarborough, E. and Tanenbaum, E. (eds) *Research Strategies in the Social Sciences* (1998) Oxford: Oxford University Press

Schiller, D. (1986) *Theorising Communication* Oxford and New York: Oxford University Press

Schlesinger, J. (1997), in Sreberny-Mohammadi, A. et al (eds) *Media in Global Context: a Reader* London: Arnold

Schumpeter, J. (1962) *Capitalism, Socialism and Democracy* New York: Harper & Row

Scollon, R. (1998) *Mediated Discourse as Social Interaction* London and New York: Longman

Searle, J.R. (1969) *Speech Acts* Cambridge: Cambridge University Press

Semin, G.R. and Gergen, K.J. (1990) *Everyday Understanding* Thousand Oaks, London, Delhi: SAGE

Sennett, R. (1998) *The Corrosion of Character* New York: Norton

Severin, W.J. and Tankard, J.W. (1992) *Communication Theories: Origins, Methods, and Uses in the Mass Media* New York and London: Longman

Shankar, S. (2001) *Textual Traffic* New York: State University of New York

Shattuc, J. (1997) *The Talking Cure* New York, London: Routledge

Shaw, M. (1994) *Global Society and International Relations* Cambridge: Polity Press

Shell www2.shell.com/home

Shepherd, D. (1989) 'Bakhtin and the reader' in Hirschkop, K. and Shepherd, D. *Bakhtin and cultural theory* Manchester: Manchester University Press

Sheriff, J.K. (1994) *Charles Peirce's Guess at the Riddle* Bloomington and Indianapolis: Indiana University Press

Shotter, J. (1993) *Conversational Realities* Thousand Oaks, London, Delhi: SAGE

Shotter, J. and Gergen, K.J. (1989) *Texts of Identity* Thousand Oaks, London, Delhi: SAGE

Sim, S. (1992) *Beyond Aesthetics* New York, London, Toronto, Sydney, Tokyo, Singapore: Harvester Wheatsheaf

Simons, H.W. and Billig, M. (1994) *After Postmodernism* Thousand Oaks, London, Delhi: SAGE

Simms, J. (2000) 'Our actions speak louder than words' in *Marketing* London: Haymarket Publishing

Slayden, D. and Whillock, R.K. (1999) *Soundbite Culture* Thousand Oaks, London, Delhi: SAGE

Smith, J.K.A. (2005) *Jacques Derrida: Live Theory* New York, London: Continuum

Sorlin, P. (1980) *The Film in History* Oxford: Basil Blackwell

Sproule, J.M. (1997) *Propaganda and Democracy* Cambridge: Cambridge University Press, 1997

Spybey, T. (1996) *Globalisation and World Society* Cambridge: Polity

Stallabrass, J. (1996) *Gargantua: Manufacturing Mass Culture* London: Verso

Stam, R., Burgoyne, R., and Flitterman-Lewis, S (1992) *New Vocabularies in Film Semiotics* London: Routledge

Steinburg, D.L. and Johnson, R. (2004) *Blairism and the war of Persuasion* Cambridge: Lawrence & Wishart

Stephens, P. (2001) 'Vulnerability of a superpower' *Financial Times* London 5.1.2001

Stevenson, N. (1995) *Understanding Media Cultures* Thousand Oaks, London, Delhi: SAGE

Stevenson, N. (2001) *Culture and Citizenship* Thousand Oaks, London, Delhi: SAGE

Storey, J. (1999) *Cultural Consumption and Everyday Life* London and New York: Arnold

Stubbs, M. (1983) *Discourse Analysis* Oxford: Basil Blackwell

Tallis, R. (1988) *In Defence of Realism* Lincoln and London: University of Nebraska Press

Taylor, P.M. (1999) *British Propaganda in the Twentieth Century* Edinburgh: Edinburgh University Press

Tedesco, J.C. (2005) 'Issue and Strategy Agenda Setting in the 2004 Presidential Election' in *Journalism Studies* 6, 2 2005 pp. 187-201

Tetzlaff, D. (1991) 'Divide and Conquer' in *Media Culture and Society* Thousand Oaks, London, Delhi: Sage

Therborn, G. (1980) *The Ideology of Power and the Power of Ideology* London: Verso

Therborn, G. (1995) *European Modernity and Beyond* Thousand Oaks, London, Delhi: SAGE

Thompson, J.B. (1990) *Ideology and Modern Culture* Cambridge: Polity Press

Thompson, J.B. (1995) *The Media and Modernity* Cambridge: Polity Press

Thomson, O. (1999) *Easily Led: A History of Propaganda* Guildford: Sutton

Thornhill, J. 'ADB adds battle with poverty to profit and loss account' *Financial Times* London 5.1.2001

Tilson, D. (1993) 'The Shaping of 'eco-nuclear' publicity' in *Media, Culture and Society* vol 15 no. 3 July 1993

Tolson, A. (2006) *Media Talk: Spoken Discourse on TV and Radio* Edinburgh: Edinburgh University Press

Toynbee, P. and Walker, D. (2001) *Did Things Get Better?* London: Penguin

Trask, R.L. (1999) *Key concepts in language and linguistics* London: Routledge

Trenaman, J. and McQuail, D. (1961) *Television and the Political Image* London: Methuen

Tuchman, G. (1974) *The TV establishment: programming for power and profit* Englewood Cliffs, N.J: Prentice Hall

Tumber, H. (ed) (2000) *Media, Power and Professionals* London and New York: Routledge

Turner, E.S. (1952) *The Shocking History of Advertising* London: Michael Joseph

United States Deptartment of Labor on Corporate Citizenship edcivic@libertynet. org

United States Green Party www.greenparty.org

van Dijk, T.A. (ed) (1997) *Discourse as Structure and Process* Thousand Oaks, London, Delhi: SAGE

van Dijk, T.A. (ed) (1997) *Discourse as Social Interaction* Thousand Oaks, London, Delhi: SAGE

van Dijk, T.A. (1998) *Ideology* Thousand Oaks, London, Delhi: SAGE

van Leeuwen, T. (1999) *Speech, Music, Sound* London: Macmillan

Varney, D. 'Managing Corporate Citizenship: a Business Perspective' speech to Royal Institute of International Affairs, 8.11.1999

Vice, S. (1997) *Introducing Bakhtin* Manchester: Manchester University Press

Viney, L. (2005) 'It's time to turn the light on BP' in BP Magazine, Issue 3, 2005

Wagner, P. (1994) *A Sociology of Modernity* London and New York: Routledge

Warr, J. (1992) *A Spark Amongst the Ashes*

Watson, J. and Hill, A. (1989) *A Dictionary of Communication and Media Studies* London and New York: Arnold

Weisburg, (2000) 'Scalable Hype: old persuasions for new technology' in Andersen, R. and Strate, L. *Critical Studies in Media Commercialism* London: Oxford University Press

Wernick, A. (1991) *Promotional Culture* Thousand Oaks, London, Delhi: SAGE

Williams, K. (1997) *Get me a Murder a Day!* London and New York: Arnold

Williams, R. (1988) *Keywords* London: Fontana

Williamson, J. (1978) *Decoding Advertisements* London and New York: Marion Boyars

Wilmshurst, J. (1985) *The Fundamentals of Advertising* Oxford: Butterworth Heinemann

Wood, G.S. (1991) *The Radicalism of the American Revolution* New York: Vintage

Woodiwiss, A. (2001) *The Visual in Social Theory* London and New York: Athlone

Worsley, T.C. (1970) *Television: the Ephemeral Art* London: Alan Ross

Wrong, D.H. (1979) *Power: its forms, bases and uses* Oxford: Blackwell

Young, J. (1999) *The Exclusive Society: social exclusion, crime and difference in late modernity* Thousand Oaks, London, Delhi: SAGE.

Zeitlin, F. (1990) in Winkler, J. and Zeitlin, F. (ed) *Nothing to do with Dionysus?* New Jersey: Princeton University Press

Zizek, S. (1994) *Mapping Ideology* London: Verso

Zizek, S. (2001) *Belief* London: Verso

Index

Note: Bold page numbers indicate illustrations; numbers in brackets preceded by *n* refer to footnotes